On This Rock

by

Peggy Long

Upline® Press

First printing July, 1999

ISBN 1-890344-10-9
Published by Upline® Press, MLM Publishing, Inc.
106 South Street, Charlottesville, VA 22902
tel. 804-979-4427, fax 804-979-1602
Printed in the United States of America

Cover design by Tom Bellucci
10 9 8 7 6 5 4 3 2 1

Contents

DEDICATION and GIFTS GIVEN

To my parents and all parents
who gave us the gift of our first breath of life. It is up to each of us to make it count— this is not a dress rehearsal.

To all the great master networkers
before me who have given me their gift of blazing the trail as passionate purposeful pioneers.

To my two sons: *James* and *Jordan*
who give me the gifts of patience, forgiveness, and unconditional love.

To my family
who have stood by me with their gifts of caring, understanding and love through times of joy and loss, times of abundance and lack.

To my awesome network team
who give me their gifts of commitment, integrity, leadership and inspiration— daily.

To *Tina Howell*
who gave me her gift of listening, during 40 hours of recording, and her gift of empowerment.

And to my friend and mentor *John Milton Fogg*
who gives me his gift of mastery in editing, his playful spirit and his gift of leading network marketing to the next level. You're the greatest, John!!!

FORWARD

On This Rock I Stand, and World, You Will Adjust. That's Peggy Long, in a sentance. (And it's about the only sentance that could ever do Peggy justice!)

Want something accomplished— something *big*? Peg can do it. Once she takes a stand for some thing or somebody, the deal is a done one.

I remember when Peggy stood up at an Upline® Masters Seminar and said she would have 30 new Lifetime Subscribers by the end of weekend. I thought she was nuts. I told her so. We'd never had more than 10 people make that thousand-dollar commitment at one time before.

By Sunday night, we had 32.

Peggy made it happen just because she said so.

On This Rock I Stand . . ., indeed!

This book is one of Peggy's commitments. Peggy said her purpose was to write a book that could take anyone who was willing to do what it takes to the very top of this business.

By now you should understand what it would mean to you to match your commitment to Peggy's.

Peggy Long is a Leader. A woman leader. Kind of a combination between Mother Teresa and Ma' Barker. Powerful and Empowering. Tough love. No B.S.— ever! She's a been there, done that Network Marketing success story— a top income-earner, business-builder, trainer's-trainer, leader-maker. The kind of person who, if she was your partner and she signed-on with you committed to help you achieve your goals and aspirations, you'd know beyond a shadow of a doubt that nothing, *nothing!*, would prevent you from achieving the success of your dreams.

With Peggy as your partner, you are unstoppable!

And with this book, you've got a powerful partnership with Peggy Long. And that, my friend— and I speak from proven personal experience— is like money in the bank!

On This Rock . . ., gives it all to you. While other books content themselves with how to approach your Network Marketing business, Peggy's covers how and who to, and why, and where, and when to, and what to have, do and especially *be* to assure your success.

On This Rock . . . can certainly be used by beginners, but I think it's advanced stuff. Peggy covers the material others leave out. (And I suspect it's because they don't really know.) Peggy knows. Peggy knows, because she's done it. Not once or twice. Hundreds, even thousands of times.

Peggy stands (and shoots) arrow straight. Integrity is her middle name. She's someone you can count on. She's in action. Committed. Powered by intention.

Peggy is strong as she can be (and soft, too.) Peggy doesn't let things get to her. And in action, she is something to see.

And most important of all, Peggy's power is duplication. What she knows and what she's accomplished is of little use to her unless she can empower you to have, do and be the same. She's all about results, partnering with you to get the results you're after in your life and work.

Peggy's worked hard so you can work easier.

Peggy's worked smart so you can work smarter.

And if it's not fun, she won't do it.

Now, that's what I want in a business partner. That's what I want in a life partner. Peggy's both for me. And when you read *Like A Rock* . . ., Peggy will become both business and life partner for you, too.

Enjoy *On This Rock* . . . and your growing page-by-page partnership with my friend and colleague, Peggy Long. I promise you, it will be one of the most valuable and empowering relationships of your life!

—John Milton Fogg

Author of *The Greatest Networker in the World*™ and *Conversations with The Greatest Networker in the World*™

Founder of Upline® and *Network Marketing Lifestyles*

PREFACE

Please read the following selection at least three times before starting this book. It encompasses the essence, philosophy and practical exercises I use in coaching leaders of leaders in network marketing.

The Master Game

Seek, above all, for a game worth playing. Such is the advice of the oracle to modern man. Having found the game, play it with intensity— play as if your life and sanity depended on it. (They do depend on it.) Follow the example of the French existentialists and flourish a banner bearing the word "engagement." Though nothing means anything and all roads are marked "No Exit," yet move as if your movements had some purpose. If life does not seem to offer a game worth playing, then invent one. For it must be clear, even to the most clouded intelligence, that any game is better than no game.

But although it is safe to play the Master Game, this has not served to make it popular. It still remains the most demanding and difficult of games and in our society, there are few who play. Contemporary many, hypnotized by the glitter of his own gadgets, has little contact with his inner world, concerns himself with outer, not inner space. But the Master Game is played entirely in the innter world, a vast and complex territory about which men know very little. The aim of the game is true awakening, full development of the powers latent in man. The game can be played only by people whose observations of themselves and others have led them to a certain conclusion, namely, that man's ordinary state of consciousness, his so-called waking state, is not the highest level of consciousness of which he is capable. In fact, this state is so far from real awakening that it could appropriately be called a condition of "waking sleep."

Once a person has reached this conclusion, he is no longer able to sleep comfortably. □ A new appetite develops within him, the hunger for real awakening, for full consciousness. He realizes that he sees, hears and knows only a tiny fraction of what he could see, hear and know, that he lives in the poorest, shabbiest of the rooms in his inner dwelling, and that he could enter other rooms, beautiful and filled with treasures, the win-

dows of which look out on eternity and infinity.

The solitary player lives today in a culture that is more or less totally opposed to the aims he has set himself, that does not recognize the existence of the Master Game, and regards player of this game as queer or slightly mad. The player thus confronts great opposition from the culture in which he lives and must strive with forces which tend to bring his game to a halt before it has even started. Only by finding a teacher and becoming part of the group of pupils that teacher has collected about him can the player find encouragement and support. Otherwise he simply forgets his aim, or wanders off down some side road and loses himself.

Here it is sufficient to say that the Master Game can NEVER be made easy to play. It demands all that a man has, all his feelings, all his thought, his entire resources, physical and spiritual. If he tries to play it in a halfhearted way or tires to get results by unlawful means, he runs the risk of destroying his own potential. For this reason it is better not to embark on the game at all than to play it halfheartedly.

- Robert S. DeRopp

I've had this quote for over 34 years, but I don't remember where I first found it. When times are tough in my personal or professional life, I read this again and become more committed to my life and network marketing being in the domain of the "Master Game."

INTRODUCTION

I grew up in a little town in the Illinois farmlands. We lived in the Windy City of Chicago during my elementary school years, and moved to Arizona when I was 13. I thought I was going out where the cowboys and Indians lived. I remember feeling very afraid of moving out West.

My father was a minister and I had a strong Christian upbringing. I had a supportive, caring, greatly empowering home life, although we were quite poor financially. I remember how my mother, bless her soul, would make me two new dresses every year. I used to be embarrassed when I went to school, because they were handmade, but . . . that's where I came from.

I always had a desire to do better in life. After high school, I went to college in San Diego. I raised miniature dachshunds and golden retrievers to get through college. I worked and I earned a scholarship, too. I got married during my senior year, and when I graduated, I was eight and a-half months pregnant. Nobody thought I could ever graduate.

I was in that marriage for about 13 years and had two wonderful sons, James and Jordan. My husband was also a minister and I basically followed the same path with him as I had with my father— until it was time for me to move on from that relationship.

After the divorce, my life took all kinds of new turns and twists. I invested a great deal in my personal growth, earned two masters degrees, and came really close to getting a third one, as well— all as a single mom. My interests were in education and social psychology, and I enjoyed working in that field for ten years.

Yet I still felt there was something else, something more. As I said, I've always had a desire to do better and be more in life.

In 1976, I took a personal growth course called Psi World Seminar. "Psi" is the 13th letter of the Greek alphabet, and it means "the unknown." That particular "unknown" turned out to be a powerful piece of self-development for me, and that seminar was the launching pad into a whole new direction for my life. I was able to unleash and unlock more of my true personal power than I'd ever imagined I had in me.

With what I learned, I was able to tap into universal truths— ideas such as win/win (it is more powerful to let both sides of an issue win that to defeat someone); givers gain ("it is more blessed to give than receive"); mind over matter; to think is to create (our thoughts are the blueprints for our lives); leadership has a price. I'd always recognized these truths existed, but never really knew how to effectively use them in my life. Because of the Psi World Seminar, I was able to learn visualization (picturing each detail of desired results), affirmations (positive reinforcement), treasure maps (visual reinforcement of goals), and many other techniques. Psi taught me the resources each human has within, and how to tap into them to get the best out of ourselves and all our relationships.

The biggest benefit of all for me was unlocking my personal power. Finally— and for the first time in my life— I learned to be *me* and express *me*.

As you can probably imagine, there are many heavy expectations placed on a minister's child and a minister's wife— and remember, I was *both*. As a child, when I attended a meeting or church, I would have to act a certain way to meet other people's expectations for how the minister's daughter should behave. The same thing happened when I became the minister's wife.

I really didn't choose to do that as a child; I knew I *had* to do it. By the time I married, playing chameleon had become a deeply ingrained habit. I didn't express myself fully. I would not say what I needed to say. I couldn't even feel what I was truly feeling. I would always hold myself back, and instead of being me, I changed my behavior to fit a role. I constantly fell into these "expectation traps" both as a child and a spouse. Most of the time I changed the color of who I was into being like what was expected of me.

I was the minister's daughter.

I was the minister's wife.

I was . . . who was I?

That Psi seminar made me aware of my chameleon habit. Once I saw what I was doing, I was no longer willing to hold back. I'd done that for the first 33 years of my life.

I was ready for a big change— I started working for Psi World Corporation as a marketer and facilitator of four- and five-day seminar classes, helping people to take more control of their lives. I worked with people regarding wealth consciousness, self-expression, and balancing the physical, the mental, the spiritual, and the emotional sides of their lives.

I loved every minute of it!

I traveled all over the United States and Canada with those seminars. I grew personally, made a tremendous contribution to other people's lives, and had a lot of fun. It was tough being a single mother and traveling so much, but that's what I chose to do. Those were great years— the most powerful and productive 13 years in my life. Then it was time for me to move on. Remember, I'm always desiring to do better and better.

I left the seminar field in 1989, not knowing what was next for me. I knew I didn't want to go back into traditional education, and for almost a year, I lived off my savings. I couldn't find a job. I got right down to rock-bottom.

I was in my late forties and found myself "over-qualified" for everything. I'd earned too much income in the past and was too educated. People didn't want to pay me what I knew I was worth.

That year was a major crossroads in my life. I had a son in college— at the cost of about $16,000 a year— so I decided to create a job for myself. I found a career as a sales trainer for an in-home alarm system.

You'll probably remember the product I was selling. Here's a clue: "Help! I've fallen and I can't get up!" Yup, I did *that*. I visited the homes of senior citizens or disabled people with that tremendous service. I traveled all over the western United States with that career, training many sales people along the way.

It didn't take me long to develop a six-figure income, but even as I was doing fine financially, I wasn't fulfilled. I'm a real team-player and that job required me to be the lone ranger. I worked almost exclusively with senior citizens, so I had virtually no peer interaction. It was hard work, and if someone didn't buy the $5,000 unit on the first appointment, then I'd lost the sale.

Please understand, the product was a very, *very* good emergency communication system which saved hundreds of thousands of people's lives, but it was classic pressure sales, and that's not who I am. The job was also unfair, because if I didn't make a sale that first time in someone's house, I never got a chance to see the person again. It's pretty difficult to develop enough trust and rapport in an hour or two for someone to hand over $5,000 for anything.

What's more, the very next day, the company would call and offer the very same product, to that very same person who just said "No" to me, for *50% less* than what I'd offered! The customer would buy from the company because they just saved $2,500, and I got no commission, even though I was the top salesperson for the company! I didn't like the way the game was being played— not win-win!

My father, Dr. Kermit Long— a minister who has been one of the greatest mentors, coaches and inspirations in my entire life— was 77 years old at the time. He called me on the phone and said, "I have good news for you." Ministers can say that.

I said, "What's that?"

He said, "Well, your step-mom and I have entered this new business. I want you to take a look at it."

I knew it was one of those "pyramid" things, so I told him, "Daddy, I'm just not interested. I can't imagine myself ever doing anything like *that*. People never make any money in it."

Then, my father the minister used the magic word. He asked, "Do you trust me?"

Well, I've always trusted my father. He asked me to come for an hour to a friend's house and just be open to what I saw and heard. He said, "Peggy, you've always been fair-minded. You taught that to people in your personal growth seminars for years. I can't imagine you not at least getting some first-hand knowledge before you make a decision— you know, research before you reject."

He was right, of course, so I went to a lovely home in Phoenix, Arizona. My dad and my stepmother, Helen, were there, as well as a few other people I knew.

When my father invited me to go look at the company he was involved in, I had planted my feet pretty deep in "No way." A few months before, I had gone into a networking membership service company for about a month, put $4,000 into it, and three weeks later it went belly up. I was out that money and that experience absolutely confirmed for me that MLM didn't work! It was only out of love and trust for him that I agreed to go check it out.

The company's product was an extensive line of high quality jewelry and I've never really been much into that. But I had plenty of money that December, so I decided I'd pamper myself for Christmas, do something special just for me *and* get my dad off my back at the same time. I bought a nice diamond tennis bracelet and some diamond earrings. I did hear about how an in-home business could give me some great tax benefits, but I really had no intention of making it my vocation. I signed the form, so I could get the jewelry at a discount, got a full 35% off the product and thought it was a pretty good deal.

That was all I was ever going to do with it— until the end of February in 1992 when I got downsized. The company decided to bring in six or eight new people. I was the best in the company, but they wanted to cut costs by paying lower commissions for less experienced salespeople. I was out.

The years with that company were an interesting two and a half years in my life, and even though I got downsized, that job kept my head above water financially and I'm grateful.

The company is no longer in operation today.

In any case, at that point I had to really think about what to do next. I was 50, and I knew how hard it was to find a good job at that age.

My folks had earned a couple of $500 weekly checks in their Networking business. I realized if my dad, who was then in his late seventies, could do that, maybe I could do it, too. So, I decided I would try it.

When I first started working with the business I was still pretty leery of the whole thing. I had my accountant and my lawyer go down to Tucson, Arizona, from Phoenix and check the company out. I thought, if I'm going to put my time and energy into something it better not go south or belly up on me in a few years. People trust me. People respect me. If I was truly going to share this opportunity with my friends— my closest confidants, my former seminar trainers— I had to know that it was really good. I would never lead anybody down a path of no return.

Well, my CPA and lawyer checked it out. When they saw how strong the company was and what a great opportunity there was, they came into the business with me right away! They said, "Peggy, you really don't know what you have here, do you?"

So I started working the business, but it was extremely slow at first. I absolutely was *not* an overnight success.

I actually got downsized while I was living up in Oregon. I'd been staying with my brother and sister-in-law's, Ken and Karen Long, when I got the "pink phone call." I didn't get a pink slip. I got a phone call, and that was that.

Karen, my "sister-in-love," saw that this business was something she could do, but my brother Ken was adamant. He said, "Don't you use my VCR to watch any of those videos and don't talk to any of my friends. If you do," he said, "you're ousted!"

Here's my brother who had been so supportive, who'd been there for me so many times with my boys, now against me. And I was staying in his home— wow!

But Karen saw enough value in what we were doing, and I shared with Karen that she could absolutely count on me. So Karen and I started the business while Kenny was off teaching school.

The very first week, Karen earned a $500 paycheck. She just couldn't believe it! Ken was still adamantly against it, and extremely negative and resistant. He was quite verbal about it, too. That was hard for me, but the sisters went forward.

What happened over the course of the next, oh, eight, nine months, was I found that I could easily sell people right into the business. But because I didn't understand duplication or have a system, I never showed the concept of time leveraging. I had no coach, no mentor, and I really didn't know what I was doing. I was just talking to everybody and anybody, trying to sell them in— "Buy some product, get in the business and we'll see how it works."

The company was so young then, we didn't have videos, audios, we didn't have any real training, so I was just out there "netblabbing." I was probably one of those people you hear about in network marketing that give it a bad reputation. I would talk to anybody, anywhere. That's a very good quality to have in this business, except I didn't know what I was doing— and obviously it really helps to know what you're doing.

All I did was tell people why they needed this opportunity. I did that by creating a lot of fear in people, although that's not who I am as a person. It was just that after two and a half years of operating out of that mode in the alarm business— fear is what I used to train people to use the alarms— I had simply carried that over into my new network marketing business without realizing I was doing it. I remember calling some friends of mine who trusted me, and they said, "Peggy, we can't believe you're doing this. You of all people!"

My money was dwindling. I had cleaned out my savings account by then, but I was hooked. I saw what was possible and I knew if I found a way to share this business and teach it more effectively and compassionately, bringing out more of who I am and what my life is really all about, I could make this happen.

But I was getting pretty scared. My savings were gone, I took everything out of my IRAs, and I maxed out every credit card I had. I was still going, but I was getting more and more fearful. It's very hard to go forward when all that fear is coming up.

I had five garage sales in six weeks and got down to one set of sheets, one set of towels. I sold my pots and pans. I cleaned out everything I didn't need just to survive. I even sold my original jewelry— sold my tennis bracelet for about $200 and it was worth $1,200! I did what I had to do.

I borrowed $40,000 from family and from friends who absolutely trusted me and told them I'd pay them back in a year at 12-15% interest. Hey, it was a good deal for them! But by then, I was really panicking. I thought, I'm about ready to lose my car and my house. They were the few things I had left!

In a month, I came back from Oregon to Phoenix, Arizona, once I got my sister-in-love up and started, because I had no job. I did send out some resumes, but I'd made the decision I was not going to allow anyone else to ever own my paycheck and my calendar again— no way! If I did that, they could always cut me off, downsize, let me go, and I'd be at ground zero all over again.

I was committed to network marketing, even though I was a baby in this industry and knew nothing about it. I had no real belief in network marketing to start with, and as my money started to disappear it was like, "Hey, does any of this stuff really work?"

I saw a few people earning some big money and realized that

something is fundamentally wrong with what I'm doing. They were working what I call the numbers game. They kept telling me to just keep talking to people. Just keep moving the product. Just get them in the business and, eventually, you're going to find a heavy hitter. That didn't feel right to me. I wouldn't operate out of that assumption, because people's lives are fragile and very important to me. I just couldn't keep shoving people into the system hoping some day somebody was going to wake up and run with it.

This was the summer of 1992. Our family has a beautiful island up in Northern Ontario, Canada, and I said, "I have two months." I stalled the car payments, house payments, and credit cards, and took two months to figure out a system to build my business.

The only book I'd ever read about Network Marketing was John Kalench's *Being The Best You Can be in MLM*. That was really my anchor and guiding light. That summer, I borrowed every book, tape, video, *everything* I could possibly get my hands on and took them with me to the island.

Most people thought that was a stupid move— they told me I should be out working the business. But I knew I had to get myself grounded and come up with a system that would work for me, not one based only on the numbers game. I didn't know any network marketing people, any obviously potential heavy hitters.

I spent a lot of time out on a boat and with nature and God, and allowed a source to come into me and figure out a system by reading, by studying, by praying and meditating. I was committed to this. I had to do it! I knew I couldn't go on financially the way I was. It was time for things to get better.

What I figured out in those two months is basically what this book is about.

I remembered years ago when I was involved in Psi World Seminars, a great mentor of mine once said,

"On this rock I stand and world you will adjust."

For some reason, that very powerful saying had never come back into my life until that summer, but when it did, it sure came back strong! "On this rock I stand . . ." is exactly what I started basing my business and the rest of my life on.

By the end of the two months, I had made the commitment.

Decisions can be changed, but a commitment is non-negotiable. Internally, I'd said I would never work for anyone else again, but I was up against the biggest rock-and-a-hard-place I've ever experienced in my life.

I came back to Arizona, and this is an interesting story:

I had sponsored some friends in Hawaii early in my business who had never done anything. In the beginning, I'd told them, "When you're ready, call me and I'll be there for you. You can count on me."

I got back from Canada to Arizona in September of '92, and I got a phone call from Hawaii. They said, "We're ready Peggy. Can you be over here in three days?" Now remember, I am flat-broke.

Because I put my word out there, I said, "Yes, I'll be there." On this rock I stand, and world you will adjust! When you're committed inside, the outside world will give you what you need.

The good book said, "Ask and it shall be given to you." I called Ken and Karen in Oregon, and I said, "I need a flight to Hawaii, and I need you to put it on your credit card and order $300 worth of supplies from the company and have it shipped to this address."

They said, "Are you crazy?"

I said, "Nope. I'm going. I'm going to trust my intuition. Ken and Karen, you can count on me. All this production from Hawaii will be under you." I gave them value.

My Hawaiian friends had been through the same Psi seminars I had done, and I knew them to be high integrity people— action-oriented, strong communicators, and super problem-solvers.

So, off I went to Hawaii.

When they heard I was coming, they said, "This is great! We're going to put you up in a great hotel down on the beach at Waikiki." Now, I knew that was about $175 a night, which of course I didn't have, so, I said, "That would be beautiful, but you know, I need to have a real working relationship with you. The best thing for me to do is to move right in with you and really work closely with you."

Well, she was eight months pregnant, they didn't have enough room— yak, yak, yak— and that didn't work.

Then I asked, "Who's the first person you want to sponsor and develop as a strong leader?" They told me Corliss and Marvin Tang. I didn't know them, but they knew me from my seminar work years ago. I said, "You have to get me to stay with them. Hawaii needs a leader before I go back to the mainland."

I didn't even know the Tangs and here I was moving into their house!

In with Corliss and Marvin I went. That first night, they had a barbecue and we turned it into a presentation meeting. They had no flip charts. Nothing. All we had was this great big cardboard box, and I wrote all over the four sides of it. I showed them the concept of network marketing and focused on value— what's in it for them. I explained the comp plan and leveraging time.

That night, we sponsored five out of seven people.

In a matter of 12 days, we sponsored over 300.

I got about two hours sleep each night, but— on this rock I stand, world you will adjust! We were up until four and five every morning, because I had to leave Hawaii and I wanted to have my leaders in place.

Here's something interesting: When I was in Hawaii, they all thought I was earning lots of money. They had no idea that when I arrived I had only $12 in my pocket. When someone carries themselves well— and they know that they know that they know how to teach and train this business with a system— they'reconfident, they're competent and they're clear with their communication. People are not going to ask, "How much are you earning?" I never had anybody in Hawaii ask me what I was earning.

Shortly after I got home, I went to British Columbia to move in with Donna and Jason Haugh and do the same thing I'd done with the Tangs in Hawaii. I had my Hawaiian leg established, developed another leg out of British Columbia, and then was able to go into Winnipeg, San Francisco, and Toronto and do the exact same thing. It was a simple process of moving into a home and developing one leader who then develops the next leader and so on down building and growing the organization. By June of 1993, I had became a Diamond with the company.

My first year in the business, I earned $7,000, spending well over $60,000 to do it!

My second year in my business, I was up to $215,000.

The third year, I reached approximately $400,000 in earned income, plus automobiles I earned through the company's car allowance program, cruises and a beautiful desert home. But it wasn't about the material things for me. I've had those in my life. What it was and is about, is me being able to bring myself, bring my life— bring my *contribution*— into an arena that now was absolutely working for hundreds and hundreds of other people. That's what made it work for me— not numbers, but putting other people first.

I now live a lifestyle of tremendous choices— and liberty. What liberty means to me, is being able to go where I want to go when I want to go. To do what I want to do when I want to do it. To be who I want to be when I want to be it. To have what I want to have when I want to have it. That's what liberty is. Be— Do— Have!

I can take my 81-year-old dad to Mexico, take him Marlin fishing— a dream he has always had. (And, yes, he did catch his first Marlin— at age 81.) I can give a hundred thousand dollars to the charities of my choice. I can take my children wherever I want, attend any personal growth seminar I want, I can give my time to the Upline® Masters Seminars.

I can do all this because I have the time and money— and they're both all mine.

I spend five months of the year now up at my cottage in Canada. I can get up when I want to get up. For me, it's the "rollover or roll out" business. I can work— when I choose to work— out of the comfort of my own home or cottage. I can hire someone to come in and teach me to use the computer without having to fumble around for months trying to figure it out. I have full and true choices in my life now. I am no longer that chameleon I used to be.

On this rock I stand, and world you will adjust!

Let's go start duplicating and becoming leaders of leaders!

Chapter 1

Network Marketing is the Best!

I believe network marketing is the greatest business in the world because of the choices people are able to create in their lives in so short a time. Instead of working for 40 years to reach freedom, you can do it in only four years—when you stay committed.

There are also many extra goodies that come with network marketing besides just the cash. I'm talking about personal growth, great new relationships and re-established relationships. My baby-sitter from 25 years ago, Margaret Craven, came into my business. Years ago, I trusted her to watch my children, so now she trusts our family to teach her duplication. Network marketing is not about information, it's about *transformation*. Network marketing allows people to own their businesses, their time and their lives—it gives them freedom.

It's Your Choice

People have different reasons for choosing to do this business. I've learned that it's important to know *why* each person is making the choice, because network marketing is not just a business, it's a way

OPPORTUNITYISNOWHERE
OPPORTUNITYISNOWHERE
OPPORTUNITYISNOWHERE
OPPORTUNITYISNOWHERE
OPPORTUNITYISNOWHERE
OPPORTUNITYISNOWHERE
OPPORTUNITYISNOWHERE

of life. It has a value beyond what you get from a traditional career. Since network marketing has the power to meet and surpass most people's financial expectations, in order to truly succeed, we each need to have higher goals fueling our actions. We must be stronger in valuing *contribution* than in valuing *cash* in order to be incredible leaders in this field.

Where there is no faith in the future, there is no power in the present. You need to seize every opportunity available in network marketing. I have a beautiful tile on my cottage wall that I see every day. It reads: Seize the Day!!! Are you seizing every day in your network marketing business? If not, WHY NOT?

Network marketing is the best because it *brings out* the very best in people. It brings out expanded leadership, increased confidence, excellence in communication. It brings out choices based on character.

I have a sign in my office which says, "Your choices reflect your character." Network marketing is like a mirror—in front of you all the time—showing you that what you see in yourself is what you manifest and create in the world. Network marketing encourages and supports us in becoming better people—*when* they choose the path of greatness, of personal growth, of making a difference, of contribution. All the highest, best and greatest qualities in people absolutely expand in this business.

If you don't want that, then network marketing isn't for you. Life is about choices. Most people fall into one of three categories:

Those who make things happen!

Those who watch things happen and

Those who ask, "What happened?"

Which one are you committed to being?

Living and Working Your Purpose

It took me about two and a half years in network marketing to become clear about why I'm alive on this planet. It has nothing to do with earning money. My whole value in living is in my vision/purpose statement which says:

"I compassionately create our world being abundant through my leadership, my integrity, my contribution and my inspiration."

For most of my life, I wasn't able to shine and fully live my purpose. This incredible industry of network marketing offered me the abundance of my own purpose. When I talk about abundance, I'm referring to an abundance of knowledge, an abundance of experiences, an abundance of relationships, as well as an abundance of money. I think too many people put the focus only on cash. Is that important? Yes, but it will come absolutely out of your contribution, giving, knowingness and beingness. It's so simple:

If you want to get more, give more.

It takes time for someone to develop those qualities to the point where they are integrated fully. Network marketing allows people to live life with no strings attached and nobody dictating or demanding. It's totally up to you, just like the saying: "If it is to be, it's up to me." Network marketing puts the accountability right back into the soul of the person who has chosen it.

And the payoff for that?

Time.

I frequently use the expression, "It's a just a matter of time for total money and time freedom." Time creates liberty and 100% choice in a person's life. And it truly is *just a matter of time*—as long as someone doesn't quit. You can even take some sabbaticals—many people do—and still reach money and time freedom.

The Earth Needs Network Marketing

We always talk about the United States being the melting pot, but the truth is network marketing is much more so. Network marketing overcomes so many walls and barriers between people. In network marketing, people get to know people. Prejudices are totally eliminated through the teamwork needed for success.

I have a favorite quote from Joseph Newton. He says, "People are lonely because they build walls instead of bridges." Network marketing is about building bridges between people and teams and organizations, between countries and all around the world. I believe network marketing is the bridge to co-operative, instead of competitive, business.

Just in case you don't see how time and money freedom could make a difference, read the following scenario. If we could shrink the earth's population to a village of precisely 100 people, with all the existing human ratios we have today remaining the same, it would look like this:

There would be . . .
- 57 Asians. Asia is a fast-growing networking market. Would our business benefit from worldwide expansion? Are you already there?

- 21 Europeans. Many European countries are just discovering our great industry. Is your company expanding internationally?

- 14 from the Western Hemisphere (North and South America).

- 8 Africans. Do you have something to offer people with few traditional options for wealth?

- 51 females, 49 males. Check out recent statistics on women-owned businesses and their successes. Do you know any women who are good with people and would appreciate extra income?

- 70 non-whites, 30 whites.

- 70 non-Christians, 30 Christians. Network marketing actually promotes ideas common to many religions: The value of integrity; generosity; love for others.

- 50% of the entire world's wealth would be in the hands of only 6 people (all 6 would be citizens of the United States).

- 80 would live in substandard housing.

- 50 would suffer from malnutrition. These 2 are both due to poverty. Traditional industries haven't been able to solve the problem, but network marketing is wealth-generating—enough for the entire world.

- 70 would be unable to read.

- 1 would be near death, 1 would be near birth.

- Only 1 would have a college education.

- No one would own a computer.

Do you see any way to make a difference with your business? How fortunate each of us is just to be able to own and read this book! Through network marketing, you can contribute to making our world a better place for all the people on our planet. Are you willing?

I asked myself that question again just recently when I was visiting a church in Lebanon, Oregon. The minister, Pastor Kate, really spoke to me through her sermon when she said, "Please don't die while you are still alive." I AM willing to contribute to our world, and I rejoice that network marketing brings out the life in me. I celebrate the gift of being truly alive. How about you?

The Two Kinds of People in Network Marketing

There are two kinds of people who make the decision to enter a network marketing company and this way of life. The first kind stays on the path no matter how long it takes. That's the mark of a true leader—somebody who's able to do *whatever* it takes for however *long* it takes. Those are the people who will achieve success.

Is this business a rose garden? Absolutely not! There may even be more thorns, more detours, more delays in network marketing than in many other kinds of work. This business puts each representative right up against the obstacles that have blocked him or her from success in other jobs, other careers and even in life. A leader stays the course regardless of the challenges.

Network marketing is truly a place to master your attitude. When you approach a prospect, from either the warm or cold market, you are going to be attacked by Dream Stealers. You will allow them to

pull you down and back, or you will propel yourself forward. The following cartoon is one I use in all my beginning training. I even give it to new team members to put on their refrigerators to keep them charged and going forward.

Then there's the other kind of person, the one who quits as soon as the going gets rough. They don't achieve success.

I am not one of those, and, if you're reading this, probably neither are you. Enough said.

We all know the expression, "The grass is always greener on the other side of the fence." Not true. It might look greener, because you have not planted, watered, weeded and maintained your own grass like you should. The greatest leaders and highest earners in our industry always tell you to stay with one company and make it big. Becoming a jumper or MLM junkie gives our industry a bad reputation-all that does is turn the grass brown.

If someone is very self-centered, egotistical, doesn't give a darn about other people, I don't want them in our industry. I certainly don't want them in my business or my company. I ask people questions before I even begin to sponsor them or when I work with a representative someone else has sponsored. In this business, one negative person can drag everyone down.

I'm not talking about someone who doesn't have belief—that takes a while. People can lack belief and still be positive. Their character will see them through. I absolutely believe the network marketing proverb:

This business will either promote you or expose you.

You Are Your Own Boss

Another great asset of network marketing is that you are your own boss, you are your own president, you are the CEO of your own company.

When I do monthly conference calls, I absolutely love being introduced as the president and CEO of my own company, Peggy Long, Inc. It feels good, it's factual, and it also demands that I take responsibility.

In network marketing, you are able to choose your work, your hours, your partnerships. When I was in the alarm sales business, I used to have to train people in high-pressure sales, many of whom were negative people I didn't really want to be with. On top of that, I didn't like the work I was training them to do. It was about high pressure, not relationships, but I didn't have a choice about any of it. It was all part of my job—like it or not. And I didn't!

This business encourages you to expand who you are by listening to personal development tapes and attending seminars. You can be around big players in life, people who are making a difference. If you get a little *discouraged*, it's okay. It's okay to get *disappointed* sometimes, to have delays, but it is never okay to be *defeated*. The "three Ds" are really okay, but the deadly "D" of defeat will kill your business. **God's delays are not God's denials.**

In a regular job, if you have a negative person next to you, you can't choose to leave for two days until they get over their pity party. Network marketing lets you avoid the politics of traditional jobs. You never have to watch your back to see if someone is going to stab you. The pressure of other people's demands is absent. You answer only to yourself. In network marketing, if you get discouraged, you can slow down, pull back for a couple of days and rebuild yourself. I have found that combining freedom and responsibility creates greater dedication. Without all those external demands, people in network marketing are actually more productive and more purposeful.

Here are some of Networking's Key Values:

- Be your own boss.
- Work with whom you want.
- Work when you want.
- Tax benefits.
- No commute.
- No inventory.
- No employees.
- No payroll.
- Small overhead.
- Minimal start-up cost.
- Free vacations.
- Free cars.
- Unlimited income potential.
- Completely transportable.
- Potentially permanent, residual income.

Independence, Security or Freedom?

There are big differences between financial independence, financial security and financial freedom. Let me share how I define each one.

Financial independence is not working for anyone else. You would be totally dependent on your own efforts to create your income—your own president, CEO, your own boss.

In the April 1998 issue of *SUCCESS* magazine, there was the statement that two out of three workers—roughly 73%—considered going it alone, starting their own businesses. Other percentages listed were:

- 8% want to leave their current job or employer.
- 3% don't know why, they just have a feeling or intuition to go.
- 21% want to earn more money.
- 12% want to have more leisure time.
- 56% want more independence.

Network marketing addresses all of those. We have to find those people and present our opportunity to them. They are fully awake and will say to us, "What the heck took you so long to show me this business? It's just what I want and need."

Network marketing creates a lifestyle of choices. In my experience, most people don't have that. They have to go to work, they have to punch a clock, and even if they own their business, as lawyers and doctors often do, they're still trading hours for dollars. They are not leveraging their time; they're not working with a whole group of people where everybody's skills, everybody's talents, everybody's efforts support everybody else in having time freedom and money freedom.

Financial security is something many people have. Many of them are also independent. Professionals have money, and most of them have planned for their retirement, as well as their present needs. Unfortunately, many of them are also burned out. They have to keep working to maintain the income their plans and arrangements require. Most have employee costs, high overhead, insurance for themselves, their employees and their business.

What do they want?

They want the real rock of network marketing—financial freedom. That means having both the money *and* the time to enjoy it—easily the most common reason for any of us to be in this industry.

It's a fun industry. I don't like to call it a job; it's more than that. It's a fun way to be. Of course, there's tremendous work involved, but it's still great fun.

To Achieve Your Network Marketing Dreams, Remember Your ABC's:

- **A**void negative sources, people, places, things and habits.
- **B**elieve in yourself.
- **C**onsider things from every angle.
- **D**on't give up and don't give in.
- **E**njoy life today; yesterday is gone and tomorrow may never come.
- **F**amily and friends are treasures. Seek them and enjoy their riches.
- **G**ive more than you planned to give.
- **H**ang onto your dreams.
- **I**gnore those who try to discourage you.
- **J**ust do it!
- **K**eep on going. No matter how hard it seems, it will get easier.
- **L**ove yourself first and most.
- **M**ake it happen.
- **N**ever lie, cheat or steal. Always strike a fair deal.
- **O**pportunities are there if we want them to be.
- **P**ractice makes permanent.
- **Q**uitters never win, and winners never quit.
- **R**ead, study and learn about everything important in life.
- **S**top procrastinating.
- **T**ake control of your own destiny.
- **U**nderstand yourself in order to better understand others.
- **V**isualize it.
- **W**ant it more than anything.
- **X**ccelerate you efforts.
- **Y**ou are unique of all God's creations. Nothing can replace you.
- **Z**ealous devotion to accomplishing your goals.

Going Back to School

Does anyone know of a four-year college where you could graduate and then retire in one to five years at better than a $100,000 salary per year? I have never heard of one. No one anywhere can come up with a college course where that is even a remote possibility.

That's what is so exciting about network marketing. You can actually learn in six months and get your belief level strong in a year.

Do you remember when you were in college and you went to the bookstore to buy your books for the quarter? They were big, heavy textbooks and cost a lot of money. You could hardly wait to get back to your room to start studying them. While you were in school, did anyone pay you for going to school? Since you went to college for four years without getting paid, since you had no hope of retiring in one to five years, then you should not be concerned with how little you have made in your first few years in your network marketing company.

Remember, when you first start, you are in school. You are in the network marketing school, and you are in your company's school. I give a *Going Back to School* handout to people, so they're very clear that this is not a get rich quick scheme.

Some people get discouraged after the first few months. I don't think they have a right to be discouraged until they have been in business for one to three years. Try letting a medical student operate on you after they have been in school just a year or two. They have to go through an internship, and that's what the first few years of network marketing is. Ask a doctor, a lawyer, a dentist, a CPA or any other professional person how long they've been practicing their profession, and their answer will be figured from the day they graduated—not from their first day in college. When you ask someone in network marketing how long they have been in the business, they will tell you from the first day that they signed their representative agreement form. You should keep track of the time you are actually in the business beginning from the time that you knew what you were doing. Compare that to a doctor, who graduated and did a full internship before going into practice.

When someone chooses to work this part time, that's okay, but they can't expect rapid development if they build in just their spare or hobby time. Working part time is five to ten hours a week which requires full-time attitude and action. It is so easy to get pulled off and not be disciplined, because most of us work out of our homes. When a networker isn't disciplined, all kinds of interruptions will cause them to lose focus. When they don't like what they are doing, or it's tough, they decide to leave their business time and read the paper, walk the dog, sweep the porch, prepare dinner earlier than necessary or take a nap.

Let me ask you this: If you are a bank teller, pharmacist, mechanic, chef or any other professional, could you get up and do all that other activity? Of course the answer is NO! As you're building for your future and financial freedom, you must keep your priorities in focus. Rick Mears says, "To finish first you must first finish." The rock to stand on is: Never let down and never let up.

The F* Words!

When someone is rushed to the hospital with a critical injury, all the medical people know it's a life or death situation. They drop any less important tasks to save the person's life. I believe you have to have the same approach to your business. I coach people in the

Critical Three that lead to death in this business:

1. Fear of Failure.
2. Fear of Rejection.
3. Frustration.

The key to treating the Critical Three so people don't quit is to get through them fast and often. That means you have to be what I call an emotional giant.

We all have the choice of being emotional jerks or emotional giants. Emotional giants face challenging situations head on. They get experience and preparation for handling the Critical Three, and the *F* words* don't get a chance to kill their business. I believe it can become as easy as turning a light switch on and off. You have to start by recognizing the Critical Three and treating them immediately.

Fear of failure ties self-esteem and self-worth to results. I don't believe a person's *self*-worth is anywhere the same as *net* worth.

I remember when I was really struggling financially. I still had self-worth and self-esteem. I coach leaders to separate results from their self-esteem and not be attached to results. Instead of beating themselves up over small paychecks, lost prospects or shaky front-of-the-room presentations, real leaders learn from each experience and move forward.

Don't compare yourself to someone who is doing "better." When you start looking for comparisons, there is always going to be someone better—and there is going to be someone worse, as well. *So what?*

My folks had a little jingle they would say to me when I was small:
There's so much bad in the best of us
And so much good in the worst of us,
It hardly behooves any of us
To talk about the rest of us.

This has stayed in my heart and mind for over 50 years and keeps me out of the trap of comparison.

Network marketing gives you the luxury of being your own gold standard, so, simply compare your results to your own best potential: Can you do better next time you prospect . . . call . . . present . . . follow up? Good! Do it! Keep moving forward.

Fear of Failure

Most people never notice someone who is doing worse than they are. They look at someone who is being and doing better in this industry, and the comparison makes them feel lesser, like a failure. The fear of failure can absolutely paralyze and freeze you from moving forward.

Most of us have learned, in everything from church to school to sports, that failure is negative. I don't believe that's true in network marketing. I fail a lot. I sin a lot. I tell people to go sin, sin, sin and then sin some more.

Sounds crazy, doesn't it?

See, most people don't know where the word *sin* comes from. It comes from the Romans, who used to compete in archery tournaments. Everybody wanted to hit the goal in the center, the bulls-eye, but not everyone could do that every time. When somebody would shoot and miss the goal, they had *sinned*, the Latin word meaning "to miss the mark."

I say you are going to fail. You are going to make mistakes. You are going to sin in this endeavor before you have the results that you deserve and desire. When someone is failing or someone is making mistakes, I know they are going forward. Only then can I— as a coach—put in some corrections. If someone is so paralyzed and so fearful of failing they do little or nothing, there's no action for me to correct and adjust. How are they ever going to move forward from there?

Look how many times a baby falls while learning to walk. Each of us landed on our diapered bottoms for a year before we were steady on our feet. It's okay with me if representatives are failing. As long as they don't fear failure, I rejoice. I think it's wonderful if they make mistakes, because then I know where to coach and direct them. Take one, take two, take three. . . . "Miss-takes," just like the movies.

Do you know how the recipe for Tootsie Roll candy was discovered? A man in Pennsylvania was making a batch of his famous chocolates. He left the factory for a while and let the chocolate overcook until it was badly burned.

"Oh my gosh!" thought the candy maker, "I have to throw away all this expensive chocolate and waste all that cooking time."

Then, acting on a gut hunch (the male version of intuition), he decided to taste the burned chocolate. It tasted so good that he started selling it as a new product in his candy store. That one "mistake" led to continuing success which has spread around the world.

Fear of Rejection

The second F of the Critical Three is the fear of rejection. We're all brought up with rejection.

From the time we are small, we learn that if we don't do something right, someone makes fun of us. I had a wonderful mother, Betty Shumway, who always did the best she could. I don't fault her for making me only two dresses each year; there wasn't money for more. But I was so embarrassed with them, and felt so rejected, that I would almost want to hide. I finally decided to ignore how I looked in my handmade dresses and achieve in other areas. I became very good in athletics and in school. I was overcoming those people who put me down for how I dressed.

Everyone can remember choosing teams for sports and playground games. One team captain said, "I'll take you," and another captain said, "I'll take you." There were always a few kids who got chosen last every time. They would decide right then that they weren't good enough, based on being picked last.

Then there are school grades. If our grades aren't good enough in school, a teacher or parent—or both—will say you need to work harder and do better. Then you feel rejected. That same pattern is absolutely carried with us as adults.

When people choose to come into network marketing, they find it's a bigger mirror than they've ever experienced in any other occupation, grade, career, or profession. You get to see your patterns quickly and clearly here. It makes us face all those old fears of rejection and programming of beliefs that we are not good enough and not really worthy of being somebody.

The good news is that the essence of this incredible industry is reaching out to each other and acknowledging the greatness in others. That's how you can change those old patterns of rejection.

The Finger of Responsibility

Before we go on to discuss the third F* word—frustration— I'd like to go into the idea of rejection with a bit more depth.

One of the most common reactions people have about rejection is pointing the finger of blame at someone else. I coach people to look at their hands as they do.

There is one finger pointing out and three coming back.

One of those fingers points to our own responsibility. Nobody can reject us and put us down without our permission—our acceptance of their evaluation of who we are.

As Eleanor Roosevelt said, "Remember no one can make you feel inferior without your consent."

The other fingers point back to us internally and externally, to our excuses and arguments. We can take things inside and beat ourselves up and put the business down. That's the internal damage. Or, we can react externally by being argumentative and defiant to the person we are sharing the business with.

The only way to become a leader and create great results is to follow the finger that points to our own responsibility. Each of the other options stops people, either externally or internally.

What I work with people to see—and what I had to work on with myself—is that there is no rejection. We just make that up. *We* bring that to the party—what Carol McCall, the great personal development trainer with the Empowerment of Listening course, would call our listening agenda. You may have your own "hidden agenda" getting in the way of your success.

My son Jordan realized this when he waited tables. He'd pop up to someone and say, "Would you like a cup of coffee?" People would say "No" or "Later" or "Yes" or "No thanks, I'd rather have tea."

Jordan saw that people were making their own choices, not rejecting him. He could have gotten depressed and negative when they turned down his offer of coffee, but he would be making up that rejection. He would be taking it personally.

When he came into this business, he decided to handle things the same way. If someone said, "No" to the opportunity, Jordan chose not to take it as rejection.

I'm fond of little reminders we can carry with us. If we each carry a Q-tip, it reminds us to Quit Taking It Personally—QTIP. It should also remind us to clean out our ears and listen better.

A friend of mine has a great little technique for times when his thinking and attitude are neither positive nor serving him. When he catches what he calls his "stinking thinking," he shouts, "STOP IT" out loud. It's a win for him internally to cease and desist behavior and feelings that don't expand his beingness and greatness.

Another tangible technique I coach people to use is to put a rubber band on their wrist and snap it whenever they become aware of their attitude being off. That little sting reminds them that a sour attitude damages them and those around them.

The rubber band also creates interest from others, and they ask about it. You could say, "I'm in a business that creates big incomes when we take charge of our attitude."

If you don't break the chains of your bad mental and emotional habits, or self-defeating hidden agendas, while you're alive, do you think ghosts will do it afterwards? Being responsible and accountable for our thinking is a rock we all need to stand on.

Mom Got Rejected, Too

My biggest business struggle with rejection started with my sons. They both resisted this business for three years. They fought me and tore me down. They thought what I was doing was stupid.

In fact, they were just concerned for Mom. They saw me not earning money, and they were afraid I was going to lose everything and be homeless. Well, they knew I wouldn't go quite that far, because I'm a survivor, but that's where their pictures were going.

That's what *they* made up. I had the choice of accepting that as rejection of me personally or simply as their incomplete view of this business. I made the choice to see it as not their cup of coffee—yet.

It's your choice to feel rejected. Rejection is not a thought, it's a feeling. Somebody says to you, "I'm not interested in this opportunity," and your heart sinks. You feel something and have a physical manifestation in your stomach. Then you have thoughts about it. Those thoughts are where you get the rejection. That's where you make stuff up. That's where you take it personally.

It's a physical sensation, a disappointment that the person is saying "No." Listening with an agenda of expectation sets you up for upset because you want them to say "Yes." If they don't, then your flood of thoughts creates rhyme and reason for why they are saying "No." We make it personal. That's the crazy part. That's where I coach people to remember Jordan's coffee/tea example. Don't make it personal—it isn't!

Feelings have no power unless we give it to them. They're just feelings. You can just as easily undo the feeling by using your mind. When you recognize that those thoughts and gut reactions have no power unless you give it to them, you can choose to wipe them away. On their own, they are nothing.

Here is a question to ask so you never experience rejection again. When a prospect says "No" or "Not now," simply ask them if you can ask a question. Most will say "Yes." Then ask your prospect, "Are you rejecting me?" They'll say, "No, of course not!" They may even tell you what is really in their way. You might learn enough to handle their concern and replace it with value.

In any case, you'll never feel rejected again. You'll know it isn't about you. The question will support you in remembering not to take it personally.

The Third F* Word—Frustration

I was so frustrated the first 13 months of my business. I was angry with myself, because I *knew* I could do this—I just didn't have a system. When someone gets too frustrated, they start burning out. They start saying to themselves, "I'm not good enough, I can't do this." Frustration, like rejection, can freeze you and stop you from moving forward.

The key to moving past frustration is to be able to communicate. A coach or a sponsor needs to be a sounding board, but people don't get to "sewer" you. I don't let anyone dump negativity on me. That's what I call *sewering*. Too many people in this industry sewer all over others. Too many of those others just say, "Oh, get over it. You know, let it go." That doesn't work any better than the sewering.

Someone who is frustrated needs to be able to release it within themselves, not by someone else just telling them to stop that behavior. How many times have we seen little children continuing their behavior even after an adult says "No"? A little child will go near a hot burner, and Mom will say, "Don't touch that! It's hot!" Until they put their little hand on that burner and feel the impact and the pain, they aren't convinced. After touching the hot burner, the child will never try it again. The pain is a better reminder than any words.

I think that can be true of developing yourself into being a great networker. There can be a lot of pain in learning not to replay certain situations in our lives. With frustration, you need to be able to communicate and see what part you played in it. How did you manifest it?

"On this rock I stand and, World, you will adjust." That can be negative. That can be positive. That can be result-oriented or not; it doesn't matter. What matters is that you see for yourself how you got burned and how not to set it up to happen again.

(I'll talk later about the ways I coach people through frustrations using questions.)

It's All a Choice

Frustration can be stopped if a person chooses to stop it. It is all choice. It really doesn't have that much to do with the upline or the company. It doesn't have to do with the product. It has to do with your being willing to go through frustration to get to the other side.

I continually ask people, "Are you willing?"

If they say "No," great! It just isn't the time for me to talk to them.

I reply, "As soon as you are willing to get through this, call me back."

I don't listen to a lot of stories, because most stories have no power and produce no results. The only worthwhile story is one that inspires or creates action in somebody. Most people, if they have a problem and get frustrated, start telling negative drama stories, and I do not listen to them. I wait for their willingness to return—that's when people start moving forward and taking accountability for solutions.

Willingness is everything—willingness to be a success, willingness to go forward or willingness to start up again. "Today is the first day of my network marketing business. This minute is the first minute of my network marketing business." That's the attitude and the action you have to take. Your willingness creates far more results than all the skills you possess.

For most people, the three F's surface often during their first year in the business. In fact, Mark and Rene Yarnell cover the Critical Three—the F* words—in their latest must-read book, *Your First Year in Network Marketing*. Whenever there is a change, major or minor, within a company, the F's usually resurface until representatives are back in alignment and rock solid with their belief. I like to use the word BE-LIVE!

The Power of Your Mind

Why does what you fear tend to show up in your life? I got the answer to this out of my 13 years of work with Brian Klemmer in the Psi seminars. Brian now has his own personal-growth seminar called Personal Mastery, and I recommend it when I'm coaching a new team member. Brian uses the concept "to think is to create." The power of our mind is so strong that if we think something long enough, it's going to manifest or be created on the outside in our lives.

Napoleon Hill talks about this in his classic, *Think and Grow Rich*. All of the greatest people in this industry work with the power of the mind. They train people to understand that we can think our success into reality. I work particularly with replacing unproductive thinking with positive thinking and taking action.

Unproductive thinking undermines, blocks, inhibits and derails your vision and results. This is a great place for taking responsibility for your own successes—we need to get out of our own way. In essence, this is a place where you can sponsor yourself. Network marketing truly allows you to sponsor yourself into success.

Daily and hourly, sometimes minute to minute, I choose to recreate a picture of my goals in my own mind. I choose to practice controlling my thought process, and because it's not easy, I have to do it continually.

Some people choose passive resistance and say, "I don't really care. I don't want to control my thinking." They experience chaos, upset, crap, junk and lack of results in their world. As within, so without. They don't take responsibility for creating all of it.

I don't have 100% control of my thought processes, although I wish I did. I have to constantly make the conscious choice to stop and alter my thought process when it is not productive, when it's not coming out of contribution and when my thoughts are not on my purpose.

Unproductive Thought

There are two reasons people undermine themselves with careless, unproductive thought. First of all, they are unaware and just don't know they're doing it. We absorb so much negativity and violence from the media—the papers, radio, TV. I won't even sit in the room when certain negative TV shows are on. I leave.

It takes intense discipline to stop unproductive, unhealthy things from coming into your mind and consciousness. When my thinking does go sour, I go back to my vision and my purpose statement. My purpose statement gets me back on focus—one of the strong values to creating your life's purpose.

Feeling rejected is an example of unproductive thought. Nobody really ever rejects us. They might say no, it might not be for them, the timing might not be right, you might not have created enough value. You might have been telling and selling rather than asking questions (and I'll deal much more with that later in this book). People allow the fear of rejection to stop them.

Carol McCall, in her *Empowerment of Listening* tapes, talks about the four groups of people we encounter. She learned this from one of her mentors, Buckminster Fuller.

Mr. Fuller said there are four kinds of people in the world: People who are asleep; people who are asleep, but stirring; people who have just awakened; and people who are wide awake.

Have you ever tried to talk to someone who's sound asleep? How about having a conversation with someone who's just coming out of sleep, but hasn't fully opened her eyes yet? Can you have a deep and detailed conversation about an important subject with someone who just woke up a minute ago?

Many people present their business and their products to people who are not awake yet. They're not conscious of what's happening in their life and in the world. Most of those people say "No." Yet the representative takes it as rejection. Those prospects are simply not conscious.

What can you do?

Go out and get more rejection. Yes! Yes! Yes!

As people come into the business, I share with them that rejection can help them learn and grow. The more rejection you experience without letting it freeze you, the more staying power you'll have. Staying power will give you results.

Can You Learn To Be a Success?

Can anyone make it in network marketing? I believe so. Education, experience, ethnic background, age and gender don't matter. I have a lady on my team who was on welfare, with two little children and a brand new nursing baby. She got so committed that she cleaned 17 houses, with those three kids beside her, to create the money for her starter-pack and products. She was not going to stay where she was. She saw enough value in the opportunity that she was willing to break out and change her life.

If someone isn't willing, we can't make it happen for them.

Can anyone be a success? Yes, but it has to do with their willingness, and it *is* always a matter of time. You must DECIDE!

- Decide to Network
- Use every letter you write,
- Every conversation you have,
- Every meeting you attend

- To express your fundamental belief and dreams.
- Affirm to others the Vision of the World You Want.
- Network through thought,
- Network through action,
- Network through love,
- Network through spirit.
- You are the center of a network.
- You are the center of the world.
- You are a free, immensely powerful source of Life and Goodness.
- Affirm it. Spread it. Radiate it.
- Think day and night about it,
- And you will see a miracle happen.
- The greatness of your own life
- In a world of big powers, media
- And monopolies.
- But of four and a half billion individuals,
- This is the new freedom,
- The new democracy.
- This is the new form of Happiness.

(Adapted by Erik Rasmussen from Dr. Robert Muller's *Decide to Network*)

Why Should *You* Choose Network Marketing?

In addition to the time and money freedom this industry gives us, part of your reason for being in network marketing should be to become—notice how I use many words with *be*: *be*gin, *be*come, *be*ware—a greater human *be*ing than you are today. That's the nature of the business. Personal growth is inherent in network marketing. Expanded leadership, improved communication, becoming a better contributor to other people and communities, acknowledging other people, having more abundance of confidence—that's part of the gravy that comes with this industry.

When you sponsor others, you need to know if these are things that they would choose. They need to be willing to explore this and have it be a part of their new business—leadership, commitment, *be*lief, integrity. Have these conversations and communications with a brand new representative, and then you can start coaching.

Usually the money and the time freedom are the first benefits people see. That's what wakes people up and catches their interest. But this industry is far, far more than that. That needs to be explored very early when they become a representative so they understand that there is going to be a life-learning process and a lifelong relationship.

A powerful team of networkers in Oklahoma says it like this:

"They come in the business for the time and money.
What keeps them in the business are relationships."

The moment we start our relationship with a prospect is our best opportunity to build a strong and lasting foundation for partnership and friendship.

Commitment to People

In time the strongest reason people choose network marketing is the commitment to other people. You are going to be making a difference in people's lives. You are going to be a point of light. You are going to be like the little pebble that's tossed into a lake and causes ripples. The stronger and more committed a person becomes in this industry, the stronger their ripple. The pebble becomes a rock. Rocks move mountains and rocks create wealth for others and self.

The greatest leaders in networking have causes that are higher, more powerful than any single person. They give their time and money to charities. Building wings on hospitals. Establishing scholarships. Volunteering in schools. Prison ministry. Homeless shelters. What is your favorite?

You don't have to know exactly which causes to support when you first come into the business, but you do need to be open to the idea. You need to be willing to think beyond filling your own immediate financial needs, to look for a higher calling to keep you on the upward path of network marketing.

This industry offers many kinds of success. We have many people in this industry that don't need the money. They're already financially set up. They are coming in for totally different reasons. Perhaps they need an arena of support, of personal growth. Perhaps they need a place where they can contribute. We have millionaires in this business who are tired of however they created their money before. They want their own schedule. They don't want a clock. They want to work when they want to work.

This industry is totally about empowering and making a difference in supporting people into a purpose in life. Network marketing is your path to your purpose. You know when someone has a purpose for living—they become much clearer on the choices they make. They know immediately if that choice positively affects their purpose or if it's detracting from their purpose. Choices and decisions become simple when you make them from your purpose/vision statement. Then you stay on your path of life.

- What is life?
- Life is a gift. Accept it.
- Life is an adventure. Dare it.
- Life is a mystery. Unfold it.
- Life is a game. Play it full out.
- Life is a struggle. Face it.
- Life is beauty. Praise it.
- Life is a puzzle. Solve it.
- Life is opportunity. Seize it.
- Life is loss. Experience it.
- Life is a song. Sing it.
- Life is a goal. Achieve it.
- Life is a mission. Fulfill it.

Part of what I do is toss huge rocks into that body of water that is also a body of life. I commit to creating a ripple effect on more and more people. I look for others who want the freedom to toss rocks with me.

I can teach anyone how to do it, they just need to be willing.

Are *you* willing?

Network Marketing and the Canada Goose

If you've watched Canada geese migrating, you probably asked yourself, "Why do they always fly in a 'V' formation?" It has been discovered that the flapping of wings "lifts" the air, making flight easier for the geese forming the "V" behind the leader. The formation allows the geese to fly 71% further than a goose flying solo.

- *Conclusion #1: People moving ahead together in the same direction reach their goals faster and more easily because they count on each other.*
  When a goose leaves the formation, it feels the full resistance of the air and has to work that much harder.

- *Conclusion #2: We need to team up with people who share our goals. When a goose is tired of leading, it slips back in the formation and another goose takes the lead.*

- *Conclusion #3: The results are much better when everyone shares the harder tasks. The geese honk and make noise to support their leaders.*

- *Conclusion #4: Our leaders need to hear our support. When a goose is sick or wounded and leaves the formation, two others follow it to protect it until it recovers. Then the three geese form a small "V" until they catch up with and rejoin the original group.*

- *Conclusion #5: If we stick together, we can all reach our goal.*

Do you possess the wisdom of the Canada goose in building your team? Which conclusion will you add to strengthen your flock?

Chapter 2

Prospecting

Prospecting is simply opening the door for somebody. Rene Yarnell says it beautifully: She calls it lifestyling and friendshipping; relationship marketing. Initially, prospecting has nothing to do with whether you're going to have an appointment later to share the business. It's just finding out if somebody would be awake and open to more possibilities in life.

Friendshipping "primes the pump," as Zig Ziglar puts it, for introducing people to the industry. Just as old-style water pumps have to be vigorously primed before any water comes out, so must your well of prospects be primed before you get into a steady flow of new representatives in your organization. Stop priming, and that flow stops, too.

When I start a public presentation—or even a private one-on-one—I simply say, *"If you want something you have never had, you must be willing to do something you have never done."* I ask for a show of hands if they agree with that. Prospecting, for many people, is doing something they have never done before, it takes them "out of their comfort zone." I prefer to call it "going into a challenge zone." The challenge and risk of prospecting takes boldness and courage. Until you're out risking and sharing yourself with other people, you'll never have or be all you really want or are able to be.

The loneliest and unhappiest package is a person all wrapped up in him or herself. Prospecting has nothing to do with you, it's all about giving to another human being. You must build your belief that you are a master prospector, because you will never accomplish more than your belief level says you can. That is why belief is one of my four cornerstones of duplication, which we'll go over in detail in Chapter Five.

Prospecting is the Backbone of this Business

To me, prospecting is like tennis. Just as a tennis player who does not serve well won't often win, a representative who does not prospect well does not win big in network marketing.

Susan Fogg and I were talking about Napoleon Hill's book *Think and Grow Rich*. He uses the concept "find a need and fill it." That's exactly what prospecting is, to find a need and fill it. To make it easier to remember, Susan used its acronym, FANAFI—Find A Need And Fill It. That's prospecting, finding out what somebody wants in life. What is missing in their life? How can we can fill in that blank with the opportunities of network marketing? It's not right, wrong, good, bad. It's not even looking for a result. You are just finding a need and then you'll fill it by then having an appointment. I call it going out FANAFIing, and that's a very big part of your business.

I use the acronym PIP: We must *Prospect* and then we must *Invite* and then we *Present*. Priming the pump is to be PIPing all over the place. Prospecting, Inviting, Presenting—that's what will build a very strong business. It absolutely has to start with prospecting, friendshipping, opening relationships with new people.

One of the greatest books out there is John Kalench's book (in fact, I just reread it), *Seventeen Secrets of the Master Prospectors*. He is phenomenal in that book, giving people lots and lots of ideas on how to become a better prospector, because that is the backbone of our business. Most people don't put enough emphasis on it, or learn their skills, learn the art of it, so they don't build a solid, lasting business. Even if you are successful and have a large income, I believe it is still important to prospect, to keep your tools and mastery on the cutting edge.

There is an old saying, "Use it or lose it." Many people stop prospecting and want to just manage and monitor their downline. Then they lose their skills and their passion. They lose their availability to just reach out and open the door to somebody. The person who prospects the most is going to win the most in this industry.

What Do You See?

When I teach people about prospecting, I show a picture that includes two different images— an old hag and a young lady. I want to know how people see that picture, whether they see the old hag or whether they see the elegant lady. It all has to do with their own perceptions.

Representatives each have their opinions, agenda and attitudes about prospecting. Pointing out parts of the picture so they see it in a new way is like flipping the light switch. It's a matter of choice of how people look at it. It's a matter of what their internal dialogue is.

If they say, "Oh, this is hard, I'm no good at that," that's how it will be. If to think is to create, then that's what they are going to continue to create outside. There is a part of me that would love to just prospect, prospect, prospect and then sponsor, sponsor, sponsor. It's a skill and an art I have chosen to develop over my lifetime. Not just prospecting for network marketing, but anywhere in my travels over my life, meeting new friends. That's what prospecting is.

The formula I use to coach strong leaders and create lasting income is:

70% prospecting and retailing products
30% duplicating and training the system

Look at your time and see what percentage you are truly spending on prospecting. Little prospecting, little business; a large time allotment to prospecting yields a large business.

Prospecting on Purpose

Randy Ward says, in *Winning is the Greatest Game of All,* that prospecting in the network marketing industry is an accelerated game of life. It adds intention to activities we would do anyway, giving value to our "small talk." I notice for myself that the times when I don't feel like prospecting are the times I'm off my purpose. My purpose keeps me always able to make a new friend and to open the door. And that's what it takes.

If you are avoiding prospecting, remember that it really has mostly to do with your perception. Are you expecting it to be a pleasant experience? Is it going to be a down experience? Is it going to be uncomfortable? Are you going to be judgmental about meeting new people? Are you going to have an internal dialogue of opinions about prospecting? Are you going to have listening that does not empower and encourage you to go forward? Did you forget QTIP? Keep your thinking about prospecting positive and empowering so you stay on purpose.

They're Everywhere

By the time someone is 18, they know over 500 people on a first-name basis. The problem is recalling them all. They're in our memory banks, it's just a matter of pulling up those names. Most people will be able to think of 20 or 30 names without much trouble. From there it helps to have something that jogs your memory, and most companies include some kind of memory jogger in their start-up and training packages.

Beyond those people you already know, you bump into people all over the place. Whether it's the grocery store, the line at the bank, the doctor's office, it doesn't matter where you are, you are around people. There is, of course, that old three-foot rule: If someone is breathing within three feet of you, open the door. Become a friend. Whether it will go anywhere doesn't even matter, but you're keeping your ax sharpened, keeping your skills honed. I'm constantly prospecting just to keep the art really working well for me.

With a cold contact, someone you just bumped into, you know when the rapport is there. I encourage people to practice cold prospecting over and over again, because **Practice Makes Permanent**. It then becomes very natural, free flowing and fun. It won't involve any struggle or effort, and that's the key to prospecting. Practice enough so that you feel no struggle, no fear and no negative or "not okay" feelings. You are just going to meet somebody when you're out in your everyday world.

We need to have awake people for this business, and remember that some prospects are not awake, yet. If you just want to have a ball, get yourself a partner and go to a mall, go somewhere, to an airport where there are a lot of people, and play a game. The object of the game is to ask questions of as many people as possible, to get names and phone numbers for sifting and sorting later on the phone. You can treat the person who has the most names and numbers to lunch, a cup of coffee or a good network marketing book. You can make a game out of it with two or three of you, or you can do it alone, which I do lots of times when I'm out in the world.

See the people around you without prejudging their value and potential. Sandy Elsberg, a good friend and author of *Bread Winner, Bread Baker*, says, "Every sparrow knows an eagle and every minnow knows a whale." You might bring someone in and question if they have the tenacity to do this business, but all they need to do is share it with a few people who share the business with a few people. In time, one of the whales or one of the eagles will decide to lead the way to success, and who knows— the sparrows may know enough eagles to take your business soaring.

Make a Friend First

Coming back to my Arizona home from California, I was sitting next to a lady on the plane. I really wanted to settle back and meditate, to relax and deal with the challenges of delayed flights and my busy schedule. The lady next to me found a pair of glasses on the floor and asked if they were mine. If I'd been thinking only about myself, I would not have said more than, "No, they're not." But I noticed the lady had an accent. I simply said, "I noticed your accent—where are you from?" She told me she's from New Zealand.

I had been there two years ago and I love her country. We talked all about New Zealand together. I found out about her family. She asked about my business. I just briefly said what it was—it's about helping people earn more money, have a better lifestyle and travel the world.

She said, "Wow! I'd be interested in that."

I said, "Well, New Zealand isn't open yet with our company, but if you'll give me your name and number, I will contact you when it is."

I gave her a wonderful little brochure, *Business is Booming*, to take home and read. That was prospecting, but I made a friend first. I simply asked a question that put the focus on her. I don't know where it's going to go, but I did agree to call her or write to her and send her some company information when New Zealand opens. The Scouting motto is "Be Prepared." Always be prepared to share your business, whether by audio (talking business card), brochure or product samples.

I also let her know that I have a commitment to come back and spend four to five weeks in New Zealand in a lovely camper and visit. She said, "When you come down to where I live, please call and we'll show you around the city."

If I'd been unwilling to prime the pump, I wouldn't have a new friend, I wouldn't have a volunteer guide to part of New Zealand, and I would have missed a potential leader.

Please keep in the front of your mind: *Any* time, *any* place, *any* one, *any* where. We can never leave a stone unturned. By using the ANY, you will contact the MANY!

Your Warm Market

That meeting on the plane was cold prospecting, making a stranger a friend. Prospecting your warm market is a little different. The prospect there is someone you know, family, friend or acquaintance. The friendshipping part is already done. Some simple, easy approach examples are: "I'm doing something new, and I thought of you immediately. Let's get together." Or, "I'm working with a millionaire who's teaching me her skills and knowledge. I'd loved to share with you how she amassed her fortunes."

I have a whole selection of ways someone can look at this business.

Once they have agreed to take a look, I'll say, "That's super. I'm not trying to sell you on anything. It's going to be totally your choice. I'm not trying to push you. I'm not trying to recruit or sponsor you into anything. I'm just asking you to be open to the possibilities of what's there for you in your life. If you had unlimited time and unlimited money, how would your life be different?"

You see, at this point, the goal of prospecting is to cause people to expand their thinking. Once they have agreed that they'd be open to looking at possibilities to enhance their life, then I'll say, "Listen, you know there are a number of ways you can do this. We can get together over coffee. You can come out to my house. I'll pop in a video and it usually takes about 50 minutes to show you how you could earn your extra money. I have a very simple book that takes about 35, 40 minutes to read. I have audio tapes, for when you are in your car, about how to escape the rat race, or a seven—minute one on how to have more sizzle in your life, and a super tape called "I've Finally Had Enough."

I let them choose. When they choose, from day one, how they want to look at the business, they feel in total control. That's what you need to create for them, for it to be totally their choice how they are moving forward in the process.

Running Interference

Before we go further, I want to emphasize that I don't think we have the right to *interfere* in anybody's life. We have the privilege and the responsibility to *intervene,* so their life will be more abundant.

Interfering is just telling somebody what to do; what this industry is; what the company is; sell, sell, sell, tell, tell, tell. You seldom sponsor a competent and willing business-builder if you're just selling and telling.

Interfering means invading somebody's privacy. Intervening means drawing somebody out, so they communicate what's important to them. What's next for them in life? What's missing? What is fulfilling?

People who interfere are usually just ATMs, automatic "teller" machines. They tell you everything they know.

People who intervene show what is possible through communication and drawing a person out.

I have a plaque on my office wall that simply says:

> *To Peggy Long in appreciation of your commitment to showing us as opposed to telling us what it takes to make things happen.*

I request that you take a minute to replace my name with yours and read the whole saying again out loud. I'll wait.

Intervening is showing, but with a tremendous amount of listening. To hear what matters to someone else, you often have to listen for what is unspoken.

When someone says, "You have to sit down with me and look at this," that's interfering. Intervening says, "There's something I think might really assist you in earning more money or having more time to enjoy. I'd like to give or mail you a tape, have you listen to a five-minute message on my toll-free line, and then sit down together to see if it's something you might be interested in."

When calling a prospect to follow up on initial interest question, simply introduce yourself again and say, "Is this a good time to talk? I want to have a conversation with you. Is it okay if I ask you some questions?" You always need to get permission to ask questions. Otherwise, you are interfering. This way you are simply intervening, and there is agreement on both sides about the communication.

Each time you interact personally or professionally with someone, remember to keep that person's well-being foremost in your mind and heart. The question becomes, "What's good for the prospect?" When you are thinking, "Is the prospect going to make money for me?" you set up a lose-lose result. When you are focused on contributing to the prospect, the business and the income is a natural outgrowth. Keeping an attitude of contribution is not always easy, but it is essential for your success.

Be Here Now

The phrase "Be here now" is so important in our personal and professional lives. *Be here now.* So many people have another agenda when they are talking to somebody about the business. We need to train our minds, hearts, spirits and souls to just be here now with each person or activity. It creates much better results than any hidden agenda or rote response ever could. Being here now means being in true dialogue, not running your monologue. When you are fully present with someone, it lets them know they are important. That's what is going to come out the strongest. We need to see every prospect with a *Most Important Person* sign plastered on their forehead. If you keep seeing that as you're talking to them, as you're relating to them, as you're asking questions, they are going to feel it, and what they feel is going to move them forward.

Asking questions shows tremendous respect. True prospecting and true communication never involves manipulation, convincing, or bribery. If a representative is just cramming all kinds of data and information down a prospect's throat, they won't be interested or listening. The how-to's, the compensation plan, the product, the company, the officers, network marketing—not much of that actually makes the difference to somebody coming in the business. It depends on how they feel about you.

Something I ask in training is, "How many of you are married or in a committed relationship?" Most people will raise their hands. "Did you marry that person for how much hair they had, their shoe size, the color of their eyes, what kind of car they drove, where they went to school? You probably married that person because of how you *feel* about them." That's a perfect example of how people follow feelings, they don't follow facts.

By letting the prospect speak with you instead of talking at them, by giving less information and drawing them out, you let them know they mean more to you than eye color or shoe size. Developing the ability to "be here now" will benefit every area of your life and business—it's not just for prospecting.

Initial Interest Questions

I'm going to go over some of the Initial Interest Questions. I have them memorized, so when I bump into someone, I might say, "I teach financial freedom; are you interested?" They say yes or no.

If they say yes, your only task is to get a name and a phone number, not to say anything else. You're playing a game with yourself to find out how many names and phone numbers you can get. You and your team member play for only an hour. You should be able to develop a list of at least five to ten names and numbers. That's your only task or goal with Initial Interest Questions.

You just say, "I teach financial freedom. Are you interested?" If they say yes and want to know more, then you say, "Great. What I need to do is just take your name and phone number and I'll get back to you in one or two days. I'll call and talk with you in the comfort of your home. It will take only three to five minutes on the phone and we'll see if you really are serious about your financial freedom."

If a person acts very reluctant about even giving you a name and phone number, they might not be open enough to do this business. It's your choice to get a name and a phone number anyway. Do *not* give them your business card on these Initial Interest Questions and contacts, because that gives them an opportunity to call you and cancel.

Here are some more Initial Interest Questions you can use:

- I help people pay off their mortgage quickly. Are you interested?
- I show people how to earn trips and cars. Would this interest you?
- I teach people how to have a better and richer life. Are you interested?
- I show people how to get out of the rat race. Are you interested?
- Would you like to retire in three to five years?
- Would you be interested in possibly earning $10,000 to $40,000a month in the next three to five years?
- I help save children's lives. Would that interest you?
- I support people in maintaining great health. Could yours improve?

Many people are willing to offer you their participation if you request it as help. You might set out to do a leadership or financial planning survey to open conversational doors. Some representatives set up wealth-building seminars and invite people to attend after the first phone call.

Get some of those questions written down and memorized, and then just walk up to people and ask. If they say no, move on. When you make it a game, it doesn't matter if someone says no.

It's important to remember what question you asked to catch someone's interest. One way is to have a card, not with your name or anything on it, but just a statement such as, "Are you really prepared for financial freedom?" Write your prospect's name and phone number on the back so that when you talk with them again, you know exactly which question they answered before.

Qualifying Questions

When you call them on the phone, always ask first if it's a good time to talk. That is so important. If they are not ready to sit down for three to five minutes—if the kids are crying, the beans are burning, if someone needs to get to the post office—they won't be there 100%. It will be a cheap conversation, and that's not what you want. You want to have an in-depth, focused, honest conversation with them.

Simply say, "Hi! We met at the park (or mall) the other day and you said you were interested in financial freedom, so I have a few questions for you. It's only going to take about five minutes. I'm looking for very, very committed people, people who are serious about the question you answered. I'm accepting only a few people. I'm going to ask you to answer the following questions simply and honestly."

I make sure prospects know this business is built on integrity, it starts right now. Then I ask, "Are you ready for just a couple of questions? I'm just going to listen and write down your key answers."

The first question I ask is, "What do you really enjoy about your life or your work?" I just listen and jot down a few notes to help me remember what they share. They are going to talk very naturally because they are talking about themselves.

When they don't have any more to tell you about what they enjoy, then ask, "Is there anything you feel is missing in your life?"

This is where you really want to listen, even more carefully than before. Their answer will tell you how network marketing will be able to fill in the blanks in their life. They won't say it that way, but that's exactly what you can learn from them if you just listen carefully with no agenda or attachment to the outcome or result.

Another question is, "What do you do for fun? What do you love to do?" You want to know if they are fun people, if they like to ski, or dive on the Great Barrier Reef. Once you find out what they want to do, what they love to do, then you can tell them how this business makes that possible.

I simply say, "That's really great because if you qualify, that's one of the advantages of financial freedom. People are able to have so much more fun and do what they love to do when money and time are not obstacles."

All we are doing is creating value for the prospect.

"Describe the perfect job or work for you." Please listen for the number of work hours, whether they want to travel, how they prefer to dress, the kind of environment they want to be in. They'll be good with this, but you still need to be ready to ask more questions to keep them thinking. You might ask, "What could be some advantages of working out of your house? What would be the best qualities or characteristics of a boss, supervisor or manager?"

Listen closely to the qualities they mention, because those preferences will also tell you how they work. Think of the sayings "Like begets liking," and "Birds of a feather flock together." The qualities that are really important to a prospect are usually the qualities that prospect would bring to this business.

Next, I want to know if they're open to working the business. I ask, "Would you be willing to work part time, five to ten hours a week, for the possibility of earning $500 to even $10,000 or more a month in the next one to three years?" Notice that I don't make a promise about how much they *will* earn. I tell them what is *possible*, but the choice and the effort have to be theirs.

I ask them to describe the qualities of a best friend. The qualities that they bring up—compassion, forgiveness, caring, listening, trusting—are the qualities that build a tremendous partnership in network marketing. It's important to hear their thoughts and feelings about friendship.

If someone says, "I want a buddy who can go out to a bar and drink me under the table," I would question if that person has qualities that are going to make a difference in someone's life.

Someone might say, "One of the qualities I like in my friends is caring about others less fortunate. We work on projects for the American Cancer Society." You can reply, "Great! That's part of what I want to show you. In network marketing, once someone is totally debt free, set up for retirement and comfortably able to do and have anything they want, they have a new perspective. All the masters in this industry will tell you how vital it is to have a purpose bigger than yourself."

If you read *The Richest Man in Babylon*, you'll discover the laws for becoming wealthy in the world. In Babylon, citizens practiced certain disciplines in order to become very rich, and tithing— giving 10% of one's income to a cause— was an important one. A 1984 Gallup poll found that 87% of people who had disciplined tithing habits never had serious financial worries.

Are you ready to tithe? I acknowledge my parents for instilling the value and habit in me from my childhood. Billy Graham said, "I dare you to try to out give God." I dare you to take the challenge of tithing. Don't forget to find out your prospect's attitude about giving, too.

Close with, "What about these questions caused you to think about what you're doing with the rest of your life?" Listen, once again, to hear if your prospect is truly open for this business. If the questions were more annoying than thought-provoking, your prospect isn't ready or awake to new possibilities for life.

Should You Continue With This Prospect?

As you've asked these questions of them, you've gotten a sense of what is important to them in life. You've heard what's missing, what could be better, and you've discovered what personal qualities they value and what effort they are willing to make.

What if the person answering these questions has never thought about these issues before? The gentle questions open them up to other possibilities for life, which is really what network marketing is about. What representatives need to really be aware of is the question: Is this prospect stirring and awaking, or are they fully awake?

How they respond with their answers will let you see if this is the kind of person you truly desire to have as a partner. Can I still work with someone who is just waking up, but still has passion, excitement in their voice while answering my questions?

Yes— as long as they're willing to continue to have communication and continue to get knowledge and information about the industry.

If they are unwilling, then it's a waste of time. It's like these people are not awake yet to what is really happening for them in their lives.

They're on a treadmill and they don't even see, feel, acknowledge that there could be other— and better— possibilities.

With short questions over the phone as we've discussed, you can spend minutes rather than hours finding out which category they belong in. This is a productive way to keep you from experiencing rejection. What happens is that a lot of representatives just want to get in front of somebody, anybody, and show them the business. The person says "No," because the representative hasn't done their homework. It takes diligent homework to find out if a person is up to even looking at other possibilities for them in life.

It's your choice now whether or not to continue with the prospect. Do you want to spend an hour of your time presenting the opportunity or having them on a three-way company prospecting call? Do you feel this is not the kind of person you want to work with? Project or promising person? You decide.

A Quaker Greeting

Back in the time of William Penn, there were many Quaker villages in what is now Pennsylvania. In the center of each of these small towns was a well where people congregated and where strangers were met when they first arrived.

One villager—usually an older man—was given the job of Village Greeter. Here's what he would do:

Every visitor would always ask him the same question: "What are the people like in this town?"

His job was to ask in return, "What were the people like where you came from?"

If the strangers replied that the people where they came from were sullen, unhappy, not very friendly or open, the Greeter would shake his head and say, "They are the same here."

If the strangers replied that the people where they came from were warm and happy, open people who cared about each other and made friends easily, he would smile and say, "They are the same here."

What we put out comes back, and how we are in a relationship is how the other person is going to be. It's like a mirror image, a reflection.

Really listen and hear what they have to say. Let them know that network marketing is about making a difference, it's about being a point of light, it's about empowering people to become greater than they are today while being paid to do it.

By doing the Initial Interest sorting and sifting, you're going to have exactly the information you need to make your decision quickly. You are in control. You decide if you want to take this process further.

This system works with teams all over the world. Most representatives need a check-list or a sketch-script to help them sort effectively. Once they go all the way through the process, from the Initial Interest game in the mall to the sorting questions on the telephone, they know if someone is serious enough to go the next step. It isn't a matter of begging or hoping or wondering if someone is willing.

If a prospect is not someone you want to sit down with or have on a prospecting call right away, or if the prospect seems unwilling, just say, "Call me back within a week to see if this is something you want to explore further" or "I really appreciate your time. I'm not sure right now if you're the kind of person I'm looking for. I develop leaders who create financial freedom and time freedom for themselves and others. If you *are* that kind of person, then we should have another conversation." Give them your phone number. If they call back, they prove their interest by making the effort. Follow through by setting up an appointment to present the opportunity. Save your best energy and efforts for the best, hottest, most open communicators—the ones you want to meet immediately for an appointment, presentation or prospecting call.

Your PIPing will be easy if you keep asking questions and really listen to their answers. The less we talk, the more we draw people out, the more they are going to be coming forward with us in a natural progression— "Over-Talk and Bore; Under-Talk and Score."

Ask, Don't Argue

Some representatives get into arguments with their prospects, because they are too attached to the idea of convincing someone to join. Some people become data dump trucks. They get too busy with facts to pay attention to what the prospect wants to know. Most prospects have a very limited range of what they need to hear. They're not even interested in the other information until they find out an answer for their own, personal "What's missing?"—what possibilities this business would offer them.

If someone says, "It sounds like you are into one of those pyramids," many networkers *react* by becoming defensive: "It isn't a pyramid! Pyramids are illegal, and the FTC checks them out and shuts them down. It's all a matter of policies and procedures, and where they fail to blah, blah blah." A belligerent recitation of facts doesn't answer the unspoken question, "Is this a pyramid; is it legal?" You can't effectively answer that to your prospect's satisfaction until you know what they think a pyramid is.

It's better to *respond* with, "I don't think I am in a pyramid. They are illegal, and I'd never be in anything illegal. But what do you think a pyramid is? Can you tell me what you think a pyramid scheme looks like? What would you watch out for?"

The prospect may have heard the word pyramid without any context. They may just really want to know how stable the company is.

The more you let your prospect talk, the more you know how you need to respond. If you react, you lose your power and purpose. The conversation is one side against the other, rather than a partnership in learning. Johnny Keller offers a great phrase in his *WMLM* interview for Upline®: "Turn down the heat and turn up the volume." Turn off the heat of your reaction to a prospect and turn up the volume on what that person is telling you.

If someone is responding, they are bringing forth exactly what they need to know in order to move forward in the conversation. The response allows both people to participate at the same time and learn about each other.

Positive Value Questions also enable the representative to help the prospect recognize and obtain what it is they want for an answer. Questioning and listening allows you to truly find out what the benefit, the value, is for them *specifically*.

Start with one of these Positive Value Question Openers:

- Could you get excited about...
- How about increasing...
- Wouldn't it be terrific if...
- Could you see the value of ...
- What is the benefit of...
- Why would you look forward to...
- Doesn't it make sense to...

- Isn't it reassuring to learn...
- Why is it easy to see...
- Are you ready...
- When would you like to...
- Where would you like to...

Then follow with one of these (or something tailored to your company):

>...earning $500 extra a month part time?
>...earnings of $500-$2250 a week?
>...other people helped build your business?
>...offering great products at discount?
>...being paid to use the phone?
>...earning money by being healthier?
>...setting yourself up for extra retirement income?
>...having more time and money?
>...saving children's lives with safe products?
>...leverage your time with lots of people's efforts?
>...that upline support is 100% free?
>...your business will grow faster when everyone works as a team?

Why would it be nice to work at your own pace?

How would you like to be earning dollars while you're sleeping or on vacation?

The Vocabulary of Network Marketing

Before we go further, I want to share my strong feelings about the vocabulary we use in our industry. I believe, for myself and for networkers as a group, that we need to use proper and consistent vocabulary in prospecting. Vocabulary is a specific language, and every profession has one, but I think we need to avoid jargon and speak the real English language.

Here's an example of why it doesn't work to speak jargon around people who aren't yet in your business: I'm selling a rental home I own and I have asked some old friends who are real estate agents to sell it for me. They were speaking with a vocabulary that I didn't even understand. I said, "Just slow down, make it simple, and make it plain." Words don't work effectively if half or more of your audience doesn't understand what you're saying.

I'm going to suggest some words that I'm committed to supporting our industry using.

Number one, I choose to use the words network marketing or network distribution, not multi-level marketing. There is a stigma about multi-level marketing. Why not let it go, and use the one that more and more writers favor? *SUCCESS* magazine uses network marketing or network distribution. So does *Upline®*. Get rid of multi-level.

Of course, more and more compensation plans are not multi-level anymore anyway. If it's the binary plan, there are no levels, there are no breakaways. Multi-level does not fit at all in the binary, unilateral and add-on systems.

I assert that people are tired of going to meetings— any meeting. Rather than inviting someone to a meeting, better words to use are *presentation, event* or *preview*. That's really what we're doing. A lot of these people have been to one or two meetings in the day, and the majority of meetings in a lot of industries are absolutely unproductive and utterly boring. We're not having a meeting. When people have a meeting, there is an agenda and people have input. In a *presentation, event* or *preview,* someone displays or explains what is available for the guests invited.

An incredible book on this subject is Brian Biro's *Beyond Success.* He goes through some tremendous ways to have successful presentations and coaching sessions.

Another thing I can't stand to hear is when people say you are going to make a lot of money. I don't use the word *make.* The only two places money is made are federal mints or in counterfeit rings. We are not involved in either of those. The word that I suggest network marketers use is *earning.* With the word *earn* comes the connotation that something has to be done; there has to be action, there has to be some movement.

I coach many people and companies to get away from the word *buying* and use the word *purchase*. Rather than saying, "I'm going to go buy a new dress," try "I'm going to purchase a new dress." The word *purchase* is much softer and connotes personal responsibility.

I am blatantly against using the word *recruit*. I can't stand it. The word *sponsor* has so much more clarity. Recruit sounds like "be all you can be" and join the army. They always talk about recruiting people. That's not what we are about in this industry. We're about sponsoring people into their own lives more, and the vehicle that moves them there is network marketing and the particular company you're with.

Another word that I don't particularly like at all and don't use in my vocabulary is the word *distributor.* So many companies are now taking the wonderful responsibility of distributing the product by UPS, Purolator, Airborne Express or Federal Express. They are the ones who are actually distributing the products. The correct word, the one I coach people to use, is the word *representative.* We are really representing a company, we're representing some products, and we're representing an industry.

Going back to another word that absolutely makes me go wacky is the word *closing.* We are not closing anything. We are *opening.* The word *close* is part of the selling vocabulary. I prefer we're *finalizing their decision.* If we are closing, that's more about how skilled we are, and how great we are, and how much we can do something to close somebody, and that's selling.

In finalizing their decision, the question I ask is, "Are you ready to come on to a very powerful team?" That's their decision. If it's a more quiet, shy person, I might say "Are you ready to be on a very supportive team?" If it's a strong, professional person: "Are you ready to be on an action-oriented team?" If it's someone more analytical: "Are you prepared or are you ready now to come on a team that is clear, takes action and has a great system in place?" That assists them to finalize their decision.

If they say, "No, I'm not ready," okay, super. "Would you be willing to share with me what it is that you need to know for you to finalize your decision?" That is not a closing. I am not doing it *to them.* Closing is doing it TO someone else. All you're really doing is asking a question to see what the next step or the next forward movement will be for them.

Another word you cannot use is the word *investment.* That word can get us in all kinds of legal trouble with the attorneys general and Federal Trade Commission. This is not an investment. Many new reps will use the word investment and totally jeopardize their business, their sponsor's business and the company's business because that's a legal word that we are not to use. Rather than saying investment, we simply talk about working to earn money, which is different from investing.

Most companies are also getting rid of the phrase *marketing plan*, because who really markets this product? *You* market the product. You're a network *marketer*. That's what the company pays you for—for marketing their products. Companies usually have a *compensation* plan, because that's how representatives will receive payment for the work that they do. We are compensated for moving product to customers.

Nobody can be paid to recruit anybody and that's why some companies have been shut down, because they are paying to recruit. The product MUST move. The only legitimate compensation is based on the movement of product.

I was in California doing a presentation and met an outgoing, vivacious lady named Charlene. I was asking her some questions, and she said, "I don't think I'll come in, because I was burned once." She had been with a company where she just gave them a lot of money and there was no product exchanged. She said, "How do I know that there is going to be a product here?"

I said, "Because you are going to sit down tomorrow with your sponsor, who you trust, you are going to order your product and it'll be shipped right to you. You should have it within two to five days. You can see all the product we have."

People must have product in their hands, otherwise it is an illegal pyramid. The product must move in order for the representative to be compensated. The company helps us by creating marketing materials so we don't have to on our own. In fact, many companies have a legally binding agreement, on the independent rep form, that you will not go out and create your own materials, because that jeopardizes the entire company.

I know that if all networkers shared a common language— as doctors have a common language, or plumbers have a common language— it would make our industry so much stronger, and we'd have fewer divisions or differences between companies. If we could be aligned in our language and how we communicate about the industry, it would be so much easier for all of us to present this opportunity with integrity and clarity.

"What's In It For Them?"

Let's say you're prospecting a woman, and she's already told you about her three teenagers. You need to know if having more time with her children would be of value to her.

You might start by asking, "What is your schedule like with three teenagers?" Your prospect starts talking about the hectic calendar of the kids going here and there, to soccer practice, to church camp, selling Girl Scout cookies, raising money for cheerleading uniforms.

You say, "All that sounds really tiring."

She replies, "Actually, I love doing things with my kids. I just run out of energy by the end of the work day, and there is never quite enough money to go around."

Did she just tell you exactly what network marketing can do for her?

All you have to do is ask, "Can you see how additional money would assist you in having more time with your children? Tell me, how would that work for you? I have a safe product that could give you more energy. Would you want to use it and see results for yourself?"

As she starts talking again, it might occur to her that the oldest child will soon be driving. Might a new car make the whole schedule easier, especially if someone else pays for it? What about the insurance for a new young driver?

That whole conversation was about letting the prospect talk about things that were important to her. You don't need to convince her or persuade her about any of those things—she already values them. Questions simply got her started. The rest is letting her own thoughts crystallize into her reason for action.

When the other person is talking, sharing, verbalizing and communicating, more and more of their needs, more of what they want, more of what is missing in life are going to come up. Your questions keep their thoughts flowing.

I have a sheet that just says WHY across the top, which you can use to help your prospects finalize their decision on their own, without pressure from you. It also lets you to know their priorities. Sometimes I just hand it to a prospect and say, "Why don't you look over this list and check the ones that you feel are the most important or most interest you." This is especially useful for any representatives who need a little help in the art of asking questions and creating value. The WHY list is a tool to get the questions flowing.

WHY?

- I want to be self-employed, my own boss. ____
- I want to be able to retire in 1-5 years. ____
- I want to do what I love to do. ____
- I want to decide if I roll out or over. ____
- I want to decide if and when I roll out. ____
- I want to decide if I go to work. ____
- I want to decide when to go to work. ____
- I want to decide who I work with. ____
- I want to decide when I have lunch breaks, and for how long. ____
- I want to decide when I go home from work. ____
- I want to decide what kind of car to drive. ____
- I want a new house. ____
- I want to own a new car. ____
- I want to choose the neighborhood I live in. ____
- I want to choose my days off. ____
- I want to choose which of the 24 hours I want to work. ____
- I want to choose when, where and how long to vacation. ____
- I want to decide when to retire and not have to take a cut in pay when I do retire. ____
- I want a way to protect my family if something would happen to me. ____
- If I break my leg, I still want my income to be the same. ____
- I want a complete house-cleaning service. ____
- I want all my family members to be able to go to anywhere as often as they like. ____
- I want someone to wash my car every week. ____
- I want a lawn and garden service. ____
- I want to give freely to charities. ____

**The most awesome thing about network marketing is:
I can't be successful unless I support *you* to be successful.**

46

Treat the WHY List as a starting point. If your prospect starts talking about family, for example, you might ask, "You have three young children at home; how do you think leadership skills will spill over into your children's learning?"

Remember to always get permission before asking all these questions. That goes back to the difference between interfering and intervening. A salesperson will interfere, they'll get right in there. A person who is sharing and responsibly sponsoring will get permission to ask the questions. That gives you the freedom to ask specific questions with authenticity and sincerity.

Let them start communicating things they've considered, but never thought were possible. We offer people the missing links to the full range of possibilities in life.

Your next job is finding the most valuable point for the prospect. There will be many things they want and value, but one will stand out above the others. Perhaps someone has a very old car that's not even safe anymore. You could simply ask, "Did I share with you that we have a car allowance where you could earn a car through this program?" If that isn't how your company does it, perhaps you could find out what their ideal car costs. Then ask, "What if you could buy that car in one to three years through this business I'm going to share with you? Would that interest you?"

What is their value?

What's in it for them? The acronym I use to remember this is WITHem.

Going for the Opening

At the very end of PIPing, there needs to be a conversation about the next step. After all, our partnership is getting started—*opening*—not closing down. I cover a few ground rules with a prospect who has passed through each of the sorting phases.

First, I let them know that I'm not going to try to sell them anything. I say, "Take a deep breath, relax, put your checkbook aside. That is not the purpose for us being together. I don't even know if it's going to be a marriage or a merger, or if this is something you want to do or if you are somebody I want to put a lot of time and effort into really developing. You have to be ready to come up to the plate, to hit a home run, so I'm not going to try to sell you anything. I'm also not going to try to recruit you into anything."

I can remember the night I went to my first presentation—I was really leery. Someone came up to me and said, "Peggy, your father's business is going to go on with or without you."

I thought that was one of the rudest, most inappropriate remarks, and I was so ticked off about it. I wasn't at all interested in whether or not it was true. And it was the truth!

Now I use that saying all the time. My success is my choice. It doesn't make any difference if someone chooses not to be part of my business—I will succeed with or without that person.

I tell others that my commitment and my success will continue no matter what they decide. It takes the pressure off them, because I'm not trying to "get them" for my business.

I can't stand it when someone says, "I'm going to *get* this guy on the team. If I *get* her, she is going to be the heavy hitter." I don't believe in heavy hitters or "getting" people. I truly don't. I believe some people do come into this business with more knowledge, more natural talent, more developed skills, perhaps even a very large background in network marketing, so their belief is already in place, but I do not believe in heavy hitters.

What I do know is we develop the committed leaders. Not just any leader, because leaders come and go. They can go into any other company, they can go into any other profession, but a committed leader will have the staying power.

People need to know that we are going to be committed with or without them. Our business is going to go on, whether they choose to come into the network or not.

Something else I might say to a PIPed prospect is, "I'm certainly not expecting you to make any kind of a commitment. You might not know enough about it yet, and that's fine."

Too often networkers say, "You just take your time—but hurry up." Some people say, "You snooze, you lose," pressuring for an immediate decision. I think it is valid to create some urgency which is not manipulation or resorting to convincing. That's kind of like a wake up call. This is urgent if someone truly wants to move into a new stage of growth and prosperity right away.

A company may have a promotion going, where people can earn more money by coming in the network or the team at that time.

Let prospects know that, but don't demand that they make a commitment because of the promotion.

It's very important that you be sincere and authentic, because people feel that. They can feel falseness, too. It's rare to feel authenticity in the business world. People get accustomed to the idea that success is built by climbing over others. We can choose to do it differently in network marketing. We need to be sincere in every aspect of our business.

On Being Sincere

During ancient Greek and Roman times, sculpting was an important art and livelihood. It took many years to create a beautiful marble sculpture. Sculptors would spend months looking for the perfect piece of stone, then, using a horse and cart, get the marble to their barn and start working on it. Once they had drawn the idea for what this marble was going to be chiseled and carved into, they would begin, and it was a tedious labor-intensive job.

Months, sometimes years, went into each sculpture. Sometimes, as the sculptors worked on chiseling the marble, they might slip with the hammer and the chisel and go too deep or chip a piece that shouldn't have been chipped. If that happened, the sculptors would take wax, and melt it with herbs and weeds and grasses to make it the exact color of the marble.

They would very gently press and pound and ply the wax into the hole. The wax looked like marble as long as you didn't look too closely or put the sculpture too near a fire.

Whenever wax was put into a sculpture, it was called an insincere sculpture. It never had as much value in the marketplace. If the sculptor never slipped or made a mistake, that piece went to the marketplace as a sincere sculpture and brought in much more money.

Being sincere means being authentic, telling the truth, not telling people just what they want to hear. Don't tell people this is an easy business—it is not an easy business. It takes more commitment than most other businesses, because people end up dreaming, eating and sleeping it. That's the truth, and people feel our authenticity when we share it.

When we are sincere and authentic, we don't have to sell. If it's a great product, the product will literally sell itself. As far as the business opportunity and them becoming a team player or a partner, when it is communicated authentically, responsibly by asking questions, by finding out their value, by being with them, then they will move forward—*if* they are open and *if* they are awake to the possibilities.

There are only basically three answers that are going to come up for you in prospecting: One is yes. One is no. One is maybe, the timing isn't good right now. Those are the only three answers.

Don't be attached to the results. That's what causes so many people in network marketing, and in life, to feel rejected or inadequate. They become attached to the results and base their feelings on the final outcome. A result is simply a result. If a representative brings extra issues or agendas to the process of prospecting, that representative risks feeling rejected, discouraged, frustrated when the result does not meet those expectations.

How do you stay authentic and avoid getting attached to results? Keep your focus on your prospect. Don't let yourself worry about your own concerns while you're PIPing. The entire PIP system is all about them. The best way I know to keep the focus on someone else is to ask questions. It works as well with friends as with strangers.

Selling vs. Sponsoring

Once somebody has prospected and invited a person, it's time to present the business. This is when it's crucial to know the difference between selling and sponsoring.

When I'm talking about selling versus sponsoring— and I need to make this very clear—I'm not talking about selling a product. Whether you're selling a health or home care product, a phone card, a website, or dog food, it makes no difference. I am discussing the issue of selling versus sponsoring in the context of how you bring a representative into the business as a business-builder.

What's the difference between selling and sponsoring? There is a very, very big difference. The first eight months in my business, I was selling people into it. I was convincing them. I was telling them what they wanted to hear. I did not have the wonderful questioning skills or arts down yet, and I was an incredible information "dumper" and "telling" machine. None of the people I signed up then did very well in the business, because I hadn't found out what was in it for them. I had *sold* them, but I hadn't *sponsored* them.

When someone is selling, they usually end up doing about 80% of the talking and about 20% of the listening. When you are asking your questions and listening 80% of the time instead talking, the prospects move themselves forward. When you are telling, you're actually pushing them back.

If someone is convincing, they are truly into selling, doing everything they can to prevail on somebody that this is going to be good for them. All that does is put up red flags between a representative and the prospect. "A person convinced against their will remains of the same opinion still." People can feel when they are being manipulated, even if they cannot identify what's going on. People will follow their feelings in making a decision. Eye contact, for example, is extremely important—"the eyes are the windows of the soul." Make direct eye contact when you're talking to your prospect. Don't have a staring contest, but look at them with the attitude "I care about you."

People need to feel that you truly care. Simply present the truth of this industry, your company and your products. One truth is that, for most people, it's going to take one to five years to start earning serious residual income. Another truth is that it takes work to achieve results— and both are conveniently left out of the conversation by people who are trying to sell someone in. Paint the picture of preparation, PPP: Paint the picture of what it's going to take to be successful. They just need to know it's going to be a process, that it takes time to establish residual income, and that they will have to "go back to school" and learn. Making income claims is not only illegal, it's misleading, because there really is no guarantee that anyone can earn any certain amount in this industry. Companies get into trouble when representatives are running around saying all kinds of stuff without being responsible. "Oh, it's easy to earn a car," or, "It's easy to earn $10,000 a month." That is not true. Telling that to someone sets them up for disappointment. We need to come from a truly caring and committed place with our communication.

Some people bribe their prospects: "If you come in now, I'll give you $50." That makes companies and the industry look absolutely horrible. In the selling world that's acceptable. All the sales in stores— come in now and get $100 off your four Michelin tires— are really bribes. I say that's okay if a business does it in the selling profession. Both the seller and the buyer know how the process works. There is no hidden agenda. In the network marketing profession, I totally disagree with bribes and pressure.

Some people beg and plead, because there might be a contest for winning a cruise or promotion for extra money. If a representative tells the prospect those kind of things—"I really need you now, because I'm trying to win a cruise"—then it's all about the representative winning instead of the prospect. I believe those conversations should never, ever come up. Yes, if there is a cruise or promotion going on and you need certain requirements or qualifications, that's your responsibility to make it happen. Please don't mix your needs into your conversation and communication with a prospect. Your desire to win a cruise or promotion has nothing to do with the new prospect coming into the business for their reasons.

When a representative has a hidden agenda that is not straight out on the table, even if it is just their desire for the prospect to sign up, they start speaking in what I call "forked tongue." If someone is pleading or begging, or if there is money involved for a contest or a qualification, it's about them, not the prospect.

People who have been sold and told are apt to do little or nothing with their business. I call these people squatters, or sitters. A squatter is a person who purchases property for a very low amount of money and just sits on a very small piece of land with no building or real estate value. If you sell people into this business, they often will become squatters, sitting on the opportunity without making anything of its value.

In order not to have squatters in your network, you need to make sure the prospects you sponsor are very clear and solid on why and what they want this business to do for them.

Selling   versus   Sponsoring

Selling	Sponsoring
Convincing	Sharing honestly
Bribes/$ off if do now	Constant prices
Manipulation	Tell as it is
Beg, Plead, Contest $$ for me	It's all about them winning
About $$$	About people's lives
Talk and Tell lots	Ask??? and listen
Information, Data Features	Value and benefits
About Seller's results	About Making a difference
Don't care who sell to	Long term Care Relationships
Over when sale is done, turn over to someone else	Ongoing process & friendships
It's a Job	It's a Life
90% about Product	Support to Win
80% seller Talking	80% listening
Little or No trust	Trust/Integrity
Low follow up/out of door	100% follow up
Fear, Guilt, sorry If don't buy	Empower to their goals
Excitement or boredom	Enthusiasm/Focus
Content	Context
RECRUITING	RESPONSIBLE SPONSORING

Be a Responsible Sponsor

One reason people get into selling is because they get too attached to the results. Whenever a person is attached to the results mentally, emotionally, or financially—I have to have this person on my line or leg or team or I'm not going to earn my car or make the paycheck—then there is a hidden agenda. The prospect feels it, but cannot identify what is going on. That's why it's so important to present your material ethically, naturally and responsibly.

Sponsoring is simply sharing honestly and with integrity. It's supporting someone to win, even if they have small goals to begin with, like a new microwave, or getting their teeth fixed. You are going to support them in reaching their small goals which will then be stepping stones to reach their next bigger goal. All you're doing is offering a present. You're offering a gift, no strings attached. The prospect is free to accept the gift or not.

Responsible sponsoring taps into the much deeper context of a person's being than selling does, with all the data and information. What someone wants and is willing to do are context. Are they willing to begin to shift their awareness, to shift their belief system for what's possible? Content is small factual issues. Context is big, important life issues, with much feeling involved.

Recruiting is content. It has nothing to do with a person's life or context or being; it has nothing to do with responsible sponsoring.

I ask representatives in training to write down what percentage of time they spend selling versus sponsoring, or said another way, in content versus context interactions.

Like most people when they come into the business, about 60, 70, 80, sometimes 90%, are into selling. That's what they think this industry is, they don't know yet about sharing and sponsoring. The more time they spend learning these skills, practicing prospecting and responsibly inviting, the faster they will begin to reverse those percentages.

As I said, in my first eight to ten months, I was doing 90% selling. Not that I wouldn't be a responsible sponsor, but I did not understand this industry, that it was really about sharing, not about selling. I was operating out of content early in my business, and it's a great joy, now, to operate from context.

When I'm coaching a new representative and listening to them invite or do a follow-up call, I will keep two little signs in front of me. One sign says *selling,* and I'll have it in one hand. In the other hand, I'll have a sign that says *sharing.* If my new partner goes more into a selling mode, I'll put that selling sign right in front of them. They know that they need to shift and change how they are communicating, how they are being with this person, to go back into sharing, asking questions.

Responsible sponsoring is about presenting a gift. It's not about getting somebody into your downline.

How to "Blow" a Sale

When I earned my first car from my first network marketing company, I went down to a dealership to order what I wanted. I only had about 45 minutes to buy the car, and had already decided which one I wanted. It was a Lexus 400SL in taupe, which is a desert color. When the salesman came out, I was very clear to him: I said, "I'm going to buy this car and I have 45 minutes to do the transaction." He told me, "You need to go out and look at it."

He didn't hear me at all. He said, "I *have to* tell you some things about it."

I had my two sons with me, and their expressions said, "Okay, how is Mom going to handle this?"

I did go out on the lot with the salesman, and he immediately opened the hood so we could look at the engine. I do not understand engines. Many people don't, and we're simply not interested in looking at them.

I said, "I'm really not interested. I know Lexus has a very high rating, and I know the engine is incredible. I would like to buy the car."

He said, "You need to know that it has an eight horse power fuel injection system that does this or that." I don't even know what all that stuff is, and he went on with all this technical jargon data dumping. Three times I interrupted him, "I really don't need to know that," and he kept just going.

Then he climbed into the car and turned the stereo on full blast. I said, "It's great music. I'm real happy with how the stereo sounds." He just kept saying, "You need to know this stereo has ten speakers, yak, yak, yak."

I said, "Excuse me, I don't need to know this." He replied, "I have to tell you." It was all about him knowing all this stuff, I mean, about how yama goochy woochy soochy stereo does this and that. I didn't care. I already knew it had a great sound system.

The salesman just kept talking, even though none of it made sense to me. He talked about anti-lock airbags, turbo windshield wipers, whatever. I said, "I now have about 20 minutes to buy the car." He said, "We can't do the paperwork in 20 minutes."

I said, "You never even heard me, all you wanted to do was to tell me all this information, all these features, all these facts, when I have already made my decision. Now you have lost this sale, because there's no time left to complete it."

This is what networking representatives do so often. They just tell and sell and break down the mechanics of the sales compensation plan and all the data about what the product will do for them and how it's going to clean out their colon or their dog is going to be peppier or their windows are going to be squeaky clean, and they don't even find out if the prospect wants to know that. Sellers don't care who they sell to, they are bent to tell any person all of the facts. All that does is push our guest or prospect further back out the door.

I did not buy the car that day, even though I told the salesman I was ready. He lost the deal. I believe that many representatives in network marketing do not have new people in their business, because they spend too much time focused on themselves and what they know rather then drawing out what's possible for the new person that will come in.

I did go back, however, and I ended up buying the Lexus. The next time I went in, I said, "I am going to buy that car, and I need to leave this lot in 45 minutes in my new car. I need to know nothing else about the car, I want no salesman to tell me anything about the car. I'm going to do the paperwork, and if you do not sit down with me now and do the paperwork, I'm going to the other dealer in town."

I did the paperwork and I drove out with my brand new Lexus that my company paid for. The salesman who helped with my paperwork shook my hand, thanked me very much and said, "I'm going to turn you over to the service department." That's what happens in selling.

In sponsoring, nobody is turned over once somebody comes onto the team or into the organization. Once the person has made a decision, that is when the ongoing process of coaching and duplicating begins. Nobody is turned over to another department or to another person to do the coaching.

Benefits Mean *Value*

Sponsoring is all about value—what's in it for them. What are their *benefits*? Randy Gage uses the word benefit very strongly. The word that I use is *value*.

If you had plenty of money, who in your life, what family members or friends, would you want to help financially? That would be the value of "plenty of money."

Selling is about the seller's results. Sponsoring has to do with making a difference in someone's life. That's why in the front of every presentation, whether it's a one-on-one, a two-on-one or a group presentation, I will always let people know, I am not here to try to sell you on anything and neither is the person who invited you here. Prospects need to hear that so they can relax and really listen.

I say, "This business is about making a difference in your life and the more that we can focus on you and the differences that you want, the more you are going to win." If someone is in a selling mode, they don't care who they sell to, they'll take anybody. They just want to get in front of somebody as fast as they can.

In responsible sponsoring, we are going to be developing a long-term caring relationship, and that has nothing to do with my results. It has everything to do with the possibilities that this person will have in making a wise decision, and in developing a long term caring relationship. And in selling, the sale is totally over when the money has been exchanged.

I greatly respect the career and the profession of salespeople. They are among the highest paid people in the world. They also spend the most money (in case you didn't know that). But if someone is a salesperson, they have a job. Network marketing has nothing to do with a job. It is a lifestyle, it's a way of leading and living your life and inviting others to lead and live their lives in the same arena of making a difference. Not just earning income, but making a difference.

How to Prioritize Your Prospect List

This acronym provides an easy way to prioritize your list of prospects. It is also useful for helping new reps to do so. I call it Prospecting for PEARLS.

P = POSITIVE

You cannot change a person's attitude in this business, and I don't choose to work with anyone negative. I don't mind a skeptical person, because all we need to do is work with them on their belief and then the skepticism goes away. But if they are really a negative kind of person, I don't even want to work with them. I'd rather not have them on the team. You are always going to be trying to straighten out their negative attitude, because that's what they are bringing in. Let's bring in people with positive attitudes.

E = ENTREPRENEUR

A great exercise to do in a training is to ask them, "Go back when you were a young kid—when you were five, seven, 12— how many of you ever sold lemonade on your street corner? How many of you had a garage sale? How many of you sold Girl Scout cookies? How many of you sold newspapers? How many of you sold your toys to earn some money?"

I can remember when I lived in Chicago, and my brother Ken and I read an ad in the big Chicago paper. We were maybe eight and ten—something like that—and the ad offered five dollars for a gallon of night crawlers. Now, we thought this was pretty cool, because we could do this on our own to earn extra money. We didn't have to be driven somewhere, and it would be easy.

We used to flood our back yard and let the night crawlers come up. Do you have any idea how many night crawlers are in a gallon? We were absolutely shocked. It took us days and days and hours and hours and hours to collect those gallons of night crawlers. When my father would go down to minister to someone in a hospital in downtown Chicago, he would deliver our hard-won gallons of worms and bring our $5 back home to us.

Even at an early age, my brother and I had an entrepreneurial spirit. When we're young, many of us have that eager, adventuresome spirit. Then, due to the systems and the behavior of schools and parenting and churches, we start getting pegged and programmed, and lose that spirit. People do the standard routine of going to college, getting a regular job and going after security, rather than allowing their great entrepreneurial spirit to soar. What network marketing does is it brings that side and that specialness and that entrepreneurial spirit back to people.

A = ACHIEVEMENT

Most people think this has to be something major and bold. No. It could be someone who won the blue ribbon for the best quilt at the state fair, because that shows persistence and patience and dedication. It could be someone who has been on the board of directors for Make-A-Wish Foundation. That shows leadership. That shows contribution.

Someone who has chosen to be a Little League coach. Someone who has led a team for a cancer walk. It might be somebody who has been a Sunday School teacher for 10 years. That's commitment. That is putting someone else first. That's passing on physical knowledge, generosity attitudes and spiritual knowledge.

It might be somebody who has won a marathon or even run in a race, because the skills and what they brought forth from themselves show they have really achieved something. Many times I'll ask, "What are some of your achievements in life, what's something you feel proud about?"

I'm not talking about money. I'm talking about things where they have brought forth their best qualities, their best traits, their best characteristics and they have achieved something special. It's okay to help and prompt them with their answers if you know an achievement that they aren't remembering. Someone who has been a foster parent might just take that in stride. It's a great achievement. I know what commitment foster parents have to take children into their home and love them and physically, emotionally, spiritually, mentally support these young human beings and then have to let them go to be with new adoptive parents or out into the world.

Find out something to focus on they feel proud they have achieved.

R = RISK

I'll ask, "What's one time in your life you took a risk and felt really good about it?"

Again, whatever they say, make it okay, because that's what they are going to ground themselves in. That's going to be their rock to stand on that you can bring forward when they need to risk more in their business.

L = LISTENERS

Remember this business is 80% listening and 20% talking. We need to be in *dialogue,* not *monologue.*

S = SINCERE

We've already talked about the importance of that. Don't con or try to sell anyone with your presentation or in your business.

When you have a new representative, sit down and prioritize their prospect list. Next to each name on the list, put whatever letters from PEARLS apply to that prospect's qualities.

There are going to be a lot of different words that come up when you prioritize this way. Some are going to be PEAS: Positive Entrepreneurs who Achieve with Sincerity. Some are going to take Risks and be PEARS. You may have a SEAL: Sincere Entrepreneur who Achieves by Listening. Some are going to be EARS. And some are going to be PEARLS.

What's important is to contact the PEARLS first, because they have all the qualities that will best create partnership for the new representative's network. This business may not be easy, but it's simple when you follow a system. Remember "K-I-S-D", keep it simple and duplicable.

Unique Prospecting Approaches

Once representatives have the prospect list done, they need to learn how to develop trust. Another word for trust is rapport. There is an old expression in this industry: "People don't care how much you know until they know how much you care." Begin that emphasis on the very first prospect call, in the first fax, with every contact you make.

1. Fax Prospecting

My team has had good results with cold prospecting using a fax machine. Here's how this system works: Open the yellow pages of your phone book and find businesses who list their fax numbers. Simply fax a questionnaire to them. If they are awake, they might fax back. If not, you have no cost from faxing locally, and you have kept priming your pump. What you put out will come back somewhere in time.

Below is a sample questionnaire:

Are You Making More Money... In Less Time?

Many thousands of people are, by starting a home-based business. Take this free test to find out how you can earn more money and have more time to enjoy life.

- 1. Are you self-motivated?
- 2. Do you like to help people who help you?
- 3. Would you like additional income now, for retirement?
- 4. Can you give five to 15 hours a week to your own business?

- 5. Do you have access to a fax machine/computer at home?
- 6. Do you pay income taxes?
- 7. Do you use ? (And fill in the blank with the kind of product you offer.)

Please complete and fax to (your fax number).

Thank you for looking at securing your future now!!!

2. Call workshops

Call workshops are an exciting and successful tool being used to coach representatives in the next important step— calling the prospects on their list. New representatives and networking veterans meet to make prospecting calls together as a group. They offer each other minute-by-minute support and coaching, and the group acknowledges each success. Our teams are seeing tremendous results and increased sales from this for several reasons including:

1. **Call workshops create an atmosphere of true word-of-mouth advertising.** Enthusiastic representatives spend time as a group sharing outstanding products and opportunities with people they know, and their positive attitude is contagious. This is the way the network marketing industry was intended to work.

2. **New representatives have positive and personal support during a critical time of their growth.** Many excited beginners crash and burn during their first few calls. If they quit, they leave their warm-market list of prospects untouched. The personal support provided in a call workshop is vital to keeping new people on course.

3. **The workshops are upbeat and positive, creating more direction, momentum, sales and fun.** The energy and enthusiasm created by a team might not be duplicated by a representative working alone. Do you remember how much trouble the little boy got into in the movie *Home Alone*? It is not much different for new representatives who make calls while "home alone." With call workshops, team conference calls, and three-way calls, no one is left to figure it out alone.

   Everyone shares in the group's success, and the resulting positive attitude comes through on the calls. Greater numbers of appointments are set, and sales are higher.

4. **All representatives have a greater success rate.** After attending approximately 20 workshops, at the rate of one or two per week,

a representative will be assured of reaching their entire list of prospects.

5. **Representatives gain a better understanding of how to work the business**. That translates into consistent long-term efforts—a major key to success.

6. **Veteran and rookie representatives alike draw inspiration from each other.** The excitement of new representatives reminds everyone that this is a fun business. The success of experienced representatives strengthens belief and confidence.

7. **Groups can set goals for each workshop, challenging themselves week to week, month to month.** The accountability of working as a team helps everyone work at a high level of production.

The call workshops I've been discussing work best if they keep a specific, duplicatable structure:

Step 1 — Preparation

Identify the workshop leader, location, date and time. Schedule three to five representatives for the workshop using a sign-in sheet.

Step 2 — Leadership

The strength of the leader will determine the success of the workshop. The leader makes sure that representatives arrive on time, each with a list of at least ten names and phone numbers. After giving a quick overview of objectives and how the workshop will be conducted, the leader is responsible for keeping it on track, keeping distractions to a minimum and recording statistics for the group.

Step 3 — Role-Play

Each representative should take a turn role-playing. Keep the invitations positive, simple and to-the-point. The leader should also have a list of at least six sample scripts with specific and different themes.

Step 4 — Making Calls

Everyone keeps a positive attitude while making calls, cheering the efforts of others and celebrating every successful call. Calls should last one to three minutes each, and the group stays quiet to respect the caller. Between calls, there is a 30 second break for positive input. The calls continue until everyone present has a chance to call 10 names on their list. Because that can take between one and two hours, teams save their breaks and discussions for the end of the workshop.

Step 5 — **Commitment**

All representatives schedule the next call workshop before leaving. They choose the location, date and time, and fill out the sign-in sheet for that workshop. Each team needs to have at least one workshop per week. Fast-growing groups really have them more often.

Step 6 — **Growth**

When a call workshop has six representatives in regular attendance, it is time to split into two groups. Continue the grow-and-divide process as your teams grow. This moves duplication very quickly

Step 7 — **Upline Participation**

After a leader has attended and organized at least ten call workshops, the next step is participating in several workshops by phone. This will allow you to organize and be involved in several meetings at once. Experienced leaders offer direction, encouragement and congratulations to each team. They also keep the statistics, which are important to both accountability and acknowledgment as well as future goal-setting.

Keep it simple and duplicatable. Have fun! It's like attending a personal or professional seminar every week and then making the calls while you are still on a high level of action and commitment. This in turn initiates a higher quality of invitation, which translates into more customers attending presentations, resulting in more sales.

I encourage you to organize call workshops— you'll see immediate results in having more business builders coming into your network. I've included more information in the back of the book to make it easier for you to plan and track your workshops.

Here is the awesome and powerful flow of the overall results of call workshops:

Build Call Workshops
   which
   Build Relationships
      which
      Build Teams
         which
         Build Leaders
            which
            Build Time Leverage
               which
               Builds Residual Income

3. Tape-deck Prospecting

I recently heard of an easy and productive way to prospect—one you may have read as an Upline® Idea of the Month. When you pull into a gas station, car wash, parking garage or similar place where people can overhear you, make sure you have a good prospecting or development tape playing in your tape-deck. Turn up the volume and have your window, or even your door (if you're doing self-serve at the gas pump), wide open.

People will often ask you about what they're hearing, or they might ask you to turn it down. Either way, it opens the conversation for you to tell them why you're listening to the tapes. Ask if they would be willing to listen to see how your business could work for them. Don't judge this one until you give it a try.

Your Dream List

After you have done the prospecting, the inviting and the presenting, another great exercise to do is to create a dream list. I did this myself before starting my business, and it really helped me find out why I would even want to consider adding more to my time platter than I already had.

Have your prospect look at it from this point of view: If you had unlimited time and unlimited money—no limits, no obstacles, you had all the money and all the time in the world—how would your life be different? How would you structure it?

Have a piece of paper and a pen and start listing the things they say.

If your prospect wants to travel, ask where. You need them to be very specific. "I'd like to go to Australia." What do you want to do in Australia? "I want to see the kangaroos, I want to see a platypus, I want to go to the Great Barrier Reef."

If they want to go to Japan, "Great, what do you want to do in Japan?" Keep writing down specifics.

If they say, "I'd like to help my mom," find out how, in what way. Maybe they want to help her get her teeth fixed. Maybe they want to give her in-home medical care. Maybe her house needs new appliances or safety improvements. Maybe they just want to give her more options for her activities. Find out.

Do they want to put the kids in private school? In Hawaii, most of the representatives are doing the business to keep their kids in private school. Find out what makes a private school appealing to them. Are they looking for smaller classrooms, more teacher time, a better curriculum?

Write down everything, big, small and in between. Maybe they want to get a microwave—they've never had a microwave before. Maybe they want to be mortgage free. You are developing the value part of vision-value-trust. What's in it for them? WITHem!

How do you create value in a prospect? What are they willing to achieve in this business? What kind of income? What qualities do they desire to expand: confidence, leadership, self esteem, communication or courage? Who are their closest friends they want to bring along?

After you have had an appointment in person, *you must know your prospect's dream!* If your coach asks you, "What is their dream?" you'd better have the answer. If you can't remember, you were either not listening 80%, or you didn't ask enough questions.

Follow-Up is the Key

When someone sells a product— and again I'm talking about a true salesperson— there is very little follow up. The guy from the Lexus dealership never called me back! Someone goes into Sears to buy a refrigerator, those salespeople don't follow-up and call the customer back. If customers don't buy right then, they walk out the door, it's no deal.

Follow-up in network marketing is the key to your financial future. In responsible sponsoring, you have 100% follow-up until the person makes a decision. Why? If I said, "You deserve a break today," what company would you name?

Right, McDonald's. McDonald's hasn't used that advertising slogan for over 12 years, but most of us still remember it easily.

If I said, "Winston tastes good . . ." what's the ending? "Like a cigarette should." That commercial is a good 20 years old.

What's my point? Follow-up is repetition to keep your name or your company name and products in the mind and memory of your prospect. We heard ads for McDonald's and Winston so many times that we *still* remember the words!

Whether it's a one-week follow-up or a two-year follow-up, there is a way to do it painlessly and have the results you want. The Bible has a wonderful verse which says, "Ask and you shall be given, seek and you shall find, knock and the door will be opened." What happens is that too many people don't ask enough, they don't seek enough new prospects, and they don't knock on enough doors. Ask, seek and knock have no time frame. It doesn't say ask 15 people and you're going to have ten. It doesn't say knock on 18 doors. I'm not talking door-to-door prospecting, I'm talking about opening the door, and it's going to be open. It just says to keep doing this and your success will come to pass in time. Your prospect will have no choice but to join you in a matter of time, as long as you want that person as a team member.

Very few people are going to join the very first night. Do people decide to marry on the first date? Rarely. There is a lot of follow-up, a lot of establishing of relationship, building trust, of building some common interest, of building integrity together.

Your Communication Pipeline

Follow-up is like a pipeline, there is a flow of constant, consistent communication. Once they have seen the presentation or listened to a company audio, offer another item of interest. Maybe a company leader is coming to town for a large monthly event. Offer to pick up your prospect, take them with you to the event and introduce them to that leader. Each contact adds to the relationship.

Have them pull up fax-on-demand or visit your company's website. Use your follow-up to help them do their due diligence on your opportunity.

Move them through the pipeline very gently. Each of the events you take them to is going to be bigger and more powerful. It's a gradual building process, with the phone follow-up and the three-way follow-up.

After they go to a small, simple in-home presentation with eight or ten people, prospects start to see what this business can offer them. Each step assists them in getting absolutely clear about the choice, and clear that it is their choice.

It's kind of like when we applied to colleges; we might have applied to three or four or five. Through the process of gaining knowledge and education and communication, we finally made the choice. The pipeline and the follow-up campaign are two ways for a prospect to make a clear choice about their coming onto the team.

My "second mom," Helen, sold insurance for years, and she used the idea of a funnel. Keep putting prospects into the top of the funnel, and some are going to come out the bottom— straight into your business. Some will be customers, and some will be business-builders.

A Follow-Up Campaign

You want to keep following up with people every single month, you need to set up a follow-up campaign. You won't know when the timing is going to be right, so if you don't follow-up, somebody else may show them a different business at the right time. You don't want to let someone else capitalize on your hard work, so you need to have an organized, consistent campaign.

I chose the word campaign for a reason. You need to treat it like a presidential campaign, like somebody running for office. Look at the time and the money they put into it. A political campaign is usually a four-year process, and network marketing follow-up can be the same. Look at the constant effort. It took five years for my niece to finally come onto our family's team. Fortunately, we don't have to put much money into it. A postcard from anywhere in the world is a very inexpensive reminder.

Start with mail as your first follow-up. It could be a postcard or short letter, but you want something in front of your prospect every month. You might not have a phone call with them, but you know it's totally insane to just contact a prospect, show them the business, and then not follow up fully. Repeating the same actions and expecting different results is insanity. After someone has seen the business, but they are not in yet, it's very appropriate to send them a thank-you note the same day as the presentation. They have given you their time to look at the business. Simply let them know you're glad they did and that you anticipate building a business relationship sometime. That's all the first follow-up should be.

You are establishing a relationship that's going to be built on trust so always leave the door open without pressure for either to call. End each note by inviting your prospect to ask you questions. Let them know the date and time of the next big monthly event. That might be enough to bring some prospects into the business— the personal touch, someone reaching out with a special effort. Don't we all love to get handwritten thank-you notes?

Let's say your prospect mentioned, on their want list, a desire to travel. You have a business trip to Hawaii to build part of your organization. You just send a little postcard and say, "This trip is a tax write-off. Look at the gorgeous ocean and mountains. I'm doing some hiking tomorrow and going snorkeling the day after. Love to have you join me in the business soon, and you can start writing postcards like this to your friends."

If you and your prospect both have e-mail, you can also send them something over the Internet. Don't make it a junky note, make it personal. Follow-up keeps the lines of communication open and builds rapport.

It's best to use a phone call as the second follow-up, within 48 hours, and the main objective is for you to show your enthusiasm and provide communication. You want your prospect to see the value of coming on your team. You can make the phone call very quick, just, "I want you to know I haven't forgotten about you. I remember how much you want to take the boys on that hunting trip. Is that still a real commitment of yours? Great. This can assist you in doing that. What other questions do you have on the products or about the business?"

Here are two interesting questions you can ask them: Who do you know that you've been thinking would be good in your business?

All prospects need to see their personal circle of acquaintance and influence. As they get their own prospecting wheels turning, they'll be making business decisions—who they want to share the opportunity with— even before they sign their papers.

The second question is: Who do you know who has the most desire to succeed? Write those names down for future invitations at a call workshop or in-home video presentation for your soon-to-be representative.

Have a copy of the 4x6 "dream" card they filled out at the presentation or one-on-one so you can ask the questions exactly to their value as they wrote it on the card. You can get clearer communication with your prospects when you know what they want out of the business and partnership. Stay away from business mechanics, compensation plan and how to's. Be very confident in your speech that they will learn those things in the excellent training provided later. Let prospects know that the first step is for both of you to know their whys or value for being on the team. At every step of the follow-up campaign, ask them if they are ready to be on the team.

Have some fun and be light with it. I'd say something like, "I'm just unwilling to quit on you. Could I touch base with you every so often? I'm not going to pressure you or push, but unless you say you can't stand to ever talk to me again, I'll keep in touch."

As long as you're not attached to the results, they are going to welcome these kinds of positive, caring phone calls. If you're still worried about rejection, ask your prospect, "Are you rejecting me?" They will say no—and they may also tell you what objections are causing them to reject the opportunity. You can then address your prospect's concerns more effectively without any further worry about personal rejection.

Read, Watch and Listen

If your prospect still hasn't said yes, the follow-up campaign continues. The third follow-up would be giving them something new to read, something to listen to or a video to watch. Before you hang up the phone on the second follow-up, arrange to talk again to discuss that item. Say, "I'll be giving you a jingle within the next three days to see what you think of the tape (or book). Would you for-sure, absolutely, no-matter-what, I-can-count-on-you watch that tape (or read A Money Making Message)? We'll talk about it when I call.

"I know this sounds like it's kind of heavy, but I just want to be sure our next conversation will move you closer to the best choice to make for yourself." Be sure you know exactly what tape or what booklet you gave out so you can refer to it. *Freedom in a Box* works great for this.

Here's what my "Money-Making Message" looks like:

A Money-Making Message

What Would You Do If. . . .

What would you do to make your life *meaningful* if you were free to do anything you wanted with your life—and money and time were no longer a limiting factor?

Think about it! Please don't *limit* your thinking with what appears to be "realistic" or "reasonable." When you have at your fingertips such an extraordinary vehicle (network marketing), ordinary people like you and me can actually achieve that "impossible dream" of being FREE!

All you need to attain your freedom and make your dream come true is have a clear vision of what you want and at least one compelling reason to commit to do whatever it takes, however long it takes, to make it happen for you.

This "freedom" is not out of reach! You can be free, too, because we have thousands that are in the process of seeing it happen for them as well! You don't have to be left out! You can do it, too! It's your turn now!

The Grim Alternative

If you keep doing what you've always done, you'll just keep getting what you've always gotten! If you do what the "crowd" does, you'll get what the crowd gets! Not very exciting, is it?

Let's take a hard honest look at the many problems of not being free (working for someone else):

Circle all that apply to you . . .

1. Fighting terrible traffic every day.
2. Feeling insignificant—your work is not meaningful.
3. Feeling trapped and hopeless in a job you don't like.
4. Feeling like a slave—no freedom.
5. Little or no respect or gratitude.
6. Underpaid and over-taxed (JOB = Just Over Broke).
7. No security; no future; no potential.
8. Stuck with having to work until you're old.
9. Insufficient or no retirement.
10. Unfair treatment, office politics, favoritism.
11. Not enough time with your family.
12. No fun! (Many people hate their jobs.)

You aren't really willing to settle for that, are you? If you lived in Iraq and had no choice, that would be one thing, but you live in civilized countries! You were destined to be free, not a slave to a job!

The Opportunity

In contrast to the "problems" of not being free, let's examine the "opportunity" that network marketing offers you:

1. You get to do something you really love.
2 You get to do something fun and exciting.
3. You get to do something challenging and stimulating.
4. You get to work out of your home and avoid the daily traffic grind.
5. You get to start part time and you don't have to go back to college.
6. You get to really make a significant difference and be "somebody."
7. You get the opportunity to give to thousands of people.
8. You get to be a part of dramatically changing the lives of thousands of people.
9. You get personal growth and leadership development.
10. You get a lot of recognition and gratitude.
11. You get the possibility of earning more than the CEO of a Fortune 500 company or a president or prime minister.
12. You get the choice of being able to retire within two to five years and maintain the same or growing income.

13. You get to enjoy the feeling of being in control of your own life (real freedom).

14. You get to enjoy the freedom to follow your true values and dreams.

15. You get to travel as much as you desire.

16. You get the freedom of being able to live anywhere in the world.

17. You get to enjoy the feeling of belonging that comes from being part of a close-knit family of people that love, appreciate and respect you.

18. You get to choose who you work with.

These points are not just possible or theoretical. They are inevitable— when you are willing to make a serious decision that this really is what you are committed to and deserve.

Keep Your Vision,
Peggy "Like A Rock" Long

The Money Making Message is an example of follow-up which really causes a prospect to think. It can be used in a fax, letter or e-mail to your prospect, and I've had super success using it. After they receive it, you also have a particular basis for communication. Ask which column was more appealing. What stood out? You can make notes on the same card you've used for all the other steps with this person. That card is also where you put down what you gave the prospect to review— video, audio, or Money Making Message.

If they need to understand the industry better, they need some education to help them know that this is a viable, powerful, lucrative way to do business. You would have a conversation and communication about the industry.

You might have a three-way call with someone who explains this industry particularly well, or use one of the credibility letters from a professional in the same field. When you have a group conference call, invite your prospects to participate. The more varied choices they can be making themselves, the better it is.

By the time you have three or four follow-up campaign phone calls, cards, conference calls and letters, you have moved them through the pipeline/funnel of presentation. You call the shots. *On this rock I stand, and, World, you will adjust.* You decide when to ask the question: "Are you ready to be a part of an action-oriented team?" By now, it's such a process and a journey for them, they know darn well that if they don't join the team, they are absolutely going to be left behind.

When a prospect joins the team, we simply fill out the application and order their starter pack and products. If they haven't come in, you continue to follow up every month until they make a decision.

What's Stopping You?

The fifth follow-up on the campaign would be another letter.

I like to use brightly colored envelopes to catch someone's attention. I just say, "I can't understand why you haven't come on the team yet. It totally baffles me. Will you share what's stopping you? Please give me a call so we can talk, or I'll give you a call."

The more you get clear with what is stopping them and the more they communicate it, the less of a stop it's going to be—for either of you.

Just keep the connection open, even if it's been three months since your first contact.

The sixth follow-up would be, "Hey, we are really moving on, we'd like to have you on the team. You've missed Barbara and Sue and Matthew, they have come on board, and you know Matt from work. Are you ready? Ready to be free? Ready to come play?" Keep asking those questions.

If they still say not yet, and you're on maybe the seven month or eight month, you just keep following up with something new. Timing in this industry and in your company is everything. Remember all I did was purchase some diamond earrings and a diamond tennis bracelet the end of December, 1991. I had no intention of doing the business. Two months later when I got downsized, the timing was right for me.

That's why as long as you keep sharing your follow-up campaign, in time, many of them are going to come around. Or they are going to absolutely say "no." If they say "no, no, no, no," then you know you can let go.

I would say, "Do you want me to keep you informed at all?" If they say "absolutely not," I'm going to respect that. "Will you keep the doors open from your side? If you ever want to know more, if your circumstances or timing change, will you promise to call me back?" Most of them are going to say "yes" to that.

The follow-up campaign and the pipeline/funnel are two ways that you can build a very lucrative business, because it's a planned strategy. It's a planned system that is absolutely going to require work. If your goal is to sign up three people a month, you're going to probably need to have at least ten to 15 people in the funnel, in the follow-up campaign. And you can have a lot of fun with that.

Sometimes if a whole group of us are together, and we all have a mutual friend who is not yet in the business, we'll just drop a little note to him. You can get some wonderful cards from Millionaires in Motion that say, "Come join the team. You're simply the best. I can't forget about you. Eagles are soaring. Are you ready?" Send something really positive on a postcard. It lets him know that other people, friends and colleagues, are still seeing him coming into the business.

Another benefit of following up is the way it keeps you in daily discipline or the single daily action. If you contact one person in your funnel/pipeline, in the follow-through campaign, it's a positive action for your business, no matter what the outcome.

We are gently leading people in through the process that leads to making their own choice. Repetition is the key and prospects are going to be watching if you do truly care. Continue to gently lead them through a very positive, powerful, productive pipeline. It has to move forward with each step your prospect takes. Stand your ground and they'll come around!

Persistence Pays

Here is a personal story from my family that illustrates why following up is so important—you never know when it will be the right timing for them.

When I was downsized and decided to work the business, I saw how powerful it was and I didn't want to leave my family behind. I had a small backup reserve I knew could carry me about six to eight months, even if I didn't receive much income from my new networking business, but I wanted to have both my sons in, even though at the time they thought their mom, aunt, uncle, grandfather and grandmother were totally crazy.

My sons couldn't believe we were doing something like this. I purchased some products as gifts to qualify my sons as representatives. They were placed in our family's network with centers they could build.

As I mentioned earlier, neither of my sons supported me at all when I first started this business. They criticized and disempowered me "for my own good." When their grandparents, aunt and uncle started earning money, Jordan said, "Well, Mom has always been successful. She's always been committed. She has always been straight, she's always called a spade a spade."

The truth is, I haven't always been successful. I've taken jobs I didn't want to be in, with people I didn't want to be around in the past. They were just income generators. What finally happened is when Ken and Karen Long— Jordie's uncle and aunt— were doing well, and Dr. Kermit and Helen Long— his grandparents— were beginning to earn weekly money, it was a wake-up call for Jordie. He was working 80, even sometimes 100, hours a week at his job in a music store. He was pumping, pumping, pumping, pumping and they kept promising him a management position. They said, "We'll even move you back to Boston, you can take over that super store. . . ." It never came to be. He was on a gigantic quota, and if he didn't meet his quota, then he didn't get his full commission. He was selling guitars, strings, drums, lights and music lessons. It took a lot of $3.00 guitar strings to meet his $40,000 monthly quota. It was absolutely horrible the way they were driving him, but he was choosing it.

Finally he said enough was enough. He wasn't making much money, he was actually receiving food stamps, because his income, even though he was working hard and making someone else a lot of money, was not enough for him to live on. (Remember, of the total real income we make for a non-networking company, 90% they actually keep and we only get 10%!)

I kept him in the follow-up campaign. I kept dropping things in the mail to him. I kept calling him. His aunt and uncle, his grandparents, everybody kept him in the funnel, in the follow-up campaign. He finally recognized that his job had no fulfillment, no future and no satisfaction. It wasn't earning him enough money, they kept breaking their agreements, and it was a mutual decision, but he really got downsized. So then he called me.

He said, "Mom, you always said when I'm ready 'you can count on me.' So I'm going to start working my networking business, and since you sponsored me, you're my coach."

I said, "Okay, Jordan, first of all, I need to set a few things straight with you. In order for me to coach you, you and I need to remove the mother/son relationship and we're going into a partnership, which is totally different. You're going to need to be a student of my coaching and not get *mother* included in that."

He said he was willing to do that, and I said I was willing to do it, too. (Here's the truth: About 95% of the time, we both did well, but occasionally mom came in and son came in. Then we would catch ourselves, and stop that communication or behavior.)

Master the Fundamentals

Let's face it, prospecting is work and it's often very tedious. The most spectacular success is not easily nor quickly won. To accomplish anything worthwhile frequently requires doing the same thing over and over again and again for as long as it takes. Winners focus on mastering the fundamentals rather than chasing every new gimmick, strategy or company that comes along.

You've probably even seen this happen many times in your own town. A new trendy restaurant will promote something, some kind of a new exciting concept and draw crowds for a few months, and then lose most of their business to the next new fad. Meanwhile, other restaurants focus on perfecting their food, their service, their dependability, their cleanliness, their convenience and their reputation, and they build a loyal clientele that keeps coming back again and again.

Sometimes we become so familiar with the fundamentals that we forget how important they are. Yet no one is so accomplished or so highly experienced that they can afford to ignore the basics of prospecting. Often the most exciting and significant results come from the most tedious effort.

Here's an easy way to remember the fundamentals— I call it STPing. STP means:
- See the People.
- Show the Plan.
- Sell the Products.

- **S**ponsor the **P**rospects.
- **S**imply **T**each **P**assionately.
- **S**ucceed **T**hrough **P**rinciples.

If you are not constantly prospecting and sponsoring, your personal responsibility to your business is standing still. You are staying stuck. Some of you aren't going to like that last statement, but look honestly and tell the truth. You'll find it is the truth

Remember your basics—prospecting, inviting, presenting and retailing. STP consistently.

Persist and you will prevail. That's the solid rock to stand on.

Chapter 3

Goal-Setting in Partnership

Once a prospect comes into the business as a business-builder, your priority should be to set the stage for developing your partnership and their goals. Goal-setting begins with initial communication and setting an action plan in place immediately. The new representative needs to know they will be in partnership with you and how that will work. Effective partnership leverages the power of relationships and teamwork— it allows more than one person to strive toward a single goal together.

Eight Excellent Sponsoring Questions

In developing this partnership and creating excellence in sponsoring, I have a series of questions for clarity.

Remember, questions are the answers. I'm going to go over some questions that you need to ask yourself when somebody has made a positive forward decision to come onto the team and be in partnership with you. Even when they don't, you need to review this list, because one of these next eight questions will show you what to do differently next time you sponsor someone. You may have gone full-out in sponsoring and you were playing to win, or you were playing not to lose, or you were just playing or you were not playing.

Partnership begins way before someone actually does their paperwork, sells, or purchases product to use and becomes a product of the product (which is a must!). That's why the follow-up, the communication and the consistency are absolutely critical. Prospects are going to be watching what you do. Lead by example. Remember these questions when you're asking for the commitment. Understand that people's responses are precious and personal, and we need to treat what they say with respect.

1. Does she have enough value yet?

Is she clear about what is going to be in it for her? Is she clear that she is going to be paying some prices in order to have all the great payoffs that are available for her?

If she is coming up with a lot of objections and uncertainties, then there isn't enough value yet. You need to go back to value— use the value list included in this chapter. Ask her, "If you had unlimited time and unlimited money, how would you structure your life, what would be different? If you had six months to live, what would be the most important things for you to accomplish?" You need to go back to value and listen and draw her out and reach her core.

2. Does he have enough information?

Prospects need to know what it's going to cost as far as the starter pack or the startup kit. They need to have the tools of the trade. If they are going to purchase some product to have available as samples or if they are going to purchase some product to be a product of the product, they need to know how that all works.

Have you clearly communicated to them the information, so they are clear this is what's going to happen, so there is no hidden agenda? If there is a training cost for your corporate training, have you communicated that to them? Have you communicated to them about additional costs and fees?

Almost all of our companies have a renewal fee, whether it's $29 or $89. People need to know all the information, so you are not throwing something unexpected at them later. Prospects must have all the information they need to know in order to finalize their decision.

3. A great leader has a strong self-image and is self-confident.

Some people buy plenty of inventory and samples. They buy some product to use and show, and this is not about taking food off of people's tables. I believe we need to responsibly sponsor. It's not how much product they start with. It's how much commitment they are bringing to the partnership.

We need to let them know they are going to need to make phone calls. They are going to do some mailings. It's going to be important to have a fax machine and be on the company or sponsorship line's voice mail as soon as possible. They need to come up with a time frame of when these will happen. They are going to need to have additional forms, videos, samples and brochures/catalogs, so they can build their business. I would rather have someone start with less product selling or purchasing it for show, so they have more money in order to really have the business tools necessary to become a big business-builder. I use the acronym RYBLAB as a reminder to Run Your Business Like a Business!

4. Does he trust you?

Have you been communicating in such a way that your prospect really trusts you? Does he feel you are sincere? Does he feel you are authentic? Does he know you are going to be there for him?

It's vital how we be with someone else, not how we do. It doesn't matter how knowledgeable we are of the mechanics and the information. How do prospects really feel about you as a sponsor or as an upline coach? You will know that by the interaction and by the dialogue going on between you. This is where the trust is built. Not you just telling. Not just a monologue. A dialogue— two-way.

5. Is this what she really wants?

If you are trying to push a prospect into the business with big money... travel around the world... paying off the mortgage... maybe this isn't what she wants. If someone doesn't have some vision— dreams, goals and desire to enrich and create a more abundant life— you can't do that for her. You need to find out if she is willing to pay the price, to be committed for one to five years in one company.

If prospects are not willing, why bring them in? Have them as great retail customers, but don't bring in someone who does not want to work the business.

Pressure and manipulation give our industry a bad name, and that's where the lower retention rate in some of our companies comes from.

Here is the biggie and here is where most people stop.

6. Have you given it 100%?

Have you done and been every single way that you can be to give this person the absolute best opportunity in making a wise choice?

This is where I find a lot of representatives hold back. They don't give 100%. They don't play to win for the prospect and for themselves.

Sometimes I'll say:

"You might feel like I'm pushing you, and I don't intend to do that. That's the last desire I have. But if you knew what I know about how great this industry is, how super these products are, you would absolutely be in the business now. Sometimes, I'm just not sure how to communicate that."

That's the truth, and you are going to win people over if you tell the truth and never make up an insincere answer. If they have a question and you don't have the answer, don't make it up. The question I ask then is, "Do you really need to have this answer in order to make a wise decision now?" About 99% of the time, they say they don't need that answer. It's just a red herring, something to throw you off. Let them know they'll learn all about that in their training.

If someone is particularly insistent, you might say, "Mark, one of my great upline leaders is here. I can go ask for that answer right now if you need it immediately and don't mind waiting a few minutes."

They are going to tell you. The more they share in their own process and progress in making their decision, the more you will become an excellent sponsor. Always look at:

> *Have you given it 100%?*
> *Where did you stop?*
> *Where were you not be as great as you possibly could be?*
> It usually all boils down to that.

7. Do you want him as a team member?

I went to another city to train some new people in my downline. I had communicated with them by phone, and they absolutely said that they were ready to go. They were responsible and ordered their supplies and a whiteboard and easel. They were ready for me to go in for five days to start the duplication process and get them ready to be leaders in their area.

When I go long distance, I move in with people. I didn't know these people, and, of course, that's always risky. I also didn't really know anyone else who knew them. They were pretty far down my organization, but they had reached up and said they really wanted to learn the business.

I said, "Okay, you're clear on the ground rules: There will be no drinking or smoking during any of the presentations or training in your house?" No problem. Okay.

I got there, and the first night they had about ten people attend the presentation. I had told my hosts we needed to be in front of 50 people in five days. I call the shots when I go into somebody's place to duplicate. Those five days can create tremendous momentum in business if you set it up right beforehand with people who are accountable and have integrity.

The first night, they introduced me, so they were moving right along the stages of learning a presentation. As I'm speaking, out of the kitchen comes a beer and alcohol cart all of a sudden. I said, "It would really assist us if you just put that on the side until later."

They said, "No, these are our friends, and we always drink when we are together."

That was a red flag. I knew I had trouble, because they had agreed with me on the phone there would be no smoking or drinking during the presentation or training. I wasn't ready to upset the applecart with the guests there, so I let them pass out the beer.

Big mistake!

All the guests came into the business that night, but they wouldn't purchase a starter pack. They said, "We're not going to do any training, we're just going to grab people and put them into this thing."

I was fairly new in the business at the time; you need to remember that. I didn't have a duplication process really in place yet. It was to be another 13 months before I truly developed mine, so I didn't have my duplication rock to stand on. They all just put money down, cash, like a $1,000 for the product. No credit cards. They signed the forms and passed in the money.

The next night there was double the number in the room. I worked with the hosts and said, "Will you keep the alcohol cart out?"

"Okay, tonight we will."

The next thing I know, double the cash on the table and out comes the alcohol cart.

I'm getting really nervous, because I don't know how to handle this. I hadn't come up against this before.

The third night we had that room packed, and I had green cash in my hand to the tune of $30,000. My new representatives kept saying, "You just send all the paperwork in. We're not going to learn paperwork, we're not going to do any training, we are just going to recruit these people in and run it like a pyramid, and buy some product."

The minute that word came out of their mouths, I thought, am I ever in trouble. I said, "This is not a pyramid. This is a legal way to do business. You need to have your forms, you need to order your materials. We don't take people's money, you need to have some product to show for this."

Just then, I glanced down at one guy's boot and there was a gun. I got really nervous. I'm not necessarily street smart, but I finally got that I was in some kind of Mafia group or something. I asked the people whose home I was in, "Are some of these people associated with the Mafia back here?"

They said, "That doesn't matter, we're just going to grab the cash."

I had $30,000 worth of cash in my hands. I had one leg that was so strong in my organization. I had developed three diamonds and 19 car earners on that leg. In order for me to earn money in my company's pay plan, I needed to have my other leg going. This was the group that was going to get my other leg going.

But . . . people before paychecks.

When I knew for sure they were Mafia, I knew the next night we would have been packed with a lineup out the door and down the street. I also knew I was in way over my head.

I finished that night, went to my bedroom and called the vice president of our company at his home. He knew why I had gone out of town, and he had been so empowering and encouraging. He knew I had done a great job with one group in Hawaii, and this group I was now training was going to be my other leg. It would give me a weekly income of $2,250.

I said, "Hi, this is Peggy. I've gotten myself in a jam. I have $30,000 cash here, and this group could absolutely get my other leg going, but I've learned these people are straight pyramid. They will not follow any of my coaching, and I'm quite sure they are Mafia people."

He said, "Peggy, you went in and you did all you could. Leave all that money there. Pack your bag and get on the next flight out."

The vice president told me not to worry about my flight. He knew I had gone back there on a shoestring, but he told me to get on the next flight out in the morning, regardless of cost. The company would cover any costs of changing my flight at the last minute.

"Leave all the money," he said, "And we will be glad to give the original couple a refund and have them out of the business."

What I respected about that company, and I pray that all companies are like that, was the integrity and the people-before-paychecks philosophy. That's so important. It was a great lesson, and if I had just gone after the money, I probably would have been up to $10,000 a month immediately. That pyramid-thinking group would have kept the leg going, I don't doubt, but I did not want to have them on my team. I did not want to have them associated with my incredible company, so I paid the price. My integrity and my company's long-term success were more important than money in my pocket short term.

It wasn't until three months later that I sponsored Donna and Jason Haugh in British Columbia as my second team. They have integrity, compassion, honesty and a background of respect from other people.

I think that's a story that really brings home a point: It's very important that we ask ourselves who we want as our team members. Ask yourself: Is this prospect the kind of person I want to have my name and reputation associated with? If not, don't bring them on your team. It will haunt you and backfire on you, your company and our industry.

There are two kinds of people in life (this applies to representatives and prospects alike): people who take charge and people who take things easy. The first are the action-oriented problem-solvers who show up as runners in a network. People in the second group are more easy going and committed. They don't want to rock the boat, so they usually show up as walkers.

One committed runner may produce as much as 20 walkers, but I suggest that you prospect for walkers instead of looking for runners. Why? Committed runners are rare. Runners often quit to run somewhere else, and you have no one as a leader in your network. If you have developed 20 walkers and one leaves, you still have 19 solid committed walkers going strong. Of course, both groups are necessary for a strong network, so don't throw your runners out the door. An equal amount of time and energy needs to go into each prospect. Just don't put all your eggs in one basket.

8. Did you listen to her?

You are going to know if you listened, because you are going to be able to feed back what it is that she said. What are her concerns? What is it that she likes most about the business and product? What is her value? What are some of her goals?

If you are not listening, you're not going to have any feedback, which is really feedforward. If prospects are not moving forward, it's because you haven't listened and you can't give them enough feed to move forward. Remember these questions when you're finalizing their decision with them. The truth is, when you answer the above questions, they are going to feel like they are in control. The they make a clear, true *choice* to start a business.

Four Personalities

There are four basic personality types, and recognizing your new reps' personalities from the start will help you be a better sponsor and establish more successful partnerships with them. Here is a brief summary of the four personalities:

Promoter

A promoter wants fun and action. Promoters want a lot of money. They earn the most money and they spend the most money. They're not very good savers, but that's something they'll learn through this partnership process in goal-setting. They are very talkative and need acknowledgment. They make decisions fast.

Analyst

Analysts want data and systems; they're very organized and detailed. They want to see the research, study, and be certain of every aspect. Dot every "i" and cross every "t" with them. They are less talkative and need patience from a coach. They are slow decision makers.

Controller

Controllers want power— they are take-charge people who need to know they are going to have their own choice within the system. Let them know how to work within a system or a controller will go out and start reinventing the wheel. Controllers are fast decision-makers and talkers who need recognition and are money-motivated.

Supporter

These are people that enjoy relationships. Supporters are attracted to the interactions and benefits of a caring team. They are less talkative, need to feel important and needed and they decide slowly.

In developing teams and partnerships, you must be clear about how to interact with different people and their unique personalities. For example, it won't work to ask someone with an analytical personality, "Are you ready to be on a fun party team?" That won't be at all appealing to them. They'll say, "I want data. I want a system. I want to know exactly what course I need to follow."

Most people have aspects of all these personality types, but in asking the questions to set up the partnership, look for which is dominant for them. If they are flamboyant, action-oriented, moving their hands a whole lot, that's going to be more of a promoter, or maybe a controller. If they request detailed information on each product, the compensation plan and the team's system, you know you're dealing with an analyst.

The Value List

I have a value list that covers all four personality types. Give this list to a prospect and ask them to check off the five that fit them best. You'll be able to see what kind of a personality they have, so you can be in partnership and coach more effectively with each individual.

__ Organization
__ Personal power
__ Financial security
__ Desire to be rich
__ Desire to look good
__ A loving relationship with a partner
__ Family
__ Integrity
__ Career fulfillment
__ Desire to feel needed
__ Personal development
__ Adventure and travel
__ Recognition and fame
__ Accomplishments
__ Personal leadership
__ Material possessions
__ Charity and church contributions both time and money
__ Relationship
__ Belonging
__ Fun and action

After someone new comes onto the team, have them write down, in order, which are the most important to them, from 1 (top priority) to 20 (least important).

A controller would want power, financial security, career fulfillment and accomplishments. Analysts would certainly be much more into financial security, organization, accomplishments and personal leadership.

The promoters desire to be rich and have fun. They like to look good. They'd like to be recognized continually, and they are into personal development.

A supporter would certainly choose relationships and family, and most supporters want to look good, they don't want to rock the boat.

It's important to know what someone, a particular sponsor or new representative, is bringing into the partnership. Then you need to operate and interact with this person on their particular values and personality style.

A strong controller may not really care what they look like. They are going to do whatever it takes, because that's how they interact and how they relate. So, they usually don't care about looking good. Whereas a supporter would care; so would an analyst.

Read Conrad Hilton's story building the Hilton Hotels. It's an incredible study of personal leadership.

Conrad Hilton said, "Success seems to be connected with action, and successful people keep moving. They make mistakes, but they don't quit."

Promoters and controllers don't care if they make mistakes, they go forward. Your analysts will need to be right. They don't like to make mistakes and neither do the supporters, because they won't look good. It's important to let them know that you know they might make mistakes, but that's okay. You need to empower them as they go forward in their duplication in the business.

Take the time— right now— to go back and rank your own values from most important #1 all the way to #20, least important.

The Right Approach Gets the Right Response

I was in Las Vegas a couple of years ago, doing a presentation. A young girl named Cindy was sitting three rows back on the corner aisle seat. She was an acquaintance, not a close friend, of a few representatives who had invited her there. After the presentation, there were three or four reps sitting around Cindy, and they were asking her questions. Don't you want more money? Don't you want financial security or financial freedom? They were focusing only on that aspect of this business.

Cindy wasn't responding. They kept going down a tunnel that was leading nowhere and getting no results. Cindy was a supporter, she was more of a quiet person, and so she started to cry. I noticed that—a leader will always be aware of what's happening in a room— and I went over and said, "Cindy, is it okay if I sit down and just talk with you as a friend?" She welcomed me, because she had a couple of controllers and promoters pushing her, and she was a supporter.

I said, "I've been listening, and it sounds to me like you don't really need any money." Tears started running down her face, and she said, "No, Peggy, my parents were killed in an accident about two years ago, and I am set up for life financially."

I said, "I'm really sorry. You probably really miss them."

Cindy said, "Yes. I do miss them."

I asked her, "What do you miss particularly?"

She replied, "I miss their friendship, I miss their love, I miss traveling with them."

I said, "How would you like to come on a team where you could travel and have a lot of people that care about you and have a support system for you?"

She said, "That's all I want. I don't want the money. I just want people to care about me."

In a matter of minutes, she was totally over the line, because I found a need and filled it. That's what partnership is. It's not leading people down a tunnel or going after the same values *you want* in your personality style. You need to go exactly where they are.

Cindy came in to the business with enough product purchased in her initial order to earn a fabulous vacation, because she wanted to travel with some caring supportive people. She did that because I found out her true personality and desires and provided her with something she really wanted.

So many reps are just pushing people in the direction of their own values instead of listening and being in partnership. Cindy was a true supporter, so she needed to come into the business for the relationships. She brought her own needs, strengths and passions to the partnership.

Know a Person's Core Values

Once someone is in the business, it's important to have them start setting their goals. The value list is a great way to discover their core values. We have people coming into our companies and into our businesses that do not need the money, but their goal for being in partnership is to help other people earn their ideal income. Or their core values might be to build that wing on the children's hospital. They want the extra money for external giving rather than for themselves.

A person's core values show up in their prospecting, in their partnership, in their goals, in their 3x5 cards and in the anchor words they choose. The entire process of their values, action, treasure maps— everything needs to be in alignment with what is most important to that person. That's true whether they are a controller, a promoter, an analyst or a supporter.

Look at yourself and get clear about which type of personality you have. The way to know best is to ask yourself: When you are up between a rock and a hard place, when you are pushed, when you are confronted, when you have a major problem, do you choose flight or fight?

A controller or promoter is going to fight. A supporter and an analyst will choose flight. It's very important in partnerships to be able to interact with each personality type so they feel protected, not confronted. You have to know yourself well to connect with other personality styles well.

When you attempt to confront an analyst or supporter, they're just going to run; they are not going to interact. They are going to back down. They're just not going to be present, and that doesn't work in developing partnerships with people.

The Treasure Map

One of the strongest things I do is what's called a treasure map. Some companies call it a vision book. This process needs to be completed within the first two weeks they're in the business.

Get a large poster board in a really bright color. Most office supply and drug stores carry a wide variety of colors, and you can do treasure map parties with a whole group of new reps. What you're going to do is to start cutting out pictures from magazines for the first part of the treasure map.

There are three parts to the treasure map. One is the *having*, which is material possessions. That is where most people start, because it seems the easiest. If they want to travel, they cut out pictures of cruise ships, the Concorde, views of Paris, photographs of the Sydney Opera House in Australia.

If owning a beautiful home is part of their dream, they cut out pictures of exteriors and interiors they think are ideal. If the goal is to be slim and fit, they would find a photo of a great-looking man or woman. They cut that person's face off and replace it with a picture of their own face to go with the strong, healthy physique. Some people cut out numbers, dollar signs and pictures of money to represent how much they will earn.

My father was 80 years old, and he had always had a dream to go marlin fishing. A year ago, I took my dad and step-mom to Mexico, and Dad caught his first marlin. He had pasted pictures of a marlin on his treasure map. They also had a picture of a hot tub, which they have now. Those are the *having* pictures.

In order to have, we must *do*. That's the second part of a treasure map. Someone might cut out a picture of a telephone, knowing that picking up the phone is an important "do." They might put down five prospecting calls a day on this treasure map. Perhaps they need to find pictures of mall-walking for prospects. The treasure map is like a goal board.

They might put down the date they're going to hit a particular level or title in a company, whether it's gold, platinum, diamond, director or executive. All companies have different levels of achievements with higher pay. They can cut those out from the company magazine.

Perhaps they are going to read three great network marketing books a month.

Perhaps they'll have a picture of a lot of people who they are committed to helping. On my first treasure map, I had pictures of my sons, my parents, my brother and sister and a few other people, and they weren't even in the business yet.

The treasure map is truly an example of "to think is to create." Most people are not in control of their thinking. It's haphazard. It's all over everywhere. A treasure map or vision map keeps people focused, keeps them on what they need to do in order to have.

We go from having to doing, and then the most important is *being*. On a treasure map, people need to cut out words about being. Perhaps someone's kind of shy. What's the opposite of shy? It might be confident. They would paste that word, and others like it, on the treasure map.

Perhaps someone has played it safe in life up 'til now. They would cut out a great big "RISKY", or maybe "COURAGE." Perhaps somebody is more withdrawn or their communication is monotonous, dull, hum-drum. They would cut out "passionate," "exciting," even "dazzling."

Some people put a great big ear on their treasure map, because it reminds them all the time that they need to listen.

The being words and pictures on your treasure map are the most important ones. Why? Because when we change, grow, expand and improve the internal part of us (our being), the external also changes. As within, so without.

I had on my map, as a big inspiration and Upline® Master facilitator, a picture of John Milton Fogg. I hadn't even met him or his great wife Susan, yet. To visualize will create results. To think is to create. After two years on my treasure map, John became first an acquaintance, then a friend *and* my collaborator on this book.

I also have had the goal of enrolling 20 new Lifetime Members for Upline® each year. Every year, I have accomplished that goal, because I see it on my treasure map and act on it daily.

Other powerful words to include are Coach, Master Duplicator, Leader of Leaders.

On my own treasure map, I have FOLLOW UP in giant, bold letters. So many representatives do not sponsor somebody because they don't follow up with them.

Even get a picture of someone you greatly respect and put it on your map. A picture of a set of keys with the word "attitude" next to them works well as a reminder that your attitude is all-important. Some people use the words *authentic* and *real*.

I'm sure you get the picture. Have the team bring their treasure maps to training so everybody can see them and they can empower each other. Team members also get ideas from others that they can add to their own maps.

A treasure map lets people know what they need to do in network marking and that there are no boundaries whatsoever. In a little less than six years in the industry, I am now on my third treasure map. I've had all kinds of challenges and fears, but my goals still keep getting bigger and bigger, encompassing more people. I have become more of a human being, a bigger contributor to others.

You Can Count On Me

These are the most important words that can come out of a sponsor's mouth: You Can Count On Me. The new representative needs to know fundamentally what's in it for them (WITHem) and that they can count on you (YCCOM— You Can Count On Me). It's rare that someone hears that said so directly from anyone, but I let people know that when they are committed, they can count on me to stay with them and lend my skills, support and coaching, so that together we can build their business. This builds their belief in the system and trust in your coaching that they can succeed.

Let Their Goals Be Their Goals

When you're goal-setting in partnership with new representatives, please do not be pushy. It's absolutely imperative that they set their own goals They'll have business goals of sponsoring, of prospecting, of inviting and presenting, and follow-up; financial goals about having and doing; and don't forget the being goals, too.

Allow their goals to be their own. When are they committed to having their first paycheck? Whatever they say, make it okay for them. It is okay to say, "Will it work for you if it happens faster?" They'll say sure. You can plant that seed, but do not change their goal. *Let their goals be their goals.* They need to choose them and own them.

In the process, be sure to communicate clearly how this is going to take work, not luck. Lucille Ball, one of the greatest comedians of all time, once said, "Luck? I don't know anything about luck. I've never banked on it and I'm afraid of people who do. Luck to me is something else. It's hard work. And realizing what is opportunity and what isn't."

Within the duplication system, you can plan exactly what it is that they need to do to reach their particular goals in sponsoring, retailing the products and whatever is on their treasure maps. The little stepping stones reached are going to create the large stepping stones which will create their huge success in time. Once they set the goals, you can show the way.

Making the Choice

When people have their own goals, then doing this business is their choice— they are *choosing* for themselves why they are going to work the business. I learned of the following choice chart over 25 years ago. It has been useful in my life and business, so please spend time with it to see where you are operating in making your choices.

Produces Results

True Choice	False Choice
-Personally Responsible	-Reactive to Others
-Uses Change as Opportunity	-Success is Not Fulfilling
-Proactive	-Let Others Choose
-Play to Win	-Play Not to Lose

Does Not Produce Results

Avoid Choice	Deny Choice
-Chooses Not to Decide	-Takes No Responsibility
-Has Doubts, Confusion and Fear	-Victim in Most Situations
-Plays Wait-and-See Role	-Not Running in the Race
-Goes for Mediocrity	-Never Fails/Never Wins
-Wants to be Right	-Not Playing

A new representative must be in True Choice. The other three choices *are* choices— like the Rush song: "If you choose not to decide, you still have made a choice"—but they will never create a serious and committed builder. Are there areas in your life where you are not in True Choice?If you have convinced or manipulated them into their goal, into partnership or into the business as a new representative, it's a False Choice, and they'll never do the business. They have to make clear choices, on their own. You need to be impeccable in your integrity and your excellence in sponsoring, and you need the same integrity and excellence in developing them into a leaders.Here's a powerful exercise I use to convey to people the importance of their personal choice. Let's say I have two ice cream cones, one vanilla, one chocolate. I ask you, "Which flavor ice cream do you choose, chocolate or vanilla?" You respond, "I choose chocolate.""Great. Why did you choose chocolate?" "Because I like chocolate." "Oh, okay." "I have two ice cream cones, which do you choose?" "I choose chocolate." "Why?" "I like chocolate, I like the way it rolls around my tongue.""Oh, okay.""I have two ice cream cones, which one do you choose?" "I choose vanilla."

"Oh, okay. Why do you choose vanilla?"

"Because if it spills on my clothes, it isn't going to stain like chocolate."

"Oh, okay."

"I have two ice cream cones, which one do you choose?"

"I'm going to choose a twist, I'm going to take chocolate and vanilla."

"No, that's not one of your choices. Which one do you choose?"

"I'll go back to chocolate."

"Why chocolate?"

"Because that was my daddy's favorite flavor."

"Oh, I see."

"I have two ice cream cones, which one do you choose?"

Now they are getting frustrated. You readers are probably getting frustrated, too, but when you get the power of this exercise, it will greatly increase your results in your business.

Back to which one you choose.

"I'm going to choose vanilla."

"The reason I choose vanilla is because it's easier to swallow."

"Oh, okay.

This exercise can go on for two or three minutes. If you have four or five people around, you do it with each person. Finally someone is going to get the answer.

"I have two ice cream cones, which one do you choose?"

"I choose chocolate."

"Why?"

*"Because I **choose** chocolate."*

This is a high-impact exercise. It is their choice; a clear and conscious choice with no manipulation, no bribing, no add-ons, no hidden agendas. By asking and answering these questions yourself, you will grow greatly in becoming a powerful sponsor and developing strong partnerships. When someone who has done this exercise with me in our partnership gets a little stuck, I will simply go, "Two ice cream cones— which one do you choose?" Then they'll say, "I choose to prospect again, because this is what I am choosing. Period. It is my choice for the lifestyle I deserve."

What Steps Will They Take?

When I'm developing a new partnership, I use a system, a formula, that lets them know exactly what they need to do to become big business-builders. It's a system that shows people exactly what the steps are, what time frame they are committing to, and communicates for action on each one of those steps. It's based on four hours a day— that would be somebody who is going to run with this business, not just be a weekend warrior, but be a daily, disciplined warrior. When you are working ten hours a week, cut the times in half. When you are working your business full time, double each time in the schedule.

I have found this to be extremely beneficial for new representatives; they see how their time will be divided to create results.

How to Be a Big Business-Builder

Follow the business plan DAILY.
Time: 4 hours a day (20 hrs/wk = half-time)

- 30 min.   Call 3 to 4 new prospects per day, 15 to 20 calls a week at call workshops and on prospecting conference calls.

- 30 min.   Follow up (calls with prospects and with your team— three-ways).

- 30 min.   Pass out or mail pre-approach audios, videos and brochures.

- 1 1/2 hr   Make in-home presentations.

- 15 min.   Read to learn and be inspired.
- 15 min.   Exercise.
- 30 min.   Listen to tapes (may be best while driving).
- Attend all presentations, training and conventions.
- Sponsor and duplicate 4+ people per month.

(Place the titles of your company's various advancement/achievement levels in the list below.)

GOALS	DATE
• Become Consultant by	_____
• Become GOLD by	_____
• Become PLATINUM by	_____
• Become car-qualified by	_____
• Become National Director by	_____

Incorporate the other parts of life into the system so that it's not just about business. Break it down into study time, into productive time, into exercise time, where they can say their affirmations over and over again, while they are taking care of their physical side. It doesn't matter what they are doing and where, but with whatever time frame they are committing to, it has to be in action and accountability.

If someone has some filing to do, or some faxing or e-mail to send out, or they have some voice-mail to respond to, that needs to be done on their unproductive time. That means after hours when it's not appropriate to call somebody. It's very important to ask someone, when they come into partnership how early in the morning they can have action communications, and how late at night, too.

I'm a night owl, and people know they can call me up until midnight. That's fine. I am not a morning person. People know that I'm not going to be calling them at 7:00, 8:00 or 9:00 in the morning. My mind doesn't click then. You need to find out when it's best for others, when they are in their peak performance, in order to work best with them. You also need to find out if there are any times or days which are completely off limits, like religious holidays or children's story hour and bedtime. Ask them directly and then respect their boundaries.

Also you need know if it is appropriate for you to phone, fax or e-mail at their place of business. If they say no, then do not do it. Only call, fax or e-mail where it is appropriate.

These are all communications for action. Set the goal and the steps early, so you're both in alignment and in agreement.

It is critical that they write their goals down and have them with them all the time. Any time they come to a presentation, they have their goals. Some people even take a picture of their treasure map and carry it with them all the time. They might even laminate it, so they can have it on an overhead and show it to other members on the team.

Team members need to circle the goals achieved in red ink on their treasure maps as they complete each one. It reinforces that they are progressing: Victory!!

The following is a checklist to help monitor successes. I suggest everyone keep a weekly meter-reading notebook and review— monthly, quarterly and yearly— the growth in doing and being what builds your network.

Success Checklist

At the end of each week, ask:

1. How many people did I show the business to this week?

   For myself   For my team

   How many three-way phone calls did I have?

   For myself   For my team

   How many call workshops did I attend?

   How many conference calls was I on?

2. How long will it take me to show 25 people the business if I keep doing what I did last month?

3. Why am I doing network marketing, and what do I want from it?

   _____
   _____
   _____

For myself:

   _____
   _____
   _____

For loved ones:

_____

_____

_____

4. Am I totally committed?   _____
5. Will I match effort and work as diligently
    as the other successful leaders?   _____
6. Have I been giving up TV time to call
    and invite guests?   _____
7. Have I been sharing the videos/audios and
    the products?   _____
8. How many new retail customers did
    I have this week?   _____
9. If I keep doing what I am doing now, how
    long will it take me to reach my goals?   _____

The AVEnue to Success

As we do this goal setting with our partners, as the coach, we need to *paint the picture of preparation* for the avenue they are going to follow. I abbreviate *avenue* and use the acronym AVE:

A— ATTITUDE

It's important that our attitude is always positive and empowering. If you are having a little attitude problem, then don't get on the phone and act like you're fine. Clean yourself up. Go to an upline person and say, "I'm stuck right now." They'll assist you to coach yourself through it, or look at your treasure map or pick up a good book.

A result-producing technique is to open any inspirational book, just at a random page, and on that page will be a solution for you to get your attitude back in check. Are you willing to use this technique the next time your attitude is off? Our attitude needs to be right on when we're coaching in partnership.

V— VISION

A great coach on the AVE to success will always have their vision in place. The vision and their values are solid as a rock.

E—EMOTIONALLY SOLID

The E stands for being Emotionally solid. Again, that has to do with belief and it comes across in your voice on the phone. Remember people can't see you, but they are going to hear and feel you. Enthusiasm is very contagious.

I have an overhead I show in training of a clown with a really happy face. He's just shining like crazy. Lots of emotion, lots of belief, lots of passion and enthusiasm. I show that to myself and the team to make a point. Enthusiasm and the emotional side of us is contagious. So is the lack of it. I have another picture of a clown with his face looking sad and his eyes drooping and his hair bouncing into his face and all over. I remind my team that people follow feelings, they do not follow facts. If someone looks like the down clown, that's the emotional place they'll share with others.

Our AVE needs to be very clear in goal setting. Almost always, when someone gets stuck, it's going to be in one of those three areas. Their attitude has gotten sour— it can be called "stinking thinking"— or they've lost sight of their vision, or their emotions, their belief has shifted a little bit.

When you have some guidelines for them to use like AVE, they can check into them and say, "Okay, it's my vision right now. I've lost my vision. I've been knocked down 12 times today." I ask, "How did you use your discipline, persistence, boldness, risking before in that goal you achieved? How can you come back to being on purpose to having your vision crystal clear in front of you now?"

The treasure map glues people right back into their value. That's another tool you can use in working with your people on communication for action and staying on the AVE.

Make It a Challenge

Developing goals and coming into partnership needs to be a personal challenge for people. It's not about easy goals. It needs to challenge them to greater heights. What you need to do, as the coach in the partnership, is inspire and hold them accountable for taking the steps to achieve their next higher goal. That means telling the truth. That means being honest to another person and not giving them any slack. That doesn't mean if they don't reach a goal that you beat them up, that means hold them accountable for where they stop and empower them to break through next time on their goal date.

I have ten people faxing to me each Sunday night exactly what their goals— their AAA or Action, Accountability and Assignments (See Appendix D)— are for the next week. The following Sunday they fax in what they accomplished. On Monday and Tuesday afternoons, for about three hours (half an hour each), I coach and work with those ten leaders I'm developing all around the country. They know right then and there they need to tell the truth to have my coaching continue.

Let's say that Linda faxed in a goal of ten prospecting calls this week, but she did only three. I don't even have to ask the question, "Where did you stop?" Linda starts communicating in partnership with me, because she is going to hold herself accountable:

"Where I stopped is I didn't break it down on a daily basis. I needed to do two prospecting and inviting calls daily. I put it off until the end of the week, I allowed procrastination to stop me. I didn't stay on purpose, and someone called and said they had a problem with the product and I got off-track. I didn't keep the goal daily and therefore I didn't create them by the end of the week."

Then I simply ask, "Linda, what is going to change *in you* this week?"

Remember: On this rock I stand, and,World, you will adjust. In communication and in partnership, people want to point that finger

outside and blame and hold someone else accountable or have an excuse, reason, justification, alibi for why they didn't achieve their goals. So the communication for action and accountability in goal setting in partnership is, "How are you going to be different this week?" I say, "Would you share with me, please, how you're going to be different, so this same pattern of not accomplishing these goals isn't going to repeat next week?"

When I, as their coach, do not stop the pattern this week, it's going to repeat the next. If Linda says, "I'm going to break it down into daily commitments. I'm going to do two initial prospecting calls a day, so that won't seem as scary as ten all at once," then I'll ask Linda, "Is that absolutely clear? Do you know what you need to do to have a different result next week? Will you need to fax me daily that you have done your two?"

That kind of coaching in partnership and communication for action assists and supports following through. Linda may not need to send me a daily report, but she knows that's an option for keeping her on track, honoring her word. Integrity is a must for accomplishing results.

They need to have a personal challenge, and we need to inspire them that it absolutely can be done.

"Are you clear that you could have done your ten last week?"

"Yes, I'm very clear."

"Great, are you clear that you didn't do them?"

"Yes."

"What was the price you paid?"

By questioning, again, they clearly understand the price they pay: No or little results.

The Three-Minute Rule

Go find yourself an hourglass, one that runs for three minutes. Turn it over every time you start a phone call, every time you answer your e-mail, every time you start an activity. Keep it where you can always see it. It will be a constant reminder, a PTD (psychological trigger device), that another minute is here, and you can make it matter or waste it. It's your choice.

It also really helps, when you call somebody in partnership, to state immediately the purpose of the call. I suggest you come up with a consistent anchor word (or phrase) and use it. Here are some examples:

"Hi, this is Peggy 'Like a Rock' (anchor phrase) Long. Is this a good time to talk? The purpose of my phone call is to let you know

… of a change on my travel schedule."

… there is going to be a conference call. Will you please note it on your calendar now?"

… we have lunch tomorrow at noon. Can I count on you?"

Your partner knows immediately who is calling and exactly what you intend to accomplish, so you can both be more effective with your time.

By having a three—minute timer on your desk, you are going to be able to stay in productive communication, not in chitchat. When we go to a professional—a lawyer, a doctor, an accountant—we don't want them sitting around just chitchatting. We want them to finish the work we pay them to do. To be on purpose and complete it. By sharing what the purpose of the phone call is and having that three-minute timer, you are able to be much more productive and communicate for action.

Many times I'll say something like, "I have three minutes right now, so let's schedule the conference call. Now, you've put the conference call on your calendar and I can count on you to get it out to your ten top leaders. I have two minutes for any questions you need to have answered. Anything you need to know?" Remember to end all phone calls with the Seven Magic Words: *Is there anything else I can do?*" Be sure to leave this partnership call with your team member feeling your support.

That keeps the call within three minutes while handling your intended result and the other person's question. It leaves more time for working your business productively. I'm going to pick up the phone and make that prospecting call. I'm going to do a follow-up. I'm going to set up a time for my next 24-hour duplication. Most people spend valuable time *majoring in the minors:* making coffee, filing, chatting about everything except their business.

I challenge all of you to have a three-minute timer right on your desk. Use it, teach your people to use it, and I guarantee you are going to see more productivity. Your people are going to have their conversations efficiently. They are going to communicate for action and on purpose, and they can do it in three minutes and have fun.

They absolutely have a ball with this.

Holding People Accountable

In partnership, communication for action is critical. In my experience, most people in any business, in families, in parenting, in organizations, in charitable causes, do not communicate for action. They allow other people to slide.

What do I mean by allowing people to *slide*?

I mean that they don't hold people accountable for their communication and their actions. How does that look when you don't hold people accountable?

Let's say I am talking to Karen and I'm coaching her on her weekly goals and her weekly commitment, and she says, "I think I'll do five initial interest questions this week."

Thinking about them is not going to accomplish it. I would say, "Karen, can I ask you a question? Does thinking mean you are going to think about it, or does it mean you will absolutely complete five initial interest questions?" I'm asking Karen to communicate in a way that will secure her action and weekly success.

Someone might say, "Maybe I'll be able to attend the training on Saturday." Those qualifiers or backdoors in communication— maybe, probably, think, hope, want, wish, like— must be stopped by the coach or the leader. If you allow people to use those wimpy words, you will not develop them into leaders. Remember duplication can be good or bad. In partnership, early in training and coaching someone, you must stop the kind of communication that does not create a result and lead into action.

Communication for action creates a certain result. Wimpy words create a lack of result. Communication for action is one of the areas in developing goal setting in partnership that is very, very important in becoming a leader of leaders. Accountability creates stability in our partnerships and income.

Another example is, "I'll probably get that done." Well, "probably" means nothing. How many of you have heard some prospect say, "I'm probably going to get there Wednesday night for the presentation or be on the Tuesday evening conference introduction call." Do they show up for either one? No.

That's why, beginning in prospecting, it's important to stop that kind of communication immediately. "Does that mean I'm going to see you there or I'm not going to see you there?" We start the partnership in communication even before they are part of the network or the team.

When prospecting, always have them pull their calendar out and write down "Wednesday night presentation at 7 pm." Let your prospect know you'll wait while they do that. "Okay, do you have it down? Great! I'll pick you up at 6:30, so we can spend some more time in the car together." The communication for action starts even before the partnership. That way, they are going to be accustomed to it. They are going to know how you're going to interact with them.

If you come across as wimpy in inviting and presenting, that's how they are going to see, hear and feel you and the business opportunity. I believe that old cliché "fake it until you make it" has some validity in regard to communication with confidence. Maintain certainty and posture in your voice.

The masters in this industry are geniuses with this, and they do not allow people to slide and back down from communicating for action. Communicating for action is going to bring about the result you and you partner have created together.

Here's an example to illustrate: A lady called the carwash she had recently visited to see if she had left her jacket in the waiting room. She asked the attendant if there was a burgundy blazer there. The attendant went to check, but returned saying, "I'm sorry, the only Chevy in the lot is tan, and it isn't a Blazer."

The lady did not communicate clearly or for action, so she didn't get the answer she wanted. It's almost as if she and the attendant were on different planets. (Venus and Mars?)

Communication for action does not mean that you are going to do the business for someone else. *They* need to become very clear in the partnership, the steps *they* are going to need to do; such as make their 100+ prospect names list and prioritize it by the PEARL method (in previous chapter). Every step in communicating for action is going to create a stronger, better, more consistent and more committed partnership.

If you leave your communication for action and the basic steps out, if you dilute it, you're going to have diluted partners and soon they'll simply disappear. We need to give them complete trust and confidence. That isn't rescuing, baby sitting or doing it for them. In communication, goal setting and partnership, I say, "I absolutely have complete trust and confidence that you will have your ten prospecting calls done this week."

You need to communicate for action and in partnership so they know that it can be done. You need to give them honest coaching. That's what is tough for a lot of people in partnership. They are unwilling to increase their level of coaching and leadership to empower and move a person further.

Is it easy for me all the time? No. Sometimes I am up against my own stuff and it would be much easier for me to back down and let someone slide, but that is not the promise I gave them. I said you can count on me that I'm going to be the very best that I can be. I need to push through, go to a higher level of interaction with other people. It is giving honest counsel and affirmation for each person. We need to correct or coach their behaviors and actions which do not assist and support them in keeping their word and achieving their goals.

"Whose Business is This?"

As you know, most companies do not use a contract, they use an agreement. It's called an independent representative agreement, not a *dependent* representative agreement. Part of coaching and responsible sponsoring and duplicating is to support the person to become *independent* fast. That means they can have a portable business. That they no longer are dependent on you as an upline coach or sponsor to do their two-on-one calls, three-way follow-ups or their presentations. Something I ask over and over again in training and on coaching calls, and if someone calls me with a problem, is, "Whose business is this?" If it's a couple, they can say ours. If it's a single representative, they say mine.

Whose business is it?
It's mine.
Is it your company's business?
No.
Is it your upline's business?
No.
Whose business is it?

It's mine.
Is it your sideline or cross line's business?
No.
Is it your downline's business?
No.
Whose business is it?
It's mine.
Is it your sponsor's business?
No.

They continue to have the words of ownership come out of their mouth. "So you have a problem, how are you going to solve it?" There is a form later you'll see in the book that's called *Getting the Monkey Off Your Back*. It's how to assist representatives in solving their own problems. That's very important. That's developing independence in a representative.

Acknowledge Them!

One of our most important responsibilities as coaches is to give them absolutely full acknowledgment, full credit, full praise when they have achieved what it is that they said they would do. Too many coaches and leaders in this industry want to keep the glory and be the hero. I don't care about the glory. I don't care about the recognition. I don't care about the acknowledgment. Does it feel good? Yes. Does it really matter? No.

What matters is that we are developing a leader to be a leader of leaders. They must be the ones that have soared to success. Acknowledge them, and then acknowledge them to other people.

Let's say that Tom is having difficulty in keeping his weekly goal. I simply would say, "Tom, I think if I shared something with you, you could gain a lot toward achieving your goal. Is it okay for me to talk with you about it?" (Get an okay that they want to hear what you're saying; it means they'll truly listen.) "You know how tough it was for Linda to start reaching her prospecting call goal? Did you realize this last week that Linda doubled her results with prospecting calls? At her call workshop, I was so proud of her leadership!"

Tom might reply that he can really relate to Linda's struggle and he didn't know about her success.

"What do you think she did differently?"

Tom might reply, "She just did it."

It's like coming up to the plate and swinging. That is communication for inspiration. Using someone else's results, someone else's story in order for another person you're coaching to listen, relate to and then duplicate. If Tom already relates to Linda, seeing her take action and accountability can show him how he can do the same.

These four steps give them a personal challenge that brings out their best:

- Inspire them to greatness.
- Give them complete trust and confidence.
- Give them honest coaching.
- Acknowledge them constantly.

"I really respect you, you keep moving forward, and that's what is going to cause you to break through the blocks or the stops."

Give them full credit, praise, acknowledgment and pass their story on to other people. Again, great lessons from the Bible and great lessons of great teachers. One of the verses says, "Let us have warm affection for each other, and a willingness to let others have the credit."

How quickly and consistently do you give credit and acknowledgment to other people? That's how you form lasting partnerships. That's how you become a leader of leaders.

"Keep On Keeping On"

When leaders are learning in partnership, once they have the skills and the knowledge, what usually stops them is really their own fear, programs and beliefs. I coach people to *do what they fear*, even though they are uneasy and unsure about it.

By taking action—picking up that phone, talking to strangers in the mall, doing the follow-up— you're going to have the power. You are going to break through. By going through your fears, you will overcome them and have more personal power plus the respect of your team.

When you have more personal power, it comes through in your communication, in your essence, in your walk, in your talk, and more people want to emulate you. Emulation means others want to have and be more of who you are. Edification means, to me, putting someone up on a pedestal and I never want to be on a pedestal. I'm always going to stay down with the troops. We're right in the field. We're in the trenches. We're in the foxhole together. They can emulate me rather then edify and put me up on any pedestal.

J.G. Holland says, "God gives every bird its food, but he does not throw it into the nest." In communicating for action and in goal setting, we cannot throw it into the representative's nest. If we keep doing all the one-on-ones, if we keep doing all the three-way follow-ups, if we keep doing all of the inviting, if we keep doing the presentations for them, if we keep doing the training, then we're throwing it into the nest of our leaders-in-training. That's a no-no in coaching.

When you keep solving their problems for them, representatives are going to become dependent and they won't feel that they have accomplished anything. You cannot give credit and acknowledgment to them. Representatives have to feel they are winning on their own before they can grow and become a greater leader. Samuel Johnson said it in another way, "Great works are performed not by strength, but by perseverance." Keep on keeping on.

I don't care how fast their results come in, how fast their cash is there, what I work for in goal setting and in partnership is the perseverance. It's the consistent consistency that every week they are setting their goals. They persist and they will become stronger, because they're going through their own fears and they are getting unstuck themselves, and then we can truly, truly acknowledge them for their breakthroughs.

Commitment in Partnership

One of the wonderful qualities of partnership is that it gives people a reputation to live up to— most people take their commitments more seriously when they've committed to a partner and not just to themselves. I came across a page on commitment in a training manual. I'm going to share this for developing partnership, goal setting and communication for action. I have my people read it aloud three times right before paperwork is completed. They can do it at home, but it must be out loud. (We've adapted it from a quote by W. H. Murry, a mountaineer who climbed Mt. Everest.)

Commitment

Until I am committed, there is always hesitancy. The chance to draw back, which is always ineffective. Concerning all acts of initiative and creation, there is one elementary truth, the ignorance of which kills ideas and splendid plans. That the moment I definitely commit myself then providence moves, too. All sorts of things occur to help me that would never otherwise have occurred. A whole stream of events issues from my decision raising in my favor all manner of unforeseen incidences, meetings, and material assistance, which I could have never dreamed would come my way. Whatever I can do or dream I can, I begin it. Boldness has genius, power, and magic. I begin now.

A simple way to say the same is"On this rock I stand, and, World, you will adjust! When someone gets stuck or they are off the AVE, the path of creation, I'll say, "Pull out your commitment page. Just take a minute and read that out loud to me now." Ninety-nine percent will get refocused, recentered, regrounded to pick up and move forward again.

A great leader is a great enabler and inspirer; they have plenty of tools in their survival/success kit to coach anybody in getting unstuck.

Remember, today is the first day of your business. It also could be the last day. How are you going to be today to begin anew? What guarantee do you have that you'll be here tomorrow to make a difference? The commitment reading, as a tool, works very well to cause a person internally to get back on track, so externally the results will start showing more effectively.

Everybody wants the prosperity and the big money from this industry. I believe prosperity is an incredible teacher. Adversity is an even greater teacher, as long as your commitment is solid through the bumps and the bruises, the changes a company goes through—the jungle, as I call it. I always learn more from my adversities, my upsets and my failures. There are times when I read my commitment page over and over again and over again.

Here's another one:

The Obstacle in Our Path

By Brian Cavanaugh

In ancient times, a king had a boulder placed on a roadway. Then he hid himself and watched to see if anyone would remove the huge rock. Some of the kingdom's wealthiest merchants and courtiers came by and simply walked around it.

Many loudly blamed the king for not keeping the roads clear, but none did anything about getting the big stone out of the way. Then a peasant came along, carrying a load of vegetables. On approaching the boulder, the peasant laid down his burden and tried to move the stone to the side of the road. After much pushing and straining, he finally succeeded.

As the peasant picked up his load of vegetables, he noticed a purse lying in the road where the boulder had been. The purse contained many gold coins and a note from the king indicating that the gold was for the person who removed the boulder from the roadway.

The peasant learned what many others never understand: Every obstacle in the road presents an opportunity to improve your condition.

Do you believe there is gold waiting for you when you handle your obstacles responsibly?

Chapter 4

Duplicating

If you look up "duplicate"in the Webster's Dictionary, you'll find that it means to make an exact copy of something. Duplication is a system based on skills, knowledge, belief, personal leadership and commitment.

Let's say you had a son or a daughter needing critical surgery and you met with the surgeon right before the operation. If the surgeon said, "I have something new and innovative I'm going to try out on your child," how would you feel? There would not be much trust or confidence. You would want a proven technique, not a risky experiment, to save your child's life.

That's what happens so often with duplication. People get a new idea and they want to use it rather than staying committed to a system. Mastery in the business comes from duplication— sticking with a system until you see the results you want. Through a great duplication system, people become leaders of leaders, and that's the *real* purpose of duplication, plus the residual income.

When I'm coaching somebody and duplicating them, they need to follow the system or I stop coaching them. I make that very clear when I get permission to coach someone. I teach about the TEAM: Together Everyone Achieves More or Together Everyone Acquires Money. Great duplication will create the residual income and the time freedom that everybody wants from network marketing. The only way to get there is remembering the TEAM and duplicating what works consistently.

Don't Rush the Process

One thing I always share with leaders is that fast cash many times leads to a fast crash. That's why, in duplication and in developing leaders, we don't rush the process. We don't want people to have their businesses crash. Someone can earn some really fast money for a year or 18 months, but if they have not passed that baton and led by example and become a leader of leaders, then, more times than not, it is going to also be a fast crash.

Pat Davis, of Millionaires In Motion, teaches a great prospecting seminar and talks about those who try to make a grandmother out of a bride. They want the finished product— commission-generating grandchildren— overnight. They forget to allow a bride to experience the joys of learning a new marriage, of growing, and grooming for the role of parent first, then grandparent of duplication. You cannot rush those vital steps, and duplication absolutely takes time. The length of time varies for each person.

That's why, with integrity, it is absolutely critical and important that we let people know this is going to take three to five years to create the large residual income and the time freedom.

Anne Landers wrote something I think is incredibly powerful, because this industry is all based on our integrity. Anne says that people of integrity expect to be believed. They also know time will prove them right and they are willing to wait. The waiting and patience builds. As long as someone is productively working their business, it will come to pass. What we put out comes back. We reap what we sow. That doesn't say when the harvest is going to come through, and that's one of the most frustrating parts of this business for the majority of people.

I would rather have 15 steady plodders than one heavy hitter. I find that those heavy hitters seldom last. They jump from company to company, trying to get in on the "ground floor." I don't look for them and I don't want them. I want to take people who have a commitment and willingness and to work with them on their belief, their integrity and their leadership to create for them the lasting—not the crashing—business.

Three Areas of Mastery
Simply put, these are a must!

1. Knowledge of network marketing, your company, compensation plan and products
2. Ability to prospect, invite, duplicate
3. Personal attitude

You coach others on the first two and lead them to the needed resources. The third, attitude, is 100% the representative's responsibility. You cannot change or force another to change their attitude. The Serenity Prayer that Alcoholics Anonymous uses goes like this:

God, give me the serenity to accept the things I cannot change, the courage to change the things I can, and the wisdom to know the difference.

Many representatives are trying to change someone's attitude and are going down a dead-end street.

Vision, Value and Trust

I work with the VVT concept: Vision, Value and Trust. A networker's vision needs to be in four areas: network marketing, your company, your compensation plan and your products. People must know the vision and be able to create that in others through their communication.

Vision is not about stating facts. I could tell you the facts that network marketing is 55 years old and in 125 countries. All I've done is given you some raw data.

Vision moves into a prospect's personal value. When you ask prospects to see themselves traveling the world for business, and writing it all off their taxes, they give that vision their own value. It may fit that vision to work through an industry that has grown and matured over 55 years— that's security. It may help to know that they have 125 countries to choose for business— that's freedom! The vision is purely their big picture, and value brings the facts home.

Ask people questions about how the vision of network marketing really truly applies to them. How would it feel to retire in three to five years— rather than 30? See what's in it for them— WITHem.

They can develop vision and value in that possibility.

The third important part of this duplication section is trust. Here is where the sincerity and integrity are critical and must be felt by the prospect. If you YCCOM (You Can Count On Me), you had better keep your word. It means less than nothing to YCCOM if they can't count on you.

Trust also involves placing people before paychecks. If prospects sense that you're most interested in your own reasons for getting them into the business, you will be paddling backwards. Their trust is an ongoing and ongrowing process with each step of their decision. It is necessary that prospects know you will stay with them in their process until they make their wise decision to be in partnership with you.

In duplication there is no time frame. It could happen in three months and it might happen in three or four years. Any great master, any author in this industry of network marketing will say that only four teams can be duplicated at a time. Too many people do what I call *shot gun,* and they just keep bringing on more and more people to duplicate. Then they get burned out and their whole system gets watered down. I don't take on more than four teams at a time, which means one leader and the whole duplication system gets passed down to the next person on the line and the next person on the line, and on and on in the network.

Personal Commitment

Commitment is crucial to the partnership of duplication. I agree to commit to certain responsibilities, and my team players agree to commit to their own set of responsibilities.

Many people say, "I'm really interested, I want to, I hope, I want, I'm ready to be a master duplicator," but there is a huge difference between interest and commitment. When someone says that to me, I know they are not fully committed. When someone is just interested in doing something, they do it only when it's convenient, easy and fits into their schedule. But when someone is committed to doing something, they will accept no excuses, no alibis, no justification, no rationalizations— only results.

When I'm duplicating someone, I work only with commitment. Hopes, wants, wishes, likes and interests have no power behind them. If you are going to really work this business, you need to put a commitment into it— not a maybe, not a perhaps, not a someday, not I'd like, I want to, I hope it'll work. I'd really like to know: Does "someday" come right after Monday or after Saturday? I've never located "someday" on the calendar.

A committed leader needs to declare their commitment aloud to their sponsor and their team. It's not enough to say "I hope to be a diamond," or "I'm planning to be a leader in my company." They need to use the word *commitment* for its strength with the people they are coaching and duplicating down the line. I request and get an agreement that they are going to make declarations for other people to hear. A winner or a leader can always tell you where they are going. They say, "I am committed to earning my car in the next year." "I am committed to being up to $2,000 a month in the next two months."

What is the difference between being positive and being a person of commitment?

Being positive is a great quality to have and share, yet it doesn't lead to results and duplication. When someone doesn't have the success through positive thinking, there is another rock that needs to be solid. That is the rock of commitment. This is a much stronger rock on which to build a foundation, duplicate and become successful. Because you say you are committed, the results, in time, will follow.

Denis Waitley uses a quote that goes something like this: Winners can tell you where they are going, what they plan to do along the way, and who will be sharing the adventure with them. Duplication truly is an adventure and process, and there is no time frame on it.

Once someone makes a decision and is clear that they have made that decision for themselves, without manipulation then I do the clarity and commitment page with them. We sit down together within 24 to 48 hours of that decision, and we start working with their foundation, their value, their "whys" to work the business.

Commitment

- 2 year commitment.
- 5-10 hours per week.
- Learn the Business — (company, comp plan, products).
- Many good reasons to quit.
    a. Returns
    b. Team players—frustration.
    c. Late shipments.
    d. Wrong shipments.
    e. Someonelse sponsors someone you have worked with.
    f. Someone will get in then get out or quit.
    g. Order from filled out wrong & want ASAP is backordered.
    h. Credit card bounced so paycheck delayed.
    i. U.P.S. loses shipment — so it is delayed.
    j. Product you ordered and want ASAP is backordered.

- Be sure you (their sponsor) commit to support them getting started & doing 3-ways
- Present for them at in homes 3 times. Then let them fly!
- Encourage them to be on training & conference calls.
- Commit to them that you will keep them informed of events/meetings ect. Have them get 800#. (ASAP).
- Call them once per week or more (minimum). 3 Magic words-YOU CALL ME!

As we discussed in Chapter Three, it's important to set the foundation for partnership early, so I need to know how each person wants to work and what I need to do to support that. I do the clarity and commitment session with everyone I personally sponsor, and the team members do it with their personally sponsored people also— it is an integral part of our duplication system.

This session involves sitting down together (or getting on the phone together, for long-distance representatives) and answering the following questions together:

Clarity & Commitment

1. What are you committed to achieving in this business?

The purpose of this question is to get the person to dream about the tangible results of their work. The answers might be: I need a new car; I need to get my teeth done; I need money to put the kids through college; my parents need special care now they're old; we need new furniture. Whatever they say is okay.

This is all about dreaming of what's possible for them through this business. Anything is fine. See it BIG!

A dear friend of mine in Winnipeg, who had some arthritis, listed a central vacuum cleaner as her first goal for her business success. That type of vacuum is much easier to use than a big push vacuum. She bought it out of her first weekly paycheck of $650.

2. What income will you create in one year, in three years, in five years?

I need to see what they think is possible for them. I don't offer them any ideas if they ask what the "normal" person can do. I'll simply say, "Do you consider yourself normal?" I don't feed people answers.

Think of the proverb: Give a person a fish and you feed her for a day. Teach her to fish and you feed her for a lifetime. I coach people to find their answers on their own instead of relying on me.

3. What will you do with your new wealth?

This question starts to show their values. They think about what they would do with money after all their needs and basic desires are handled. How do they value wealth? It might be that they have a special project or charity to fund. Investing doesn't count. The Yarnells say find a purpose bigger than you. I 100% agree with them.

4. Are you coachable with a teachable spirit?

Most people are going to say yes. Then I say, "Share with me what that means to you." We're going even deeper into contextual how I need to best coach them. Sometime people say, "I don't know if I can do that." I understand, but my question is: With coaching, are you *willing* to do that? Are you *willing* to have your closest friends, family members, professional associates, people that you meet along life's way become business partners and team members? I go right back to willingness. Few people tell me they are unwilling at this point, because they know what I am committed to creating with them.

Sometimes at this point, I ask, "How would you best be coached, on a daily basis, on a weekly basis? Do you keep your word when you say you're going to do something? Do you do it?"

If they do happen to say they are unwilling or they refuse to accept coaching, then I simply say, "At this time, you are uncoachable, and that's okay. That's not bad. I can no longer work with you right now. I'm going to wrap up this conversation in just a moment. When you become willing to be coached— call me back. I'll be eagerly waiting to continue coaching."

I do not baby-sit. I do not solve people's problems. Too many net-workers baby-sit their new representatives, which does not bring out their greatness and does not further their leadership.

Most of those who were unwilling or uncoachable call me within the next 24 hours or less. They apologize, "I was a jerk. I was really out in left field. I didn't mean to be like that. Something came up."

They know that I am there to coach them, to support them, to empower them, to contribute to them, to acknowledge them and to make a difference in their lives.

As for the midway levels of commitment— I'll try or I'll do my best— I like what John Fogg says. He calls it the *committed maybe* or the *for sure perhaps*. Of course those never happen. If someone says, "Maybe I'll try to do the business," I ask them, "When did you *maybe try* to do something else? Did it work?"

5. How much time a day, a week and a month can you give to your new business?

If it's five hours a week, great. Then I know, and we'll block it out on their calendar exactly what those five hours a week are going to be. If they are able to do two hours a day (ten hours a week) then that's going to require a stronger time commitment on my side as their coach. However much they say, there's a different impact on the coaching. Same coaching, but of course, the more time they're able and willing to put into the business, the faster and stronger it's going to grow, and I'll certainly communicate that to them.

Here's an interesting way to look at time commitments.

When you are doing/being your business on a part-time commit-ment, look at it in this light: In a regular job, could you take a long break and read the newspaper?

Probably not.

Could you talk to your mom or friend for half and hour?

Most likely not.

Could you go to the fridge and make a ham sandwich, sit and eat it, and clean up afterward if it wasn't all within your allotted lunch break?

I don't think so.

My point is to treat your part-time business seriously and work it

full-time-part-time. If your mom or friend calls and it's your business time and it isn't an emergency, let her know you'll call back at a better time for you to talk. This attitude and action is truly being a leader of yourself and your time.

6 Are you 100 % willing to give this business one to five years for your success?

This question is extremely important. Does that mean, when you're disappointed, when you're discouraged, when you're down, that you will not become defeated? I don't care what feelings they experience as long as it doesn't go into defeat. If they give in to feelings of defeat, then they'll quit. They need to know that duplication is a process that's different for everyone— I never know how long it will be before someone is fully duplicated. As their coach and partner, I need to know that they have the staying power for lasting results.

7. Can you see, with my skills and coaching, that together we can build your business?

Many people are going to have fear, unless they have a network marketing background, most people don't think they really can do it. This question eliminates the fear that they might have by reminding them of the partnership and giving them a foundation for building their belief.

I always YCCOM— I say, "You can count on me to lend my skills, support, and coaching, so that together we can build your business."

8. "Do you now see anything that isn't positive or win-win?"

I ask this directly, because if our partnership doesn't feel entirely like a positive, win-win agreement for them, they're going to come into the business without courage, clarity and conviction. I don't care about confidence yet, because that has to do with belief, and a coach is responsible for holding their belief level until they develop it for themselves, but they do need to be clear, courageous and have conviction.

By this point, 95-98% will say, "I see it as win-win." Then, we put the dates in their calendar. They'll have a schedule of the weekly home or hotel presentations, introduction conference calls, call workshops and training, and based on how much time they are able to give each week, we figure out how many one-on-ones, two-on-ones or three-way calls we're going to be able to do.

Then I give them the names and phone numbers of five upline people. The new representatives need to call the upline team and introduce themselves as new team players.

Why wouldn't I have the upline call the new representatives? Because the more responsibility and accountability the new people take, the more they will own their businesses. Each new representative becomes a leader immediately.

Have the upline team members ready to ask *why* the new person is in the business, what's the value. Speaking the answers aloud to someone else deepens the value for the new representative.

Throughout this process, I ask my new partners to choose what will work best for them— I know what kind of coaching I will give them depending on the time agreement and their accountability. Accountability is very important to duplication, and it starts with understanding our agreements and commitments from the beginning.

Being Coachable

I like to tell a story about Socrates and Plato that has to do with being coachable and willing to pay the price in duplication.

Back in ancient Greek civilization, there was a great teacher, a master duplicator named Socrates. Many people walked miles just to beg lessons from this great leader, this great duplicator, this great teacher. He was willing to give his skills, knowledge and philosophy to anybody who was truly eager— not the ones who were merely curious, but the ones who were so eager they were willing to put legs under their willingness.

One day, a very young student called Socrates on his cellular phone and said, "Hey, Soc, I'm ready to be trained, I'm ready to duplicated by you."

Socrates said to this young man, whose name was Plato, "Are you absolutely serious, will you be committed, will you follow, will you trust, will you do what I ask you to do? I will impart all of my knowledge to you if you will come forth with such willingness."

Plato said, "Of course. Of course you can count on me, Coach. I'll do whatever you say."

So Socrates said, "There is a series of tests you are going to need to take. Meet me tomorrow down at the seashore."

Plato thought, well, this is very interesting, this isn't how I expected it to go. I thought I'd be in a big basilica and have him sitting at a huge desk and coaching me, but the seashore. . . .

Well, Plato had told Socrates he'd do what he said, so he went down to the seashore the next day, and he was dressed professionally in his three piece suit. He got down to the seashore, and there is Socrates in a bathing suit. Plato thinks to himself, what the heck is going on? This doesn't make sense. What is Socrates going to do with me?

Socrates said to Plato, "Plato, come with me into the water."

Plato said, "Are you crazy? Look at how I'm dressed! I'm dressed professionally, I'm dressed to be taught, I'm dressed to learn your knowledge."

Socrates said "Come with me into the water."

He took Plato's hand and he started walking him into the water, and Plato started thinking, oh no! look at my shoes, my pants are getting all wet. This is stupid. This is a $800 suit and a $250 pair of shoes.

"I ain't going into the water, Socrates! Forget it. This isn't what I am going to do, I'll go find another coach or another teacher." And Plato left.

Socrates said, hmm, one more just bit the dust. They say that they are willing to do what it takes, to follow coaching, to listen, and to trust, and then they don't.

About a week later, Plato called Socrates on his cellular and he said, "Soc, I'm ready. I was stupid. I wasn't a student. I was concerned about how I looked and what would happen. I'm ready now."

Socrates said, "Are you serious?"

Plato replied, "I am so serious. I am tired of this rut I'm in. I have to have the knowledge, and you, Socrates, are the one who holds the knowledge."

Socrates said, "Well, I hear something different in your voice, I feel that you are ready. Meet me back at the seashore."

Well this time Plato went, okay, I'll do that. He put his Speedo on and went down to meet Socrates at the exact time, because integrity is very important.

Plato met Socrates in his Speedo down at the seashore, at the beach.

Socrates said, "Now, Plato, you told me, and I heard it come out of your mouth, that you are willing to trust, you are willing to follow, you are willing to take instruction. No matter what, I will be there for you. You can count on me."

And Plato said, "Hallelujah! I'm ready Socrates."

Socrates took Plato's hand and he began to walk him out in the water. The surf was crashing, and it come up to their ankles and Plato's eyes got a little bigger. The water went up to their calves. Plato was going, hmmm. Socrates had Plato's hand so strong and he was pulling him out through the surf. It got up to their thighs, then it went up to their waists. Socrates was so clear and he was so calm, but Plato was getting feisty and nervous and moving around.

He said, "Hey, Soc, this is . . . you know, I think I've learned my lesson. I get what this means.

Socrates said, "You haven't yet begun to get what I'm going to teach you."

They were up to over their the waists, and then Plato screamed, "Hey, Socrates, you don't understand, you don't get it, I can't swim. I can't go any further, forget it, I'm getting out of here. I don't need your lessons, I don't need your coaching, I'll do it on my own."

Plato ran out of the water and up the beach and disappeared again. Socrates, with much power and much presence, simply walked back onto the shore and went about his business.

About a month later, Socrates got a call from Plato. Plato said, "Hey, Soc, I blew it again. I said I'd trust you. I said I'd follow your coaching. I said I wanted your knowledge and your expertise. I stopped. I allowed my own fears to stop me. I'm willing to come on bended knee one more time. Are you willing to be there for me, Socrates?"

Socrates said, "I will always be there for you, Plato, but you must come up to my level, I will not go down or back to where you are. I do not live my life out of fears, Plato, I live it out of possibilities. If you are 100 % committed, meet me at the seashore tomorrow."

Plato thought, well, I said I'm going to do it. He went back to the seashore the next day in his Speedos and his old flip flops. He got down to the beach and there was Socrates.

Socrates said, "Well, my son, you're back again. I've said I'm going to be there for you. I have given you my word that you can count on me that I am committed to impart all of my knowledge, all of my skills, all of my coaching to you. Are you ready?"

Plato said, "Yep, I'm ready."

Socrates took Plato's hand and moved them into the water much faster this time. The surf hit their calves, up to their thighs, up to their waists, up to their chests. Plato's eyes were getting big, big, big. His heart started pounding and pounding, because he knew he must break through and trust where Socrates was leading him.

Socrates got him way out, the water was now up to Plato's neck, it was going up over his chin, it was going up to his mouth, and Plato took a deep breath. Just at that time, Socrates, who was a very big and very powerful man, took Plato and pushed him under the water with great strength and held Plato under the water.

Plato was kicking and moving his body and twisting, but Socrates was solid as a rock and he held Plato down. Plato started coughing and spitting and spewing under the water, the bubbles were coming out, the air was disappearing. Finally, when Plato thinks I'm going down, this was the end of it, I shouldn't trust this, Socrates grabbed Plato and brought him up out of the water.

He was spitting water. He was coughing. His eyes were as big as platters. Socrates held him and said, "Plato, when you have so much commitment and desire to learn what I have to give you and when you fight for it like you have just fought for your life, then you truly will be ready to receive all the gifts I have to give."

Socrates was a master duplicator, and he was willing to take Plato through all the steps he needed to go through in order to create that commitment, that burning desire. He proved with his test that Plato would follow all of the tests, all of the coaching that Socrates would give him.

In developing leaders of leaders, we need to let them know that this is going to be one of the toughest journeys they have ever taken. For them to have 10, 30, 40, 50,000+ dollars a month, they must follow the coaching and then pass that coaching on. As long as the caring and the compassion that Socrates had for Plato is there, and the trust is there, know that it might not look like it at the time, but in time you will become completely duplicated and completely coached to pass that baton on to the next leaders of leaders.

Play to Win

Don't play to lose, and don't just play. Make the commitment to play to win. Action has to follow personal commitment. I work in duplicating Single Daily Actions (SDAs)— action is the "Playing to Win." When I am doing my business, I am on purpose. People come up and say, "Peggy, I can't believe you ever take a break."

Yes, I take tons of breaks. I take five months off during the summer and go up to my cottage on the island in Muskoka, Canada— and, my income still goes up. But when I am doing and being my business, I have a huge amount of intensity that creates attention and commitment from other people.

That's CBC— Casualness Breeds Casualty.

Someone who has intensity and is on purpose won't create casualties around them. A great duplicator doesn't create casualties, fall out, or drop out. They know that someone is there, the coach or the upline duplicator, to stay with them 100% until they are strong enough to fly and go out on their own.

There are five levels of commitment:

- Level 1 - "I won't do it."
- Level 2 - 'I'll do it if it's easy or convenient."
- Level 3 - "I'll try."
- Level 4 - "I'll do my best."
- Level 5 - "I'll do it." (provided it's moral, ethical, and legal)

Ways we Play/Be/Do Our Business

100 %	Playing to win.
50-99%	Playing to lose.
1-49%	Just Playing.
0%	Not Playing.

I suggest you totally forget anything to do with money, because I know what I put out will come back, as the Bible says, tenfold. Of course, Flip Wilson said it very well, "What goes around, comes around."

My sister-in-love, Karen Long, made me the most beautiful needle-point that hangs on a wall in my island cottage. It says, "Life is like an echo, what you send out comes back."

The great thing about network marketing is the more we stroke it and contribute to other people, the more comes back to us. Too many people put a time frame on it and they panic if the results are not coming back in fast enough. They want to be on the fast track rather than the permanent income track. That again, is why duplication does not a have a deadline. It can, however, have a time frame to structure your effort, using the schedule from Chapter Three.

Getting Organized

Every newcomer to this business needs to find a way to get organized. The prospecting organizer I use is the *Freedom in a Box* from Upline®. They have already done the organization structure for prospecting, 3x5 box, saving me hours of running to the store and even more hours of setting up a system. All your efforts will get lost in the shuffle if you start the business in a disorganized way.

Open a checking account exclusively for your business. Any CPA or financial adviser will tell you the same thing— keep this totally separate. Remember RYLAB— Run Your Business Like A Business. A separate account keeps your records in order for taxes and other financial reports.

Start making your own library rather than borrowing books and tapes. Lead by example. When people know that you have your own library, start suggesting they create their own. It establishes the importance of ongoing learning and growth, and your silent mentors and professional resources are always at your fingertips.

As people are coming up through the system, it's important to have recorded testimonials, especially if you are working with a variety of professionals. I have letters from doctors, dentists, ministers, rabbis, CPAs, chiropractors, pilots, etc. Those letters offer great third-party credibility. People want to hear endorsements from within their own profession, and specific testimonials offer that.

I've heard young people say, "No one listens to me because I'm young." That's just part of their listening filter, but it doesn't need to stand in the way of communicating the opportunities of network marketing. Have letters of endorsement from youthful representatives. Let them be your voice to their peers.

My son Jordan Ledgerwood was 24 when he started his business, and he has been among the highest paid in the company. He's been featured in *Upline®* magazine twice. Other young people can take Jordan's article and say, "Here is a young man who has done it. I am absolutely committed that within the next two to four years I am going to have time and money freedom. I'm asking you to come on the team. I don't need you, and I'm offering you a gift."

When it comes out of that presence and power of communication, the prospect receives a clear, positive message. It bypasses issues of age or profession.

Tools of the Networking Trade

It's imperative that a new team player know exactly what duplication steps to follow. When there is a systematic format in place, it keeps things simple. Below is a checklist I use as a leak-proof way to set up a new representative to win and be prepared:

Checklist for New Representative

___ Start your prospect list (100+ names).

___ Read *The Greatest Networker in the World* by John Milton Fogg and *Being the Best You Can Be in MLM* by John Kalench.

___ Buy an appointment and address book for your business only.

___ Call phone company and have three-way calling installed.

___ Order your business cards.

___ Order voice mail through your company if they have a system.

___ Order subscription to the *Upline®* Journal.

___ Make your "WHY" List (25 reasons, large and small, for your commitment).

___ Make your treasure map (done in two weeks).

___ When your Starter Pak arrives, listen to audio tapes, watch videos, read all, policies & procedures, training materials, brochures and scan your catalogs.

___ Use and know your products.

___ Write down questions to be answered by your coach.

These are some basic tools that I require everyone I'm duplicating to get for their business. Some are repeated from above to give you more information, and I ask for a commitment for when they will have them.

1. Three-Way Calling.

It usually costs about $4 or $6 from your local phone company. You can do three-way calls and work with two or more people at a time. You can also do prospecting calls or a follow-up call after a presentation.

2. Speaker Phone.

When I'm coaching a team out of town, and I've gone in there and kicked them off, I need to be able to call in to do training and call workshops until they're flying on their own. The upline duplicator needs to call in and work with more than just one person at a time.

3. Fax Machine.

I ask people to get one as soon as possible— so many companies have wonderful fax-on-demand services, and it's a great way to keep up on vital information about new products, training and conventions.

4. A Voice Mail System.

I'm on a system which allows me to push one button and send a message out to 10,000 people. Most similar voice mail systems cost $20 to $35 per month. A voice mail system lets you call 24 hours a day and just punch in your number. You never have to answer the phone, just let voice mail handle it. If you have a new release from your company, if a new country is opening, if a new product has been added, if there has been a change in the compensation plan, a new event scheduled, you can put that on your message and send it out to whomever you choose. You just call your own number, record the message you want to go out and then people can call in and hear all about it. Voice mail distribution lists are a great way to acknowledge big success, to provide sponsoring support and to send inspiring messages. Many companies have their own voice mail systems.

I'm putting out a message welcoming new representatives aboard my team. These are people who might be 20-30,000 people down from me, but they are able to call a number and hear me or hear the president of the company welcoming them aboard. You can also have all of your key leaders on a chain of communication with the push of one button. They have it immediately and can send it to however many people they want to put it out to on their team or on their downline.

I have a huge organization in Australia, and while calling Australia is very expensive, they are just all local calls for me through voice mail. You don't get charged for long distance calls. I can very effectively and inexpensively communicate with all my people Down Under.

You can call 24 hours a day, so you don't have to worry about time zones, which is extremely valuable. From the East Coast to wherever, there are enough time zones to make scheduling tricky. A good voice mail system bypasses all of that, and all without an interrupting (or waking) ring to bother you or your people.

5. Business Cards.

My business card says "Making Life Happen!" When I hand it out, people ask what it means. They get the conversation started by responding to my card. Then on the back of the card is where the value is: It simply asks Initial Interest Questions to get people thinking. (This is not for use in the Initial Interest exercise we went over earlier. DO NOT give out your business card there.) I have a little arrow on the front of my business card, pointing to turn it over, and I just let people read it:

Concerned About . . .

- Future Job Security?
- Sufficient Retirement Income?
- Current Income?
- Children's Education?
- Excessive Taxation?
- Time and Money Freedom?
- Helping Others?
- A Truly Enhanced Lifestyle?

We Can Help

T.E.A.M.

Together Everyone Achieves More

This gets prospects (usually cold contacts) thinking about issues and values. It tests their level of awareness, and if we make an appointment, we have something to talk about immediately. Business cards are a must— generic, company or both. A company audio tape is a talking business card and is very effective.

6. *Upline*®magazine.

It's a must for the people I am duplicating to subscribe. *SUCCESS* is another great magazine, and now we have *Network Marketing Lifestyles* magazine, on newsstands. These publications keep you up to date on the industry, on tips and methods others use, on technology to help your business go and grow. Such publications are also great to give to prospects, as well as being tax write off.

7. Cellular Phone or Pager.

As serious business-builder, you will always have to be available for communication with your prospects and your team.

8. Company Business Aids.

Always have supplies from your own company on hand. It might be the starter pack, your catalogs, your samples, whatever you need from your company. If you nickel-and-dime your business, that's what you will profit from it— nickels and dimes.

9 Seminars and Company Events.

I have a list in the back of this book of personal and professional growth seminars I recommend, along with phone numbers. Everyone needs to take their growth seriously and make it an an ongoing commitment. Attend every corporate function or event that's reasonbly close to you.

Now, what does that mean?

I can remember when my brother and sister, Ken and Karen Long, came in the business. They gradually built their belief system until they asked me what the next step would be for them in their business.

I said as soon as there is a corporate event in the Pacific Northwest, I'll let you know. So I called Ken one night and said, "Well, Ken, you said you are committed to going to the first Northwest corporate training, right?"

He says, "Absolutely."

I said "It happens to be in Vancouver, British Columbia."

Ken immediately went into how long a drive that was, what it would cost, all the reasons not to go. I said, "Ken, what I heard come out of your mouth is that you were going to go to the first one in the

Northwest. You might have thought it was going to be in Portland, which is an hour and a half from you. Are you going to be committed, keep your word and be there up in Vancouver, along with a couple of your new representatives?"

He had a friend with him, and they got in the car and drove eight or nine hours Friday night after school to get to Vancouver. They stayed with some representatives up in British Columbia and attended the eight-hour corporate training on Saturday and drove home on Sunday. That told me and Ken's entire team that they were committed.

When people say, "That's three hours away, I can't get there," I let them know they are saying to me that this is not important enough. If I said, "There is a corporate event taking place in a city seven or eight hours from you. Attending that training will mean earning $10,000 a month," would you go? Of course. People don't see enough value attached to attending a corporate event if it's way out of their area, yet that's what it's going to take until an area is strong enough to have a local corporate event.

Attend your annual convention or company convention with your organization. I invite and challenge people to make a commitment of how many of their team they are going to have at the annual corporate event or convention. That is becoming a leader of leaders. I always make a commitment to bring a certain number of my people with me. Big decisions are made at major company events.

10. Dunn and Bradstreet Report.

You need to know the background of your officers, and almost all companies have to register with their own corporation commission. It's public information, so you can call your state corporation commission and get a report. I think it's about $10; Dunn and Bradstreet is about $65. By doing this, you are building your belief and getting the credibility of the company you are with to share with your prospects.

11. Will or Trust.

Add your business to your will or trust, so there is never a question of how you want it to be passed to your heirs. It also strengthens your commitment that you are in the business for the long term. Network marketing is legitimate business which you own independently. You can sell your business or leave it in your will just as you would a store or stock. Check your company's polices and procedures.

These are tools that people need in my coaching and duplication. It doesn't have to be done all at once, out of the same paycheck, but it can't be six months out, either. The time frame needs to be reasonable, and they need to commit to it. When they are earning their income, they are going to invest in their own business with these tools, these seminars, these books, these publications. That is truly leading by example, which is the basis of effective duplication.

Integrity

I have a big bolt and a nut that I carry with me all the time in my coin purse. It's what I call a PTD—a Psychological Trigger Device. Whenever I pull it out, whether I'm in a training or getting caught in airport security (it is a pretty big bolt), I remember what it means to me.

A bolt has many threads on it, and in order for the nut to be screwed on the bolt, the threads of the nut and the threads of the bolt must be in alignment. They must perfectly match in order for the bolt and the nut to have any strength to hold a table brace, a chair leg or a bumper on a car. The threads in duplication come from four places: leadership, belief, commitment and integrity.

If any one of those four threads is not aligned, the representative and the team will not have the strength of duplication. What if someone has tremendous belief in their industry, their company, their sales compensation plan and the product; they have commitment, they have leadership, but they lack integrity?

They don't follow through with their word. They miss appointments. They break agreements. These actions say to the team that they are coaching, "I don't really care." Too many people have no commitment to keeping their word or following through on what they say. In duplication, this is one thing that I am absolutely inflexible about. When I say, "On this rock I stand, and, World, you will adjust," what that means to me is that my integrity is impeccable and everyone I'm duplicating knows that.

When someone's word is broken, the nut will not go on the bolt and there is no strength. I use that analogy all the time with people. I simply ask them, "Are you out of alignment in any way on the four cornerstones of duplication?"

If they say yes, I ask, "Okay, what's your next step? What is it that you need to do, or how do you need to be to get back in alignment?" We reestablish trust, a new alignment, a new commitment, a new partnership. In duplication, this is done over and over again, until it isn't broken anymore.

I always ask in the beginning, "What does integrity mean to you? Are you a person of your word? How do you feel when agreements are broken?" This is a business built on integrity and agreement— I need to know that my partners understand and embrace that. This does not mean that an agreement cannot be renegotiated, but for me, there is no such thing as a partial commitment. There are several levels of commitment between "I won't do it" and "I'll do it" and there is nothing wrong with any of those levels, but I put *my* effort into only one: *I'll do it.*

If people break agreements with me, I don't start duplicating with them again until they get back on track with their integrity. I keep in honest, heart-to-heart communication about when something or someone is out of integrity or commitment. When we need to stop the process of duplication, it is worth it to keep integrity intact.

A great coach or a great duplicator does not compromise just to make it easier on whomever they are training or coaching. They stand on their rock and bring the leader that they are duplicating up to the next level.

This can sometimes create a lot of friction, but the team coming up through the ranks knows without a shadow of a doubt their leader truly possesses sincerity, commitment, courage and compassion. Each person is able to go to battle with anybody on the four rocks of alignment in duplication. There is no need, ever, to compromise your integrity.

Respect is Earned

Many representatives— and most people in general— use exceptions, saying, "Just this one time I'll . . ." whatever they want to rationalize doing. *Exceptions are destroyers and dampen or even drown dreams.* Any time you say, "Just this one time," you make it easier to make an excuse next time. "Just this once, I'll . . . skip reading bedtime stories to my children . . . postpone my daily exercise . . . pass on tonight's AA meeting . . . not bother being on a conference call or attending the call workshop . . . avoid my daily reading session."

You are setting yourself up to lose. You are literally breaking your word to yourself and others. You will become discouraged, even to the point of quitting. It will be easier because you have talked yourself into quitting on your commitment to yourself.

I ask people, "How many of you like to be liked?" Most people are going to raise their hands. Then I ask, "How many of you want to be respected?" Nearly everyone wants that, too. What is the difference between like and respect?

Well, who decides if someone likes you? They are going to decide that they like you based on your actions, behavior, attitude, what you do, what you say, how you dress, how you look. *They* are going to decide if they like you. I recommend people read *What You Think Of Me Is None Of My Business*. It's a great book on this subject. What I think of myself, how I feel about myself, what I do with my own life, that is my business. What you think about me . . . that's not my business. That goes along with respect and keeping our promises.

Who will decide if they respect you? You will—personally—decide if people respect you. I know you have all heard the expression, "The higher you go up on the flag pole the more your okole (okole means butt in Hawaiian) shows". That's true in leadership and in a network marketing business.

It is far more valuable and important to be respected. People are going to follow a person they respect much more than a person they just like. That's a very subtle and important shift in developing leaders and in duplicating. There are many times people don't particularly like me, but that doesn't affect me. What is more important is that I create respect from people, because I can take them to the mountain top with respect. I cannot take them to the mountain top if they just like me.

Give more than what you promised. What does that mean?

Watch your promises, your commitments, your agreements. As I have shared with you, too many people spread themselves too thin. When a leader makes a promise, that's a commitment, that is our bond, our word, in a partnership. It absolutely must be kept, because every time someone does break a promise, there is a little chip taken out of the trust. When there are enough chips taken out of the trust, you will not have someone you can work with, because there is no trust, there is no respect. Results can also create respect as long as integrity is in.

As a leader, you are someone your team counts on to keep your word. Exceptions are a big black hole in your personal accountability and integrity.

Taking Responsibility

I hear so many people say that something isn't working in their business or they might be frustrated with their company, with a change, or a product hasn't given the result they want. No company is perfect, and people forget that they are the CEO and the president of *their own* company. If there is a problem in their business, it is their problem.

Rather than saying, "Something has to be done about this," a real leader will say, "I must do something about this." They take ownership and accountability to help get the problem or the concern solved with the home office.

It is extremely important to be in partnership with the home office. Empower your home office. Are they perfect? No. Are they going to make mistakes? Yes. Are you going to get a product delivered to the wrong person occasionally? Yes. Might a check be late sometimes? Yes. Might this, might that, might this, might that—YES, because human beings (remember, we are called human beings, not human doings) will make mistakes.

When I call into the home company and someone answers the phone, I'll say, "My gosh! It is so good to hear your voice. It's been about three weeks since I've talked to you. I am so grateful for how much service you are to us in the field."

Have I not opened the doors, the channel in that person to be now more receptive to listen to what I have to say? When I state the situation and propose a solution, will that person listen to me? Of course!

A true leader will always have two solutions to a problem and not just voice a complaint. They are already going to take the time to sit down, to reflect, to write it out if they need to and have at least two solutions before calling the home office or the upline with a particular problem. The higher someone goes in a company and the larger network or team that they have, the more likely they will be to have people calling them with problems.

It's very important not to get sucked into the problem or the story.

A true great duplicator and leader of leaders does not listen to downer stories, junk and negativity. They immediately shift it, and there is a great exercise on how to do this, called *How To Get The Monkey Off Your Back* later on in the book. It gives you tools, so that you are not engulfed in negativity and problems.

Our leaders become stronger and success comes to them when they solve their own problems and their own situations. I cannot believe the people that call me and say, "I am so overwhelmed with having to solve all this stuff." I say, "Why are you solving it? Whose business is it?" If the business is yours, so is the problem. If it is someone else's business (the CEO/sponsor downline from you, for example), it's that CEO's problem. Give it back to them. Would Ford solve a problem for Chevrolet? Solving others' problems weakens the people we are trying to help. Empower them by showing them the resources to help themselves and truly shine.

Stop the Negativity

Say a representative calls and starts complaining about something. They might say, "Do I ever have a problem! This is ruining my business, costing me money, stressing me out! This just isn't working."

Here is a very simple, fast and effective way to defuse the situation. In a calm tone, simply say, "May I ask you a couple of questions?"

Now, a lot of times they are going to say, "You need to listen to this." That's when, if you already have permission to coach this person, you need to stop the negativity. You do not need to listen to garbage.

Zig Ziglar has a story about negativity: If someone came into your home and emptied three huge garbage cans full of slop, paper, cans, bottles, bacon grease and orange rinds all over your living room, on your carpet and all over your furniture, and you couldn't catch them, what would be the first thing you'd do? You would clean up the junk that was in your home and on your floor and on your furniture. You would do it as fast as you could.

This is the same thing, same attitude and action in solving a problem or a situation or a concern with a representative. *Except they need to do it.*

To start, simply ask the question, still in a very calm tone, and say,

"All I need is the bottom-line answer, I don't want the story."

When people call with an upset, with a story, it's all the emotional energy and drama that keeps them going. It's like a rat on a treadmill, they go over and over and over and over, and they have already probably told this story to four or five people. Now it's gaining more momentum and more energy. The important thing in network marketing is to go up with a problem or a concern, never to go downline. Go downline with good news. Go upline with problems and concerns.

Too many people sewer their downline team by telling them negative situations. They have a piece of jewelry break, or a bottle is broken when it comes, someone gets sick or the free phone card no longer works. All those are irritating, and some need to be handled, but they don't need to be complaints passed down the line to take downline down.

You ask for just the bottom—line facts, no energy and no upset. You might even say, "If I hear you getting upset and negative, I'm going to hang up on you." Say exactly what your actions are going to be based on what they are giving you.

If someone still launches into the story, I hang up. I say, "When you're committed to getting this issue solved, call me back." I don't have people dumping on me. They know I will assist them to solve problems, but I will not be part of the problem. I will be part of the solution, never part of the problem.

Once you have the bare basic facts of the situation, you need to direct your leader to find solutions. Keeping your calm tone, ask:

1. When did this situation arise?
2. Where exactly have you looked for possible solutions?
3. Who is directly involved in the situation and could possibly resolve it?
4. What do you feel could be two possible solutions to this situation?
5. What do you think is the best way to put the solution into action?
6. Why do you feel these are the best avenues for you to take at this time?"

This is a gentle, leading process of solving the problem, rather than saying, "Fax me all this stuff, and I'll call and solve it." Then you are not developing a leader to own their own business. By asking questions, you allow your leader to discover a solution and own it and the business.

When you have a few answers to those questions, you might say: "Knowing what you know about this situation, and seeing that you have a great understanding of what's happened, I suggest you go ahead with those solutions. Give me a call or fax me and let me know how everything worked out. The good news is, if this situation ever comes up again, you now know exactly how to handle it, right?"

Your leader gets to feel great about it, and you are both able to see the solution. I do not solve other people's problems, I simply show them a system or a way for them to own the problem and solve it. Then they are going to be able to teach their people how to solve a similar situation when it arises.

Another Way for a Three-Way

Sometimes I'll get on a three way call with the home office to work through a problem. I just say, "Hi, this is Peggy "Like a Rock" Long calling and I have a new representative on the phone. I'm just going to assist her in learning how to work through a situation with representative services, so she'll know how to solve this next time."

The situation might be a backorder or product return. It might be a delayed or lost shipment. Representatives need to know how to communicate about any and all of those issues, and I am willing to do that training once.

I coach them on a three-way with the home office, and then they never have to call me again. I get a commitment from my leader to learn during that call. "You will not need me again on any of these issues, will you?" She says, "I now know how to do it." One of the keys to success is to show your people how to solve their own problems. Duplication!

Buddy Systems

One of the things that can be very, very effective, especially for new people, is to have a buddy system or a partner. What I find is that people are more creative about problem-solving, accountable, reliable, and responsible when they are in agreement with someone else besides just themselves. In home businesses, many people are not disciplined to get up and go to their office. It might be in the kitchen, in a bedroom on a card table, it doesn't matter where the office is, they do not treat this business like a business.

Again, I use RYBLAB— Run Your Business Like A Business. By having a buddy system, you can check in every other day and see how they're doing on their goals of prospecting, of inviting, of presenting, of teaching the skills of duplication, of attending call workshops.

Perhaps I'll give someone an assignment to read Peter Hirsch's book, *Living With Passion*. I will simply say, "Choose yourself a buddy on your team where you're working so that person can support you. Your buddy will support your being more passionate."

Some buddies come up with subtle reminder signals. If one buddy needs to show more enthusiasm, the other buddy will give the signal. It takes some of the pressure off new reps who are trying to remember several new things at once.

Practice Makes Permanent

I went over to San Bernardino, California, where Jordan was living and we started with just a couple people. He was very willing to learn and mastered all the skills very quickly. He learned his two-on-ones, his one-on-ones, his 48-hour duplication, and within four days, I said, "Jordie, we have about ten people coming tonight." There were now about three or four representatives he had sponsored. I said, "Tonight, you need to be up in front doing the company part of the presentation."

I thought his gorgeous green crystal eyes were going to fall on the floor and roll away. His mouth opened up. I had let him know that he was going to do it, but now he was up against his own stuff. He said, "Mom, I don't know enough. I can't do it. *I can't do it!*"

I said, "Jordie, do you remember your agreement? You promised me, the coach, you would follow and trust the steps."

He said yes.

I said "Okay, you're going to go up and present the company."

He did it because his word was good . . . he got up . . . he botched it. He named the officers the wrong names, he mixed up their positions, he forgot the date the company started. The one thing he did was be very confident about his botching. So the feeling that the people got in the group— it was a small group, maybe ten or 12 people— was: Hey, this kid is confident. (I call him a kid, I guess that's mom coming out.)

What's the worst thing that can happen? If you're training someone and they say the company started in '91 and it started in '90, does that really matter to the guests making a decision? Absolutely not. But the presence, posture, beingness and the confidence do matter.

I shared with him, "Jordie, all you need to do is get up and be really strong about how you feel." And he says to the group, "I feel so great about this decision. This company is great." He had a lot of facts wrong, but that doesn't matter. Practice makes permanent.

I didn't care if he was perfect up in front. What mattered is he took the next step in the duplication process and in developing himself as a leader. By the third time I went to Southern California— he was starting to earn money, $500 a week— he was doing the complete presentation.

He went through a real roller coaster ride sharing the business with people. It was easier with his few friends. He had just moved to California, and so he had a few friends from work that he sponsored and a few friends that he knew from his church and a couple of sports outfits he was in, but to go out cold contacting was a major, *major* challenge— and *major* breakthrough for Jordie.

He kept PIP-ing— Prospecting, Inviting and Presenting. He had a goal to become a corporate trainer and to become a diamond of this company. I kept him right on the duplication path— the AVE and the skills he needed in order to become a corporate trainer and a diamond. He was able to do that in approximately one and a half years. He earned more in one month in network marketing than in six or seven months strumming the music store owner's pocketbook.

However, he had sat around for three years without doing anything, while half of his organization and his team was already built for him. He only had to build the other half in order to become one of the highest earners in our company.

It's been a roller coaster ride for Jordie. It's still a challenge for him, it's still a challenge for all of us. I greatly respect what he has done and he's a phenomenal coach now to other people by totally following the system and keeping the four cornerstones in alignment: Belief, Commitment, Leadership, and Integrity.

Success Breeds Success

One of your top priorities in early duplication is to support your new representatives to earn consistently for four to six weeks or months (depending on how your company pays) in a row, so they have a solid track record.

When I say earning, I'm talking about significant amounts. I know in some companies, your first check might be $7.95 for that month— and yes, that's important, those are stepping stones. But I'm talking staying at the same power with the people you are coaching and duplicating, so they have four to six consecutive weeks/months of good income. Success breeds success, or it begets success. It can keep the momentum and the magic and the miracle moving. I stay with people for four to six weeks/months until they have good income coming in.

The Drip System

Follow-up is crucial to duplication. Most people treat follow-up like it doesn't matter, but it is the most important part of our business— *the key to your financial future*. It is staying with people long enough for them to make a decision. Times change. It might be a year or two. People are watching you, and their own time and their life and their work conditions change. They may suddenly be ready for your opportunity. They may see you demonstrate the answers to their questions. That's why it's important to use the "rock to success," or the drip system, as the basis for duplicating follow-up in your organization.

Here's how the drip system works: Take very brightly colored envelopes— chartreuse, bright pink, magenta, purple, bright yellow— and handwrite a person's name and address. Don't put a return address on it, or a computerized label. You want the person who is going to be opening it to know that this isn't just general junk mail. Put a regular stamp on it, instead of using a postage meter, so they see that it's personal. Send out a letter, network marketing brochure, newspaper article or company material every month to keep your prospects aware that you are around, active and thinking of them.

If someone says, "No, it's not quite right for me at this time," simply keep the door open. Say, "Would it be okay if I just dropped something in the mail or gave you a call occasionally, just for you to see what is going on?" Very seldom will anybody just say no

The drip system is simply to put something in the mail for people, such as a notice for a new product your company came out with. We cannot be showing checks, legally we are not supposed to be out crowing about money. But, if your company prints a list of their highest earners in their monthly or quarterly journal, and your name is there, you could send that. You might send a picture of a car you have earned or purchased and simply have a little note on it saying, "Are you ready for yours?" Those show high income without illegally promising or showing paychecks.

When I travel all over the world, I send postcards to people; I take ten or 15 prospect names and addresses with me. I might send a picture of the new cottage I built last year, or a postcard of the cruise ship I'm on. "Are you coming with us next year?" You want to just keep dripping on them, and in time more of them come around than don't.

Stick With One System

What is absolutely necessary is you must duplicate your leaders 100% before they will begin to multiply— and multiply means that time leverage kicks in.

What I see with a lot of people is that they don't stay with a particular leader until they are totally duplicated. The time frames vary for different people, depending on their own personal circumstances and the hours that they are able to work their business. Something I always add in training and presentations is, "It is just a matter of time."

We don't know what that time will be. Building a network can be like roller coaster ride, until you have lasting residual income, and there can be tremendous ups and downs. You will not fail as long as you don't quit. I almost quit four times, and I'm so glad I didn't.

Stick with one system until you've mastered it and see the results you deserve.

I do lots of what I call meter-reading. It's like if a guy comes up to read your gas meter, he is going to tell you exactly what was used last month, and then you are going to get billed for that. That's the same kind of meter reading I do in coaching and duplicating people. I have my team rate themselves on their own business, their passion. They go down all the letters of passion and rate each on from one (low) to ten (high).

The **P** of passion means **Personal** commitment.

The **A** stands for **Action**, daily, also called the single daily action (SDA).

The first **S** of passion stands for **Sincerity**.

The second **S** has to do with being a **Strong** duplicator, following the System, following the Steps, following the chain of communication. "Chain of command" is an army term, a more traditional business term. I don't use that; I use chain of communication.

The **I** stands for **Intensity**, and that means staying on purpose.

The **O** of passion stands for **Ongoing** leadership and learning.

The **N** in passion goes for being very **Natural**.

It doesn't matter how they have gotten to the tens— hard work, natural talent, sheer luck. We just need to see how it's going. Meter reading helps even out the effects of the roller coaster ride.

By looking at their own businesses, the team can make their own choice of what is best for the next step. I have them list three action steps for the category where they need improvement. They choose where they are willing to expand and become better within the next 30 days. One step might be to read *The Seven Habits of Highly Effective People*. Another might be writing daily action lists and completing each item.

Then I just have them turn to someone and say, "Here's the one I need to improve, and here are my three action steps." By making the statement out loud to someone else, they commit to it more strongly.

Then I have each person share the strongest of their passion meter readings, the one closest to being a ten. "I have done my Single Daily Action every day this month, without fail. I'm now doing front-of-the-room presentations." Each person declares their recent successes to the group.

They are going forward in the areas that need strengthening, and they are acknowledging themselves on the areas where they are already excelling.

Compliments vs. Acknowledgment

The people you are duplicating absolutely need to know that they are very important. People will go to the wall to learn if they are respected, appreciated and acknowledged for who they are as people. And there is a big difference between compliments, acknowledging somebody and empowering them.

We have been taught, since we were little, to give compliments. We say, "That's a nice dress," like the dress is not on a human being. A different way to say that, which would have a much stronger impact, is, "You look great in that dress!" Now you are acknowledging the person for the choice of that dress.

Compliments are a dime a dozen, and they have no lasting power. They sound nice and feel good, but they don't generate action or commitment.

"That was a great lemon meringue pie you made. You gave an incredible presentation." Compliments are on somebody's doing, what they have done, and that feels good for a split second. To acknowledge somebody has to do with their beingness, not their doingness. The difference: Compliments are short term and content-based; acknowledgments are long term, lasting, contextual and bring people forward to interact in their business on a higher level, a higher playing field.

Let's say somebody was on the registration table at a big company function, presentation or monthly event. The leader of the presentation or one of the presenters might come back and say, "Hey, you know, Randy, Sue, Tom and Judy, you did a great job on this registration table. Thanks a lot." Randy, Sue, Tom and Judy are going to internally say, "Oh, that's nice, at least he knew I was here." That's a compliment.

An acknowledgment would be, "Randy, Sue, Tom, and Judy, do you know what a difference you made on this registration table? I noticed you had all your supplies in perfect order, you were here 45 minutes early. I know that took time out of your day, away from your family. When our guests and the representatives came through, you sparkled. You were smiling. You were right there to take care of every need they have. What a difference! They felt cared for and they felt welcomed in being here. You are the kind of people I want to spend more time with."

The difference between that acknowledgment and a compliment had to do with their beingness, their commitment, the difference they made. That will last for them, whereas just, "You did a good job on the registration table," doesn't last, doesn't cause people to want to pick up and do and be more in their business.

After somebody has made their decision— they've signed their representative papers, they have their tools they need, they have their products— then, as the coach, you need to send out a welcome aboard letter. You can make one up. Mine is a very simple, clear letter. (See Appendix B)

When they meet their milestones in becoming a gold or a platinum or a director or an ambassador, whatever your titles are as people are moving up the leadership levels, then I send an acknowledgment letter to them. Each time, it ups the ante.

Periodically, I send a special book or tape to the key leaders on my particular team. Really acknowledging them for their commitment, their tenacity and their inspiration.

It's so important that they know that I know that they make an awesome difference. I have them fax back to me the names of five people on their team they are presently coaching. This keeps me seeing the empire that's being developed by many. They send back the five names of people they are presently coaching, and I'll send a book, tape or letter from me to this new person coming up through the team.

Empowerment

This is the skill that ultimately all great networkers are able to express successfully. Compliments regard doing; acknowledgment is their beingness, the difference they made; empowerment is passing that baton on or training, coaching, teaching someone else.

Here is an example of empowerment: You would come up before or after the presentation and say, "Randy, Sue, Tom and Judy, do you know that you were phenomenal? How you met us all tonight, all of your organizational skills, everything perfect, your attitude, how you sparkled, smiled and made our guests and representatives feel comfortable! Let me ask a question: Do you feel that you know how to do a bang-up registration table for a big event?"

They're going to say yes.

"Great! Here is my challenge: If you truly are committed to being a leader of leaders, next month when we're back in town at our big event or monthly presentation, will you make a commitment with me that you will train four new people to be as good or better than you were this month?"

They will agree to it. They are reviewing everything they did— their skills, their supplies, their attitude, their action, their smiling and their passionate welcoming. They are going to pass that baton and teach four more people next month to be as good or better. That's the key— as good or better. When people are merely complimented, they think, Okay, next month you'll get four new people on the table. That has no substance, no *context* under it. All it is is *content*. It's do— get four more people to *do* this next month. There is no value, there is no liveliness, there is no vitality. They don't feel like they've made a difference. They feel like they have just been *doing* something, and, in time, they will feel used.

As you work with people and develop leaders, constantly encourage, acknowledge and empower. You can never overdo those three. That's one of the rocks in solid duplication and in developing a leader of leaders.

Be a Natural

Duplication needs to flow naturally. It should be easy going and intuitive.

Once someone has mastered duplication themselves and has the results, then they become what is called an *unconscious competent* (more on that in the next chapter). Their effort just flows, and the people they are duplicating say, "That looks so simple and easy." It took me almost two years to begin to really master duplication. I'm still learning more to make it— like they say in Hawaii— "more better."

In working with somebody, in duplicating them, work with their passion. If they are melancholy or quiet, then one of their leadership steps is to speak louder, perhaps speak faster and have a different tone as they speak, because that activates and keeps the attention of people they are training, presenting to and coaching.

I can't stand going to a presentation and seeing some representatives dragging their heads down. Work with people regarding their naturalness and their passion. They need to walk like they are earning $10,000 to $1 million a month. There are networkers who *are* regularly earning a million or more a month, you know. Will you be one of them within the next five to ten years?

They need to walk and talk like they are totally debt free and have residual income. The words need to come out of their mouth again and again in a passionate way, "I am committed to being debt free in the next two years." People need to hear that over and over and over again, so that they know that their coach or their duplicator has her own commitments and goals that she is working with and committed to.

I had the awesome opportunity to meet and learn from Brian Biro at the Upline® Lifer's Retreat. What a genius he is in his leadership and people skills! A concept he presents strongly in his seminars has to do with our energy. Motion creates emotion which creates movement forward. In call workshops, events and presentations, take Brian's advice and be sure to often include motion like raising hands, nodding heads and shouting out answers. In a training, take quick back-rub breaks. Keep the energy/motion moving to keep attention and emotional involvement in place. It will keep people at their peak in learning.

The RSVP Principle

A great duplicator leads by example with the RSVP Principle:

Read daily. Spend 10 to 15 minutes a day reading something positive or spiritual that will feed your soul, feed your mind, feed your business with new knowledge. I commit to reading at least three network marketing, personal growth, or spiritual books every month. I make declarations. I let people know what I'm reading and what I'm learning. I don't tell them to go get the book, but I do ask if they are *willing* to purchase the book. They don't want to be left behind if something I've learned is also beneficial for them.

That's what a great duplicator does. The system is the same, but can you become more proficient, more profound in your communication, in your leadership, in your actions? Darn right you can! Then you will always continue to have ongoing leadership and ongoing learning.

Study daily. I don't care if it's only five minutes. Pick up something new and do it again and again so you become competent in that area.

Visualize daily. A treasure map, psychological trigger device and your affirmations will help you keep a constant vision.

Plan and prioritize daily. A Single Daily Action will create awesome results over time if it fits into your purpose. If you are not as good with prospecting, then that's where you need that Single Daily Action over and over and over. If you are not as proficient with your follow-up, commit to a daily action of follow-up. Sit with an upline team member and listen, take notes and be keenly aware of their beingness and contextual communication.

My parents had an opportunity to spend three weeks with Albert Schwietzer, years ago, in his village in Africa. He said, "Example is not the main thing that influences lives or influences others. Example is the *only* thing."

Many people think that example is just one of the things that influences others. It isn't. It is the only context, the example of beingness that truly makes a difference.

So many people want to bypass the steps of duplication and not do the personal development and work that greatly reflects the professional results. I believe my personal growth reflects my professional results. Any master or high earner in this industry that I have ever talked to absolutely agrees with that statement. Theodore Roosevelt once said, "Do what you can with what you have where you are."

Emerson says, "What lies behind us and what lies before us are tiny matters compared to what lies within us." Becoming a more passionate and committed person about life, about business, about relationships, about knowledge, about experiences will bring out more natural qualities and characteristics that will draw more people to you. You become more magnetic to other people by honing your skills and qualities by RSVPing.

Passing the Baton

I was in Atlanta around the time of the 1996 Summer Olympics where one of the women on my networking team had chosen to assist and support the relay racers from all over the world. She told me, "Peggy, you have no idea how much time and discipline is involved. I'm not talking days, weeks, months— I'm talking the *years and years* these relay runners practice passing the baton."

That baton has to be passed so responsibly and so strongly that the next racer can take it and not lose a nano-second from their running stride. First, the batons have to be absolutely clean. Then they have powder toweled on in a special process, so the baton can be more easily grabbed without slipping. The baton has to feel the same each time the runner passes it off— not slippery, not sticky, just easy to grip and release. Each runner has a responsibility to pass the baton without fumbling it or letting it drop to the ground.

The whole thing is duplication. We are passing the baton of leadership to the person we have chosen to coach in partnership. If a baton of duplication is not passed on responsibly, then you are going to lose a step in your business-building. If you lose too many steps, you drop out of the race altogether. Don't try to pass the baton to everyone who jogs by— save your effort for responsibly duplicating leaders to run the race to the finish.

Many network marketers just keep saying yes, yes, yes to anyone near the starting line. They are ineffective in passing the baton of duplication, because their own attention is divided between the leaders and the also-rans. They end up duplicating their own indecision and lack of focus, and they seldom manage to stay in the race. Many, in fact, burn out and drop out.

To pass the baton effectively to your leaders, you have to recognize the limitations of effective coaching. People call me and say, "I want you as my coach, I want you to duplicate me." I say, "I have my four teams now. I have a commitment to them that might last two years. I do not pick up any more in between."

I have no trouble saying no. I let them know they'll be on my waiting list, but there is no commitment from me until I finish one of the other teams. When I'm done duplicating a team, it has very successful income-earners and at least ten to 20 strong, successful, high-earning leaders.

Know When to Let Them Go

Perhaps you've heard the great story about how an eagle raises eaglets: The parents spend months building a very soft, protective nest with lots of down and soft leaves. Once the eggs are laid in the perfect, cozy nest, both the male and the female sit on the eggs until they hatch. Then both parents take care of the new eaglets with careful protection and food until it's time for the babies to fly. Then the parent eagles begin to take the soft down and leaves out of the nest. They just peck them out and let them drift away on the wind.

The nest starts getting very uncomfortable for the eaglets. Sticks protrude, poking them, and the bottom gets weak and drafty. The eaglets know it's time for them to learn to fly. With the soft nesting gone, they have more room to flap their wings and get those wings strong. The adult eagles will not allow the babies to fly until they know they are ready. Once a baby eagle flies and is strong enough, the parents never return to the nest again.

Why do I share that story with you?

In my experience, too many coaches or upline duplicators hold on to a team that they are duplicating for too long. They feel successful, acknowledged, recognized, and there is a lot of satisfaction there, but unless the eaglets of duplication fly, they will never be strong. Once someone has the skills, the knowledge, and the results, I totally let them go. They know they can always return with a question or if they want to hone a skill, but once my eaglets of duplication are gone, I don't hear from them very much.

This frees me to duplicate others, but also frees them to become true leaders in their own right. It's important when people are fully duplicated to put them out there so that they can be recognized as *the* leader for their network. When I was doing a duplication tour, a nice man in Sydney, Australia, gave me a button to wear, saying that I "truly exemplified" what it meant to him. The only thing on the button was a big "#2." It means put others first and yourself second, and I wear it often. Allow your leaders to be "#1's."

Once representatives are fully duplicated, they no longer need me. They are now the leaders of the leaders that they are duplicating on their team. Corliss Smith Tang, the key leader I duplicated in Hawaii, always uses the phrase that captures it perfectly: "Let them go and they will grow."

Don't Think Small

The Mitsubishi Company, the great technological corporation that makes cars, TVs, sound systems and more, has a philosophy that is absolutely awesome. When there are too many mistakes along the assembly lines, if their production is not up, if the sales are not up, if there are too many people missing work, when the entire company is becoming casual and lackadaisical, the president will shut down every plant, every administrative office, every accounting office, every assembly line and every delivery section.

The company intercom reaches every plant and every area, so the president will get on the intercom and say, "Attention, I want you to know that our great company will always forgive you for making mistakes. But I also want you to know that I will never forgive you for thinking small."

The president then shuts off the intercom and sends everyone back to work.

That says to me that it is okay to make mistakes. It is okay to sin, to miss the mark— the bulls-eye, the goal. It is not okay to think small. Not in developing leaders, not in solving problems, not in working for your success and financial freedom.

IMAGINATION

A Mind Once Stretched by a New Idea
Never Regains its Original Dimensions—Oliver Wendell Holmes.

I don't tolerate thinking small. I bring people up to the level I have reached so far. I do not go back down to lower levels. I always approach situations with solutions in mind, not problems.

We all know John F. Kennedy's famous quote, "Ask not what your country can do for you. Ask what you can do for your country." Why not take it home into our own business?

- Ask not what my company can do for me.
- Ask not what my downline can do for me.
- Ask not what my products can do for me.
- Ask what can I do for my company, what can I do for my downline team, what can I do to make anything I endeavor to do much, much stronger.
- That's bringing it home.

- That's taking accountability.
- That's being a leader of leaders.
- The author Kurt Vonnegut gave a commencement address at MIT in which he gave four strong, simple keys. He said, "I want to address the graduating students. I want the parents to listen. I want the future students to listen. I want the president of this great institution to listen. I want the grandparents to listen to this. I want the nieces and nephews to listen to this. I want every faculty member to listen to this. I'm going to suggest four things for you that will cause you to lead a very exciting, productive, passionate and purposeful life:

- *Do something daily that you risk. Get out of the rut and risk.*
- *The only race we have is the race with ourselves.*
- *Do not be reckless with other people's hearts.*
- Do not allow other people to be reckless with your heart."

His address sums up this chapter perfectly and simply. It doesn't matter if you are a marathon runner or if you are a sprinter, what matters is that you stay in the race. Risk daily, the race is only with ourselves, don't let anyone be reckless with your heart, and don't be reckless with other people's hearts. Those are simple, strong rocks to stand on that will create a great person and a great leader in this industry.

Finally, a little story from *Readers Digest* that illustrates how duplication works.

In good weather, Mark always lets his yellow amazon parrot, Nicky, sit on the balcony to get some fresh air, up on his 10th-floor apartment balcony. One morning, Nicky, flew away, much to Mark's dismay. Mark searched and called and yelled for the bird, but Nicky didn't come back.

When Mark returned from work the next day, the phone rang, and the caller asked for Mark. The caller said, "You are going to think this is crazy, but there is a bird outside on my balcony saying, 'Hello, this is Mark.' Then he recites the phone number I just called and says, 'I can't come to the phone right now, but if you will leave a message at the tone, I'll call you right back.'"

Nicky's cage had been kept in the room with Mark's answering machine, and Nicky duplicated exactly what Mark had put on his message.

People are going to copy you, good or bad, without being much different from parrots. They will duplicate you.

Chapter 5

Personal and Professional Growth

I know my success is a direct result of my personal and professional growth and development, and I believe that's true for all other successful people. If you look at traditional professions— doctor, lawyer, CPA— they put time and money into their initial education and continue to educate themselves throughout their careers. Why? Because their earnings are directly related to their expertise.

Why would it be any different in network marketing? We just don't have to pay $30,000 to $50,000 to go to college, and we can even earn money during our "freshman" year. It is important to communicate to new representatives right off the bat, "You are going to need to spend some money on your own development." I ask them, "How much have you ever spent on your personal growth or your professional growth?" Most people haven't even thought about it.

Let them know, "In the next four or five years, you might be spending $4,000 to $8,000. If that will bring you $10,000 a month, or a million dollars a year in five to seven years, would you be willing to do that?" No one has ever told me that they would be unwilling to spend $4,000 to earn $1 million a year. I ask the question and open the door and see if they are willing to walk on through.

I agree with my friend Rita Davenport, the president of Arbonne, who says that at least 2% of your earnings should go into your personal and professional development as an investment in growing your business.

What's the Difference Between Personal Growth and Professional Growth?

Personal growth is developing and refining the attitudes, actions and vision we bring to all aspects of our lives. It involves communication and interaction with loved ones as well as colleagues and prospects.

Professional growth has more to do with developing knowledge, belief and skills in the field of network marketing.

Imagine getting a master's or doctorate in becoming a better human being. That's the aim of personal growth, and I continually work towards that goal. That's why I greatly recommend the Upline® Masters and Lifers Seminars and Brian Klemmer's Personal Mastery seminars.

Yes, I did complete my first Carol McCall listening course July 24, 1998. WOW! I received more than I paid for. It was a perfect time in my life to participate. Notice I didn't say attend.

On July 14, 1998, the network marketing company I had given my best and all to for over six years declared bankruptcy, much to my shock and surprise. I received a phone call from the president simply telling me it was over. What do I do next in my own life and as a leader of an enormous TEAM?

I never looked at another network marketing company during my commitment to my first company. I knew about many great companies and made a decision in four days to join 21st Century Global Network and its president, Mark Yarnell, whom I've known as a fellow Upline® Master.

As you can see from the dates above, there were only ten days between that and Carol's course. It was at a time in my life when I was ready to experience letting go of the loss of the old and prepare myself for the excitement and challenge of the new. Carol was a gentle master with me as she knew I was in an extremely vulnerable time of my life's journey. I got clearer that now I needed to up my ante 100% to be on my life's purpose: To compassionately create our world being abundant through my leadership, integrity, contribution and inspiration. I actually added the word compassionately while in her course.

Susan Fogg was my 90-day follow-up listening partner, and she was an anchor to me on many of the phone calls. You're the bestest listening partner, Sue.

I highly encourage all of you who haven't experienced Carol's work live, to set that as a goal. I have committed to taking her Possibility of Woman course in 1999. Yes, I completed the Women's course. Awesome! My "Ph.D. in life" is an ongoing program. Is yours?

I find, for myself and the people I coach, that when we better ourselves personally and professionally, our results proportionally reflect that growth. There are a lot of millionaires around, and many people who earn a lot of money. Externally, that looks good, but if they're not also millionaires on the inside, they probably have very little joy or gratitude in their life. Think of Howard Hughes or Christina Onassis: Their billions didn't buy them happiness. Now, think of Malcolm Forbes and the delight he took in entertaining himself and his friends.

Many people think they're doing well, but they're really just surviving. If you dig down to the truth, you find they're suffering physically, mentally, spiritually or in their relationships. If they take, and *use*, personal growth courses, they can turn their energy and consciousness into success and celebration rather than living in survival mode. *Suffering is optional!*

I believe in a higher power. It doesn't matter if you call it source, energy or God, but what I know through interviewing and talking to hundreds of people is that anyone who has been very successful believes in some form of a higher power. I got my guiding light from my father. I'll always treasure and share my faith.

Personal growth can show up as increased confidence, expanded leadership, improved communication, developing a deeper spiritual side— meaning being of service, that's all that spirituality means.

Notice how all those areas of personal growth spill over into professional growth. Does improved communication help in business? Is it a professional advantage to be a confident leader? You bet!

Are You Willing to Change?

You know life changes, and it's important to be able to flow with the changes, not to fight them. Remember it's easier to ride the horse in the direction it's going. Go with the flow.

Before the end of World War II, there were few VCRs, televisions, channel changers or video stores. There was no direct distance dialing or call waiting or answering machines or photocopiers. No dental floss, automatic washing machines, automatic transmissions in cars. There were no electric typewriters. There were no franchises of any kind. No fast food outlets. No fax machines. No car phones. There was no space travel. There was no Kleenex™, no paper towels. No calculators. No desk top computers. No synthetic fibers. No

Velcro™. There were no suburbs. There were no malls. There were no additives or preservatives in food. There were no digital watches. There were no microwave ovens. There were no diet soda drinks, credit cards, bank cash machines. No wind surfers. No snow mobiles. No weather forecasts. No x-ray machines. No aspirins. No penicillin. No birth control pills. There were no lasers, no CDs, no Walkmans™. No one had run a four-minute mile. Everyone thought scaling Mount Everest was impossible. No human had walked on the moon.

In the last 50 years, look at how our world has changed.

Do you have any idea what is going to happen to network marketing as it continues to change and move around the world with leaders like you?

The point is, none of this was here before, but now that we have it, our lives are much simpler. When network marketing continues to grow around the world with integrity, excellence and partnership, we are going to become the industry that changes and transforms the way business does business *every*where.

I'm going to suggest to you that this is far, far bigger than what you even see today. In the six years that I have had the privilege— and I consider it an absolute privilege— to be an ambassador of this industry, I have never had a greater opportunity to serve than I have right now. I am able to reach out and touch so many lives through the entire network and industry. I serve my life's purpose of abundance, through sharing leadership, living with integrity, contribution and leading by inspiration.

You have to be willing to adapt to change and also willing to make changes in your own life in order to grow. That, of course, isn't always easy. A common place where this comes up in our industry is around public speaking. I've had so many people tell me, "I won't ever speak in network marketing." It's one of the biggest fears people have. The people who refuse to consider changing that attitude will never be able to do it, but those who allow themselves to step out a little bit at a time, it's not more then a month or two and they are out doing part of the presentation in front of the room. Perhaps they get involved in ToastMasters, which is a great, inexpensive way to take those first steps towards confidence in public speaking. With each step there is a solidness underneath. Each step forward will create a stronger foundation for the next step, even if it seems scary and shaky at first.

Here's an example of a change I've made personally: When I first started this business, I called it a game— kind of spun off what Randy Ward uses in *Winning Is the Greatest Game of All* (which I suggest you read). Because I have such a strong, duplicated team, they were all using the word game, too. I can remember the president coming up to me at my company's convention in 1996. He said, "Peggy, can I ask you something? Do you really feel that what you are doing is a game?"

I stepped back a little bit and had to run it through my filter— through my thinking system— because I had taught tens of thousands of people to use the word game. When I really stepped back and looked, I realized that it is absolutely *not* a game, this is a lifestyle. This is about making a difference and about sharing a business and a product. It was hard for us to stop using that word, but we did it!

Jim Rohn, a great leader and trainer, simply says, "Unless you change how you are, you will always have what you got." Your success is going to equal how willing you are to change and to grow.

Your Walls of Attitude

I have a jagged piece of rock on my desk that's about two inches by three inches and maybe an inch high. It has some pink writing on it, but I can't figure out what it says. It's a piece of the Berlin Wall, and I keep it on my desk to keep me focused, keep me on purpose. My joy, responsibility and privilege is to support other people in breaking down their walls. How many years did the Berlin Wall stand? It used to seem permanent, and yet the structure's been torn down. The same thing can happen with all our walls between human beings. It doesn't matter how long we've had them.

Most of us were brought up with programming to create walls that *seem* to protect us. They're designed to keep out anything that might hurt. The problem is that they also keep us in. In becoming a great leader and having a purpose in life, we need space to shine, to grow, to be vulnerable. Walls are too limiting to give us that kind of space. Personal growth and professional growth help us break down our walls.

How do you break them? With constant, daily discipline. It's sharing or declaring with other people what it is that you are committed to making happen, to creating, to manifesting in your life. Share those only with very positive supportive people, because there are dream-stealers out there.

Many people think personal growth is a bunch of hogwash or brain washing— a waste of time at best, potentially dangerous at worst. Most of those people have never even been to a class, but they think they know it all. Know-it-alls would rather steal your dream and throw it away than see you learn and grow. I don't have much use for such people.

I have tremendous value for people who know that they know that they know. What does that mean? That means that they are able to tap into a higher power, an intuition, a force, a god, a guiding light. That's like a super consciousness. They are able to draw it up to the subconscious and then put it into action in the conscious world, the world where we spend 95% of our time. "To know that I do not know" is the beginning of wisdom.

Your ATTITUDE, not your APTITUDE, determines your ALTITUDE!

Your Supreme Power

People wonder why life isn't as great as we know it could be. It's partly because they operate mainly out of their conscious mind. This part of our mind is the least powerful and creative place to operate from. It is our reason and logic, and this is an important part to use. However, the subconscious houses our intuition, feelings, creativity programs and our five senses. Of course, there are positive and negative programs, and they all stay in the subconscious.

By the time a child is four or five years old, 50% of programming is planted. By age eight, 80% is firmly in place. In relationships, we operate as eight-year-olds most of the time. Ugh!

Can you imagine an adult acting and talking like a five- to eight-year-old child? Yet adults respond with their programs through their five- to eight-year-old child feelings. They react out of old habits, unthinking patterns and unserving programs.

Some of these are:

- I'm not good enough.
- Lack consciousness.
- I'm unlovable.
- Playing it safe, not risking.
- I'm not open.
- People won't like me.
- Not worthy.
- Interrupting others.
- Not important enough.

These show up in low self-esteem and self-worth. Until we choose to enroll and fully participate in a seminar to change these programs, attitudes and habits, we will keep the same communications and actions in relationships and in our business. We will continue to lack the awareness we need to grow and develop.

The super-conscious—the power, the force, the light, the energy, God, whatever you want to call it— is the supreme power to tap into. It gives us the option to make careful responses, break old habits and achieve even greater personal goals. It's a source of higher knowledge. So I listen to someone who knows that they know that they know.

Their actions are aligned with what they say they are going to do and be. It may take the form of integrity. It may be wise choices that propel them forward versus negative choices that cause them to stagnate. Washington Irving said, "Great minds have purposes, little minds have wishes. Little minds are subdued by misfortune, great minds rise above them."

Great minds know, little minds are know-it-alls.

Why is it so important to know the know-it-alls from the super-conscious? It's all part of the awareness that helps you break down walls. Know-it-alls will put back every brick you take out of your walls. You don't need that. You need support and encouragement in your growth process.

John Wooden, who coached UCLA basketball to 10 successful seasons, says it's "What you learn after you know it all that really counts." I love that. Are you open to know there is a world of knowing awaiting you?

When I was growing up, I learned relatively little prejudice. It was fine with my parents for me to marry a man of another race, any race. That was okay. But I was raised that I could not marry a

Catholic and I could not marry a Jew. That program carried on into my adult life.

After my divorce, I decided that belief was very limiting. Any wall is extremely limiting. I decided to change that. I thought, "I'm single and what if I met somebody who was Jewish or Catholic and we grew in love?" (I don't believe we fall in love, we grow in love.) What if we both wanted a commitment? I had a wall or a barrier there, so I went to the Jewish temple and I studied the Torah. Also—every Sunday for six months—I went to the Catholic church, so I could experience that firsthand. I decided within myself that I could marry either a Jew or Catholic. I broke the wall that separated me from people of those religions.

My parents never intended to put negative limitations on me. In their belief, you simply didn't marry interfaith. My belief is different, so that was a wall I chose to eliminate. It was a whole-year process for me, and it probably would have taken even longer if I had not been aware and disciplined to break down that wall.

What does my attitude about marriage have to do with network marketing? I now have so many incredible Jewish friends, and Catholic friends, and Hindu and Muslim friends in my network. I might have missed those relationships if I hadn't handled my prejudice against interfaith marriage. I might not have been able to be an effective coach had I not changed my beliefs.

Wealth Consciousness vs. Lack Consciousness

One of the most important paradigm shifts to make, on both the personal and professional levels, is from lack consciousness to wealth consciousness. Most people have a lack of wealth consciousness—most of us aren't taught about that in our formal education or at home. We can become masters of the Three R's, but, really, how often do we use those R's to achieve wealth? I have an extensive and expensive formal education, but it didn't make me wealthy. I had to develop a wealth consciousness that had nothing to do with my college degrees.

What is lack consciousness?

Lack consciousness is seeing "not enough money" as a permanent state, as your fate. "I'll never have enough. I can't pay my bills this month. I'm tired of living like this. There is no way out. My parents were like this and I'm following in the same mode."

When lack consciousness goes shopping, it always looks at the price tag not the value or how much pleasure it gives. When lack consciousness eats out, it always looks on the right side of the menu before making a choice. It bases decisions in life on lack of money, lack of time and lack of abundance.

When someone has a lack consciousness about cash, they need to do some studying and learn how to break the pattern and the belief systems of poverty. I see a huge difference between being poor and being in poverty. I have been poor as far as money is concerned, and maybe so have you. To me, being poor is simply a condition that can always be changed in time. Poverty is a mindset that has to do with lack, and it's tough to change. Sometimes impossible. That's where public subsidy begets public subsidy. It's a program that gets passed on in generations.

Some people have a lack consciousness in relationships. They think they can never have a good relationship. I had the privilege of working with John Gray for almost two years. He's the author of *Men are From Mars, Women are From Venus* (I think that title is very accurate) and a tremendous man. I learned a lot about relationships in his course and by working with him. If someone has a lack consciousness in leadership, then they need to take some leadership seminars. They should read books by tremendous leaders like George Washington, Winston Churchill, Golda Meir, Gandhi, Mother Teresa, Stephen Covey, Oprah Winfrey and John Milton Fogg.

Lack consciousness doesn't have that much to do with the size of a paycheck. It has to do with the scope of a person's thinking. Napoleon Hill uses this concept over and over again: To think is to create. If people's thinking continues to be one of lack, that's what they're creating. It's a perpetual program and a belief. It goes on and on and then it gets passed on to their children and to their children's children. That's where so much of the world is today.

Do you know that in fact our world is truly abundant? We have enough food on this planet to feed everyone. We have enough money. We have enough wealth in the world. So why are people poor, starving, desperate? It's because most people are operating out of lack, thinking there is not enough. By changing to wealth consciousness, you and I can make a difference.

Wealth consciousness involves being totally open and willing to receive. Are you open to abundance? That might mean better relationships, more money, richer experiences or greater knowledge. Wealth conscious people think in abundance and talk in abundance. They make declarations to their friends and family what they are going to manifest, create, make happen in their lives over and over again. They read the books on wealth consciousness, like the *Seven Laws of Money* and *The Richest Man in Babylon*. Babylonian society was the richest, most civilized in the world for years and years and years. They developed a long-lasting society based on wealth consciousness.

Last Christmas, I received the most unusual gift from my dad and second mom Helen. It was a picture of a pig, a pregnant pig, no less. It said a pregnant pig was being shipped to a small village in Africa. This one pig, when the piglets are born, will feed an entire family. When the piglets get big and have more piglets, they must be given to another family in the village. In a short time, there will be enough pigs to take care of an entire community. Each one teach one. Isn't that duplication?

Almost monthly now, I give chickens, cows, goats or rabbits to one family, and the natural multiplication of these animals will feed an entire village. The organization I work through is called the Heifer Project, and it's been around for 40 years or more, waging a campaign against lack consciousness. Until there are enough visionaries committed to breaking this cycle of lack consciousness, the pattern will continue.

With knowledge and education, when someone is willing, lack consciousness can be shifted. It's not an overnight process. It's going to take some time and conscious effort and thinking. It takes awareness to stop a program of lack that has been going on for 20 years, 40 or 60 years.

I've studied many of Katherine Ponder's books, especially *The Dynamic Laws of Prosperity*. She deals very strongly with how to shift a lack consciousness into a wealth consciousness. Brian Klemmer's Personal Mastery Seminar is another resource. I've participated in and led that seminar 30 to 40 times, and so did about 50 of the high-income earners I've coached. In my lifetime, I've invested close to $70,000 into professional and personal growth— and that doesn't include two and a half master's degrees.

I am listening and applying a series of relationship tapes by Ellen Kreidman, Ph.D. I know that I will always have room to grow. When we add spice and renewed commitment by continuing to develop ourselves, then our relationships expand. I am ever conscious of the increased abundance available in all relationships. Are you?

I mentioned that I had a tremendous home upbringing as far as support, empowerment, caring and spirituality, but I was raised financially poor. It wasn't until I was 34 or 35 that I even really knew about lack consciousness versus wealth consciousness. It was through a seven-day, $2,500 seminar that I became aware of it and learned I could do some things to change it. The next year, I tripled my income by changing my thinking from lack into abundance, and I purchased my first home.

I have absolutely changed from lack to wealth consciousness in my life. If I can do it, you can do it— definitely. Wealth consciousness really is just an awareness of all that is available, already within your reach. You have the power in you to change your history and create more self worth and abundance in all areas of your life.

There are some people who truly desire and will be committed to breaking out of this mindset to create new wealth in network marketing— they will welcome the gift you offer. Just don't chase poverty conscious people for months in hopes that they will become wealth-thinkers. You'll have too big a project on your hands.

Where You Get Your Fire

I use a little story to remind myself and my leaders about the continuing importance of personal and professional growth.

A man was lost in the woods on a very cold snowy day. He needed to get inside because he was literally freezing to death. He finally stumbled across a little mountain cabin, its stone chimney dark against the falling snow. As he went in, he thought, "Thank goodness it has a fireplace!"

The man staggered over to the hearth and commanded, "Give me heat."

Nothing happened.

The man wanted some heat like crazy, so he said, loudly, "Fireplace, give me heat!"

Still nothing.

The man pounded on the mantel and screamed, "Give me heat! Now!"

The fireplace finally said back to him, "You give me wood, and I'll give you heat."

Personal growth is the wood that fuels our productivity fires. More wood means more heat, more steam, we can be more, we can give and contribute to more people. Most people run around in life and in their network marketing company wanting to get, wanting heat from the fireplace of their upline, downline or sponsor. GET GET GET—ME ME ME shoves teams or friendships away. They don't want to BE with someone so self-absorbed.

That type of person doesn't have enough inside to start a fire; they have no heat to give. So they are always drawing from other people rather than filling up their own internal heat. Personal growth heaps wood on those inner fires—enough to drive the engine of development, contribution and success.

The Seven Positive Attitudes

The Seven Positive Attitudes are a wonderful tool for advancing your personal growth. It's one I use to remind myself of who I am committed to being in my relationships, and I highly recommend adopting these Attitudes as the basis for the partnerships you create in your business, as we discussed in Chapter Three. They will be a tremendous source for your own growth in the process. The Seven Positive Attitudes are

1. Caring

A caring attitude acknowledges one's responsibility to respond to the needs of another. To care is to show interest or concern in another's well-being. The more you care, the more you are naturally motivated to fulfill or support others. Caring is also an acknowledgment of what is important to a person. Caring for a person shows that you consider them special.

2. Understanding

An understanding attitude validates the meaning of a statement, feeling or situation. It does not presume to already know, but gathers meaning from what is heard. An understanding attitude starts from not knowing and moves towards validating what is being communicated.

3. Respect

A respectful attitude acknowledges another's rights, wishes and needs. It yields to the wishes and needs of another, not out of fear, but through acknowledging the validity of those needs, wishes and rights. It is a heart-felt consideration for the well-being of another person. Respect is the attitude that motivates one to truly serve another.

4. Appreciation

An appreciative attitude acknowledges the value of another's being and behavior. It acknowledges that another person has enriched one's well-being. Appreciation is the natural reaction to being supported. (Respect is generally confused with this attitude. This is because when we greatly value or appreciate someone, naturally we respect or yield to their values or needs.)

5. Acceptance

An accepting attitude acknowledges that another's being or behavior is received willingly. It is not a passive, overlooking or slightly disapproving attitude. It does not reject, but affirms that another is quite enough and is being favorably received. To accept a person does not mean that you believe they could not improve; it means you are not trying to change them. Acceptance is the attitude which forgives another's mistakes.

6. Trust

A trusting attitude acknowledges the positive qualities of another's character; i.e., honesty, integrity, reliability, justice, sincerity, etc. When trust is absent, it is common that people consistently jump to the wrong and negative conclusion regarding a person's intent. Trust gives every offense the benefit of the doubt. Trust says there must be some good explanation. Trust grows in a relationship when each partner recognizes that the other never intends to hurt but seeks to support.

7. Love

Love is a connecting, uniting, sharing or joining attitude. Without judgment or evaluation, it says, "We may be different, but we are also alike. I see myself in you and I see you in myself." On a mental level, love is expressed through understanding. It acknowledges a sense of relatedness. It says, "I relate to you in this similar way." On an emotional level, love is expressed through empathy. It acknowledges a relatedness of feeling. It says, "I relate to your feelings. I have similar feelings." On a physical level, love is expressed through touch.

Each of these attitudes offers a different facet of development, a way to grow. You could choose to focus on one attitude each week, keeping that attitude at the forefront of all communications. Will you accept this challenge for your growth?

Echoes and Affirmations

We have a lot of mountains and absolutely gorgeous lakes here in Arizona. Canyon Lake is about two hours from Phoenix. It's a large man-made lake surrounded by gigantic canyons. In one spot, there's a very narrow channel, probably only 60 feet wide, with huge cliffs on each side. I can remember going up there in a boat and yelling into that channel just to hear the echo from the water and the mountain walls.

When we speak, we put out a message into all the human canyons, and an echo is going to come back. Mother Teresa said, "Kind words can be short and easy to speak, but their echoes are truly endless." Remember Flip Wilson's saying, "What goes around comes around"? On the other hand, if they say, "Oh, I'm not confident," that's exactly what is going to come back to them. It's a universal law that's been around forever, it's nothing new.

Affirmations are a tremendous tool for changing your negative echoes into positive echoes. A good affirmation is detailed, specific and in the present tense. It is not a goal, so it has no time table. It is just an affirmation.

Affirmations are very powerful for all areas of life. If someone has a goal to lose weight, they might have a great big sign (like the one in my house) which says, I Am Healthy And Slim. I must see and hear that message, so every time I go by my sign, I read it out loud. Of course, exercise goes along with that, but I'm setting the positive thoughts deep into my mind even when I'm not exercising. The conscious mind keeps planting the seed into the subconscious mind.

Too often, without meaning to, people build walls that keep out success. If I sat around thinking, "I'm fat and out of shape. Guess I'll always be that way," how effective would my exercise be? I'd be building a wall between me and my own health. Our thoughts are as powerful as our actions.

Two Ways We Learn and Change

When we experience something which triggers powerful emotions, alter our behavior in order to repeat or avoid the emotion. Emotion is one of the greatest teachers. Remember the child and the hot burner? The pain and emotional distress made more difference than the mother's repetitive warnings. Our adult experiences of divorce, a loved one's death, or job loss are similarly powerful forces for change in our behavior.

The other way people learn and change is through repetition. Repetition is easier to work with than emotional experience. By doing the same thing over and over again, you establish new thoughts and beliefs. Affirmations are among the most powerful ways to start personal change, and they work through repetition.

Affirmations always start with "I AM." This I AM is one of the most powerful, truthful concepts in all history. It comes right out of almost every spiritual teaching.

Here are a few examples of affirmations:

- I AM an Awesome Prospector.
- I AM a National Marketing Director.
- I AM Earning $10,000/$100,000+ a Month.
- I AM in a Powerful Passionate Relationship.
- I AM Driving a New Red Lexus SL400.
- I AM a Tither.
- I AM a Leader of Leaders.
- I AM 125 Pounds and Healthy.
- I AM an Upline® Lifetime Member.
- I AM a Great Mom/Dad/Grandpa/Grandma.
- I AM Full of Passion.
- I AM Financially Free.

I coach people to get a lot of 3x5 cards and write their affirmations on them. Put a card on your desk. Put one on the dashboard of your car where you can see it while you are driving. If you want to be really bold and ballsy, take lipstick and write your affirmation BIG on your bathroom mirror. Use red lipstick. Red is emotional and vibrant—you will see your affirmation every single day as a big, bold statement.

Even when I'm fishing, while I cast out my lure, I say my affirmations. Become conscious of all the pockets of time throughout your day and use that formerly "dead air" for saying your affirmations.

Read your affirmations aloud— repeat them passionately every morning and every evening, repeat them while you are waiting on telephone hold. Write them out over and over and over and over again, instead of doodling. I will promise you that they work as long as you work them.

State your affirmations OUT LOUD and EMOTIONALLY.

Most people feel foolish doing that. When I'm walking down the street or going into a mall, rather than just looking around at the trees and thinking about that blouse I want, I will be saying my affirmations. I'm not shouting them out, I'm just repeating them for myself to hear.

But sometimes I do shout them. A whole bunch of us will go to a park or beach and we'll just shout our affirmations. It doesn't hurt anybody. It does cause representatives to expand their comfort zone and deepen their belief. People at the park or beach come and ask what we're doing, so at times it even turns into a prospecting event. What the mind can see and believe, it will achieve.

About 15 years ago, I was given a gift that I see every day in my home. It is a positive reminder for me of what can be done, and it is, literally, a *can* which has written on it: **When I can't, God can.**

So true, so true. When I'm wrestling with a big challenge, I see my "God can" and I feel more at ease and trust the process.

Shoot for the Moon

Many years ago, there was a very young boy growing up in Ohio, and he was very sick. He had extremely bad childhood asthma and couldn't go to school. He spent many, many hours, days, weeks and years in his bedroom, because if he moved much, he would start coughing and having asthma attacks.

The little boy's mother would go into his bedroom often in a day to check on him. Many times, she would see him with a Tinker Toy or a pencil or a crayon clutched in his little fingers. He would start with it set against the floor and then stab it toward the ceiling, as far as his arm could reach. He made little bursting, exploding sounds the whole time. His mother finally asked, "Son, what are you doing?"

The little boy replied, "I'm going to the moon."

She was a very wise mother, not a dream stealer. She didn't tell him the moon was too far away, or that he was too sick to go. She simply said, "I believe you could do that."

For years, the little boy would turn every pen, pencil and twig into a rocket bound for the moon. Do you know who that young boy was?

Neil Armstrong, the first man on the moon.

He saw his goal daily, he acted it out over and over, and years later, he took the educational steps to reach his goal. From his youth, he had a vision that he would be the first man on the moon. By seeing it and believing it and acting on it, he achieved it. It's a great example of an affirmation at work. If we see and say and act our vision, we will achieve it.

It's not an overnight thing. You can start seeing small changes. Other people start acknowledging you for it and you go, "Hey, this stuff works!" I usually suggest people have at least five affirmations in different areas, not just their business. The business might be a little slower. Perhaps their health is better or perhaps their spirituality is improved or perhaps their relationships are more open and honest. Affirmations absolutely work, even at different speeds, and only when you work them.

I can remember when I was going to buy my first house and I didn't have the money for it. I made an affirmation, a declaration that I was going to do it. I had to go through eight real estate agents to do it, because they didn't believe it was possible, but I bought my first and perfect house just as I said I would, against every odd in the book. On this rock I stand and, World, you *will* adjust.

Remember the three-minute rule? That came from a personal growth seminar many years ago with Brian Klemmer. He asked us each to bring a small egg timer with us—a three-minute egg timer. You can get one at any hardware store or supermarket. The seminar exercise was designed to make us see how precious time is—time is our most valuable asset, and wisdom is how you use it. If you have a dream, don't plan to start pursuing it down the road, start now!

How well are you using your time, especially the time that you are giving to your business? I have a very large hourglass on my desk right now. I turn it over continually during the day as I'm working on the phone or returning my voice-mail messages or sending out e-mail or doing some coaching of a particular leader. I can see how the time is going from one part of the hourglass to the other, and it keeps me very focused and very much on purpose. Every minute is precious. My hourglass reminds me that time is not an infinite resource. I have no guarantee of tomorrow.

Whitney Houston sings an inspiring song, "One Moment in Time," which is great to play at training. Give yourself and your team reminders of how precious time is to you and your business—and to your prospects. I also use a little verse to teach people the value of time:

Another Minute

Another minute just went by. Maybe you used it to learn something or to work towards a goal or create or to enjoy. Maybe you used it to say thank you or to make a difference in the life of somebody. Or maybe you just let it go without making the best of it while it was here.

And now this minute is gone forever and you can't get it back.

And so it goes day after day after day.

There are millions of things you can do with each minute. And in those minutes life is lived, dreams are pursued, great cities are built, beautiful art is created, magnificent machines are designed, families are strengthened and businesses grow. And every minute is the opportunity to jump on the road to success and fulfillment. It all depends on how you use it.

Another minute is starting right now. . . .

Models, Mentors and Coaches

Another powerful tool is modeling, which we touched on briefly earlier. When somebody wants to grow or expand in a specific area, then they need to find a model for success in that area.

Let's say that somebody has a goal of earning $10,000 a month in this business. They need to find someone who has made $10,000 a month—that $10,000-a-month person is the model. What does that person do, say and manifest? How could you model that behavior? Modeling is imitating the actions, skills and communications of success to reach success. If you model someone who makes $2,000 a month, does that help you reach $10,000 a month? Not likely! If you want to know what your income is going to be in the next year, look at the ten closest friends you have today. Are they living in wealth consciousness? Will they make $10,000 a month this year?

I can go back in my life and see how true that was before I chose to break down my wall of income and be around people who had created the kind of income I was committed to creating. Modeling is finding somebody who has what it is that you plan to have and doing what they do and being how they BE. Your model may be available in person, in a book, on tape or on video. If you are able to be with your model in person, ask questions, listen and learn all you can from their experiences and knowledge.

I didn't have a model or a coach I could talk to or a hands-on mentor for my business. I had what I call silent mentors. They were authors, seminar leaders, speakers on audio and video tapes. I couldn't ask them questions, but I could learn from them. By studying and reading and finding out what a person does, how they behave, you can model them. Some have no idea they're my mentors, because I haven't met them yet. I've "known" them through media or perhaps by talking to someone else who knows them.

That's how I learned this business. I was in the business two years before I met John Kalench and over four years before I met John Milton Fogg, who have been my two strongest silent mentors in this industry.

I have mentors in many different areas in my life now. My father has been a spiritual coach for me. I have relationship coaches. I love to talk to people who have wonderful, incredible, awesome 30-, 40-year marriages. I love to find out what's worked for them, what they are working on now, what are their keys to success. I have financial coaches, personal growth coaches. Do you have coaches in various arenas?

We talked earlier about professional growth and public speaking skills. Most of us need to find someone who has great public speaking skills to model. Get some of their tapes. Repeat what they say. Modeling helps to make those shaky first steps easier, to build rock-solid foundation.

You can model attitude, you can model leadership or public speaking, you can model a master duplicator or prospector. This fall, I'm going to have a physical mentor— a personal trainer who will come to my home and work with me. I can afford that now and I have the time. My strongest contribution is leading by example in all walks of my life.

Pretend you have the head and heart of someone you greatly respect. This person has the personal qualities or networking expertise you are committed to developing in yourself. Talk, walk, think, act and BE like the person you respect. This technique really works! In time, you will add those desired traits to your own beingness and business. I request you do this exercise for 30 days to see how you feel, how you relate to prospects, how you interact with those you are coaching. Are you up for this request?

I get about 20 calls a month from people on my team who want me to duplicate them. I am only good enough today to take on four teams at a time for 100% duplication. Since I learned by reading books by Randy Gage, Jan Ruhe, Sandy Elsberg, John Milton Fogg and John Kalench, I decided to make it easier for people to model me by writing this book.

I've invested time and money reading at least 100 books on this industry in the six years since I've been in it. There is not a book I read where I don't learn something and where I can't find something I can model that will make me become more competent and of more service to other people.

It is valuable to your team to share the book or video you are reading or watching. Share at least one good insight that you have gleaned from it. By sharing your value, you will create value for others to invest in themselves by reading or watching the same material.

I have wanted to write a book my entire life. It has flashed in and out of my conscious thinking for years. Even before network marketing, I had a varied and exciting life. I worked in the hills of Kentucky with hillbillies. I've started schools for drug users and dropouts when nobody was working with them. I've worked in prisons and rehabilitation centers. I've traveled all over. If my life and experiences can inspire or teach anyone anything, then I need to share it and be a point of light.

I had the privilege, when I was about 13 or 14, of marching with Martin Luther King, Jr. We had tomatoes and bottles and rags thrown at us! I was about eight rows back from Dr. King, but I could see him up there. He was walking proud. He was walking tall. He had a purpose for that march. I needed him as a model. I'd get hit with something and I would become very fearful. I focused on Dr. King as he and his main leaders linked arm and arm and walked, the black and the white together.

I said, "I'm going to walk just like him." I modeled Martin Luther King. I was walking with strong steps and my head held high. Instead of walking in fear, I was walking in faith to make a stand for something. I truly believed that our country needed to change. By modeling Martin Luther King, Jr., I was able to act on my belief, in spite of my fears.

I am so grateful that I now have many, many female models in my life and business. I'm learning from them in regard to leadership and the woman's role in network marketing. I will always model someone who gives more than I do, who has more than I am today. That's what a model is.

I choose to model people with personal power, people with passion, people who are phenomenal communicators, people who are successful, people who are making a difference with their lives. I don't want to model someone who is a millionaire five times over if what they are doing in their life is not making a difference to other people. I have no need to model anyone whose *heart is in their wallet.*

Who are your models? What areas of your life and business are you choosing to expand by modeling now? Let your team know who your models are and what you are committed to learning from them.

Resources to Support You

Resources to support your personal and professional growth are abundant in this industry. Look in the magazines for network marketers: *Upline®; SUCCESS; Entrepreneur.* There are so many seminars out there: Upline® Masters Seminar and Lifer's Retreat, Brian Klemmer, Carol McCall, Brian Biro, Bob Proctor, Tony Robbins.

I will not recommend a seminar, personal or professional, unless I've been there first. That's part of my leading by example. I have my favorite seminars, and those are the ones I most often suggest to people I am coaching and to my own team and other network marketing friends. Then we can be in alignment with the learning from the seminars.

At the same time, it's important for me to keep learning and growing from new experiences. Your personal development is important to your business, and it affects the personal development of people who look to you as a coach and mentor. That's why I commit every year to go to two personal growth seminars. It's a personal commitment that I made even before I became involved in network marketing. What's the next seminar you can do for your growth?

Hands-on learning absolutely makes a difference. Being in an environment of support, of caring, of gentleness, of empowerment, of joy, of celebration— whether it's one day, four days or a whole week— produces much higher and lasting results than reading a book or watching a video. Seminars combine emotional involvement and repetition. Most people aren't disciplined enough to get that powerful combination from audios, videos or books.

Where do you find great seminars? I ask people. Some of my mentors are people who have been in this industry much longer than I have. When John Fogg asked me to be one of the masters on the Upline® *Womans Tapes*, I was awestruck and extremely humble about it, because I was young in network marketing. The other five women masters had been in the industry for 10 to 27 years! I was so eager to ask them what classes they'd taken. What books were they reading? I acknowledge them for being open and willing to share with me.

I even ask that question *before* I'll sponsor somebody. What was the last book you read? I love to sit down with a good novel on an airplane every so often or if I just need to take a break, but I need to know if people are also delving into something deeper than that. Someone might say, "I just read a good golf book."

I could get judgmental: "Why would you waste your time reading about a game!" Instead, I try to find out more by asking, "Why did you choose to read that?"

"One of my goals is to be more mentally disciplined in the game of golf."

Then I understand the reason behind it, and reasons can be very valuable. Mental discipline can apply just as well to business as it does to golf. Personal development comes in many forms, so I look for them and ask plenty of questions.

Do I have some things in my life that aren't perfect? Well of course

I do. I think that when I no longer have challenges, when everything is perfect in my life, I'll be in another time and another place. I like this world, so I'm not ready to check out or move over, but I continually look for ways to grow beyond whatever challenges I face right now.

I consistently rely on the tools and techniques I'm sharing in this book.

Make It Play

One of the most fun kinds of personal growth is play, and I believe it's important for a team to play together sometimes— not just work. I went out to dinner the other night with a couple who are in our company. We didn't talk shop. We just played together for an evening. That makes our working relationship stronger. It's just like the old saying, "The family that plays together, stays together." Network marketing families need to play together— social events, barbecues, acknowledgment parties and treasure map parties.

I have a drinking mug that was given to me years ago, and for some reason, it's a cup that's never broken. It says, "Love what you do and do what you love." I love doing and being a network marketer— and it's not work. It's play. It becomes glowing. It becomes very natural and free-flowing for me.

I can't say I never get tired. If I'm out on the road for a while and I've taken on a lot, I come home physically tired. Sometimes I get mentally tired, too. That's when I need to slow down and renew myself. I'll do that through, of course, getting a good night's sleep, but I almost always will also pick up a good book. I check into a positive, spiritual book that will refill my soul fast.

I take four to five months off each summer and go up to our 4.5-acre family island. I just built a beautiful new mortgage-free cottage up in Canada. When I'm with all my family up on the lake, I fish, I read, and I garden. I've never been a gardener before, but now I have a wild flower garden up there, and I just go crazy with the weeds in it. To me that is playing. It's important to have that balance in life and always pull the weeds in our businesses.

Most of the time, though, I don't feel that network marketing is work. I wish we didn't call it net*working*. We should call it net*playing* that pays and relationship marketing.

Sometimes I teach new representatives about netplaying. That's part of their professional growth. I have a wonderful representative over in California, Deni Cooper, who lives right on the ocean. In the morning, we'll get up and we'll just walk down by the cliff and talk about nature. We don't even talk that much about business or work. That is playing to re-energize. I'm rejuvenating my soul and my spirit, so that I can go and work very intently. Deni plays and rejuvenates in the morning, so she creates the results in her work the rest of the day and the evening.

I've heard a story about two women out chopping wood for their fireplaces. They each started the day with a sharp ax and a big pile of uncut wood. One woman worked all day without stopping. The other stopped chopping once every hour and went away for ten minutes.

At the end of the day, the woman who worked steadily had a large pile of chopped wood, a few blisters and a backache. The other woman, however, had a *huge* pile of fireplace-ready wood and no blisters or aches.

The first woman finally asked, "How can you have more wood chopped? I worked steadily, while you took a ten-minute break every hour! What did you do?"

The second woman replied, "Every hour, I sharpened my ax."

Play keeps your work-ax sharp. Recreation keeps your ax sharp.

Personal and professional growth sharpen the ax of our ability. The results of our labor are greater, and we avoid the blisters of worry and lost focus.

I get so excited I almost jump for joy when I see people's personal growth expand. No child is born distrusting or prejudiced or shy. We learn those things and hold onto them until something or someone comes along and says, "Hey, there is a better way, let me lead you down this path." That's what personal and professional growth is— a path to something better in our lives.

Chapter 6

Personal Leadership

The first and best step to developing leaders is to become a true leader of yourself. This is a step many people in this industry leave out, and they aren't willing to pay the price to grow in personal leadership. They become duplicated, do the business and earn money, but mostly on only their own driving efforts. Let's say you are driving your car, and you stop to go into the store. The car also stops because you are not behind the wheel driving it. This is what happens when a person is driving his lines or legs. He stops— business stops.

By not developing leaders of leaders, they end up doing the business all on their own and not passing that baton. As long as they stay busy, they'll earn good money fast, but then they start getting burned out. They start getting tired. They start saying, "Where in the heck is this leveraging of time? This isn't happening for me." Most of the time they are operating out of ego, and the need for recognition and cash. It's all about "me" rather than empowering, appreciating, raising the excellence in other people. Become a true leader yourself

Leadership Comes from Within

John Maxwell has some tremendous material out there, and two of his absolutely awesome books on leadership are *Developing the Leader Within You* and *Developing the Leaders Around You*. Most people want to get their hands on *Developing the Leaders Around You*. Bypass the Leader Within, but we must all develop our personal leadership first.

I believe the wonderful, simple concept in the Bible, "As within so without." Coach people to start developing the leader within. Develop personal mastery of your attitude, your inspiration skills and the hands-on knowledge. Let the wonderful leader within come out and shine before you start Developing the Leaders Around You.

John Maxwell comes from a Christian context, but if you come from a different faith—Buddhism Hinduism, Islam or Judaism—don't let the Christianity stop you from gaining what's available. These are two books I highly recommend.

Being a leader is a choice. *Choice, not chance,* determines your destiny. The choice is simple and it's always in your hands. You can either stand up and be counted *on,* or lie down and be counted *out.*

What It Takes To Be a Leader

As I've said before, being has nothing to do with *doing*— in fact, great leadership involves doing less and *being* more. Many can **teach,** but few can **reach**. The following are the eight key elements in developing your leadership state of being which are the reaching bonds which connects people:

1. Contribution

If someone does not choose to be an incredible contributor, they may be a leader of themselves, but they will never be a leader of leaders. If someone is having difficulty contributing, reaching out and being there for other people, I will give them special coaching. I often recommend The Tao of Leadership, by John Heider, as a superb coaching tool.

The idea of contribution can be extremely difficult for people who come from the traditional business world— especially men. Ego must be out of their beingness totally. The truth is men and women operate differently in many areas, and network marketing mixes us all together. Men tend to come from numbers, they come from action, and they are more like hunters— they're going out to conquer, to do it, to "bring home the bacon," so to speak. That's been in their consciousness, their upbringing, their belief system, forever.

Women tend to be more nurturing. They tend, overall, to be more patient, more understanding and better listeners. A man will want to solve the problem. Men are fix-it machines. Someone calls on the telephone and says, "Hey, I have this problem with a late order or a wrong order . . ." or whatever the situation might be. A man often will go straight to solution, rather than allowing people to briefly express themselves and resolve the situation on their own (one of the skills people need to learn in order to grow).

In developing a leader, how I work with a man and how I work with a woman is sometimes different. Network marketing gives us the opportunity to work with all kinds of people, from all walks of life, all ethnic backgrounds, all educational backgrounds.

We need to accept potential leaders as they are, without any prejudices about what they can do or be. Gender, race, education, personal history, age— none of these makes a difference in network marketing. Don't we all know incredible stories about someone on welfare, a non-English-speaking immigrant, a 77-year-old minister (my personal favorite) or a disabled person who has made it big in network marketing?

Our true aim needs to be service, with financial success in second place, not first. Wealth will absolutely come when we are of service and contribution to others. Contribution is the thermometer of our love for mankind; paychecks will follow.

2. Honesty
   and
3. Integrity

A true leader's state of being has to do with integrity. People throw this word around glibly and lightly, but it is vital to being a leader and earning the respect of others.

Integrity has to do with being true to yourself. That means when you make an agreement, you keep it in every way. If I say I will be at the meeting with a set of overheads, my integrity gets me there on time or a little early with each item I agreed to bring. Integrity means if you have made a commitment, it is a done deal! That is real integrity, and a true leader needs to be constantly setting goals and commitments and reaching them.

Integrity is completing what you say you are going to do without any excuses, rationalizations or justifications. Leaders do not come from explanation. They come from I did it or I didn't do it, period, end of story.

One of the few things you can keep while you give it as a gift is your integrity. (Another is your love.) When you break your word to yourself or to others, you break your trust, something very difficult to mend. When you keep your word, it is priceless.

What's the difference between honesty and integrity? I'm going to go over the difference here, because people think they are the same thing, and they absolutely are not. Honesty is what we do or say to other people. Honesty is external, while integrity is internal. It's amazing how some people can be true to themselves and not true to other people.

Abraham Lincoln said honesty is the best policy. That man led a very incredible life, and he certainly led by example. Integrity and honesty need to be constantly strengthened and developed for both ourselves and other people. They become magnets to people around us.

4. EnthusIASM: I Am Solid Myself

The fourth element of a true leader's state of being is a person who has enthusiasm. The last four letters of enthusiasm are i-a-s-m. The first four years in my business, I said i-a-s-m meant, "I am sold myself." I changed it about two years ago, and i-a-s-m now means, "I am solid myself." I am unshakable, I am unsinkable, I am unstoppable— On this rock I stand, and, World, you will Adjust.

That goes back to "As within, so without." The way a leader develops on the inside will absolutely show on the outside. When it is not showing on the outside, in results, production or new leaders emerging, then they may not be 100% filled with enthusiasm.

Years wrinkle the skin, but lack of enthusiasm wrinkles the soul. In network marketing, it's our souls and spirits which attract others to us.

Another enthusiasm is for you to BE network marketing. This industry is about changing the way business is being done on our planet. Be this industry and live it daily, no matter where you go or who you are in front of— you are the example. We are the ambassadors, the messengers of this industry.

Many people in this industry say, "Oh, I'm so excited!" They play excitement songs at the rallies and jamborees. To me, enthusiasm and excitement are two different things, and I don't operate out of excitement. The difference is that excitement is driven by external motivators, while enthusiasm comes from within yourself.

Here's an example to illustrate the difference: People go to a football game or a hockey game or any kind of a professional sport, and as they are driving to the game and talking in the car, the excitement is building. "Man, the Jets had better beat the Broncos." As they talk about it, they are stoking all the excitement inside, and they carry that into the stands. There people are cheering and yelling and screaming and booing. Everybody is excited, because when the players are on the ice or on the floor or on the field, their activity generates excitement in the crowd.

When the game is over, it doesn't really matter who won or who lost. Within a half hour of leaving that stadium or that arena, the excitement level is gone.

In network marketing, a lot of people and companies are on this excitement trip. I personally disagree with it, because excitement is externally driven or generated, so after a person leaves a rally, jamboree or a rah-rah, jack-them-up, juice-them-up, send-them-out event, it will not last. Excitement is only temporary.

A true leader's state of being is one that doesn't need motivating from anyone or anything outside themselves. Richard Brooke says it so well in his book, Mach II with Your Hair on Fire! He says motivation must come from within. If it comes from outside, it won't last. He points out that the meaning of the word enthusiasm itself is, "the spirit within." We need to bring out that force, that power, that spirit. When you are authentic and sincere on the inside, your enthusiasm shines and shows on the outside.

With enthusiasm, your team will keep their belief constant, regardless of what happens in their business. Think of the steam kettle: Even though it's up to its neck in hot water, it continues to sing! Are you a complainer or a singer?

A true leader's state of being never needs anyone else to motivate it and pump it up. It's be-living your vision, your purpose. Other people will see this enthusiasm. Once we are solid ourselves, it does-not matter what happens around us. It doesn't matter if one of the key people in your company decides to quit. It doesn't matter if the company changes the compensation plan. It doesn't matter if they drop a product. None of that matters. That's all external. What matters is your internal integrity and your enthusiasm, the be-living your business to the very fullest. Enthusiastic people are happy and smiling, and it's contagious.

Smiles is the longest word in the world: There's a "MILE" between the first letter and the last. That's long enough to last well beyond all the external concerns of day-to-day business.

5. Creating Leaders of Leaders

The fifth state of being a true leader needs to master is the ability to pass the baton of leadership to the next person on the leg, the team or the line.

How do you know if you are passing the baton responsibly?

First of all, real leaders identify themselves when they are ready for the baton. They'll be calling, e-mailing, faxing or voice-mailing often. They'll be asking, "What can I be doing next?" They are the self-starters who motivate themselves, but we'll go into that in more depth in Chapter Seven.

The way to tell if you have passed the baton responsibly is to watch the results of your duplicated leaders. They are with your company for two, four, 15 or 20 years without wandering to the "greener grass" (ho-ho-ho) of another company; OK their results (don't worry about the time frame) show wealth and lifestyle, and there are newly duplicated leaders on a steady basis; their integrity and belief are rock solid, then you've done your job as a leader of leaders.

Let me quickly remind you one more time about leaving a company for the greener grass on the other side of the fence: The grass is not greener. It just looks that way, because the person hasn't stayed on their own side of the fence to plant, water, weed and harvest. All the great networkers I have known have said, "Start and stay with one company." If the company gets shut down, that's a different story. Under those circumstances, it's fine to relocate to a new home. Just don't be one of the network marketing junkies who give our industry a bad reputation. They cost all of us a tremendous amount of respect, they lose face with their old company and, many times, with the company they jump to, and they're usually not very successful in the long run.

My view, and that of most industry masters, on working two or more different networking companies at one time is that if you chase two rabbits at once, you're going to lose both of them. I do feel it is fine to purchase products from other companies if yours doesn't offer those items. I do that myself. Wait! Wait! Please don't call, fax or e-mail me asking me to use your products. I have what I need at this time. Thanks anyway!!

Be like a postage stamp— stick to only one company, one system of duplication, one vision until your goals and commitments are achieved. That is what a visionary leader does.

I met a wonderful friend through the Masters seminars: Her name is Carolyn Wightman; she lives in the Florida Keys and is a Lifetime

Subscriber with Upline®. I got to know her during last year's Upline®
events in San Diego, British Columbia and Dallas. She has been with
Shaklee for 27 years!

I am always so eager to sit with Carolyn and ask her questions and
learn. I have only seven years experience in this industry. She says
she has been asked all along to jump to other companies, but she
agrees that's not the solution. Carolyn Wightman has been a great
inspiration to me for her staying power and what she has created in
her network and company.

6. Communicator for Action and Inspiration

The sixth element of a leader's state of being is that they communicate for action or for inspiration. These are forms of communication that make a difference— much of the communication we hear
has no impact or purpose at all. Communication for action would be
like what we shared in the last chapter on empowering someone to
pass that baton and having new people trained at the registration
table. Communication for action means that you are moving people
forward in alignment with their purpose.

Here's an example: I call Deni, a committed leader in Washington,
to let her know of a new four-minute phone message on our hottest
product. I give her the number to call and tell her what the message
regards. Then I say, "Please listen to this new product knowledge."

What did I do? I very nicely made a request with no communication for action. Communication for action would be, "Do you have
just a minute to listen to exciting news I have for you? Do you have
a pen and paper? Good. Please copy down this phone number. I'm
requesting that you call and listen to the hot new four-minute message on our product. Can I count on you to listen within the next 24
hours?"

That communication requested their action, but there's still something missing. That's right, I still don't have an agreement from
them. Once they agree to listen to the message, I can communicate
for further action by asking, "Once you have listened to the message,
will you please call my voice mail and leave me a short message
about how you will use this new knowledge with your team? By
when do you agree to leave that message? Great! We are both in
agreement. You can count on me! Can I count on you to do what you
say you will do? Super! I love working with you because you are
100% accountable with your word."

Communication for action always has a time table on it. You produce and make happen what you say you are going to do. Then you ask the follow-up questions: "I know I can count on you— right? Is your integrity impeccable in having this to me when you said?" Because they say yes, they are accountable and will make it happen.

Many people do not communicate for action. They just say e-mail, call or fax me, and they don't mention by when they need it. Someone who communicates for action makes a declaration to other people what they are going to do, and by when.

I have an absolute commitment— not a goal, a commitment— to be at National Marketing Director, the highest level in Legacy USA, (the company that merged with 21st Century Global), by July 31, 1999. I have made it very clear what my commitment is and then communicated it for action on my time frame. Actually now achieved, May, 1999. Ahead of commitment.

Communication for inspiration lights up another person. It's the communication that will last in someone's memory and heart. Many people talk about the weather, politics, sports, with little quality or in-depth communication and no inspiration. My particular story, the introduction to this book, was not too inspiring when I was in the middle of it— no money, about to lose my house and my car, borrowing close to $70,000 to stay in the business— that was not inspiring to me then. Now, years later, I believe it is an inspirational story for other people.

When you communicate for inspiration you are speaking belief, not doubt. Too many networkers believe their doubts and doubt their beliefs. This benefits no one. When doubts are shared down-line, they create flickers of concern and worry. Too many flickers will put out the flames of inspiration, and you will have a stalled or totally stopped team.

7. Being an Emotional Giant

The seventh aspect of a leader's state of being has to do with becoming an emotional/mental giant, not an emotional/mental jerk.

I'm going to be very open and honest with you here. I used to call them emotional giants or emotional midgets. One day, I was sharing this at an event and I looked out into the group and there were about four or five of the small wonderful people called midgets. I just wanted to fold! I wanted to crumble, because that had never entered my mind. I immediately changed the vocabulary from saying mental or emotional midget to mental or emotional jerk.

Adjust when it serves and supports the greatness in others. A great leader will change something that has worked a long time as soon as it becomes a necessary, especially when it could hurt somebody else.

I want to apologize right now to all of the wonderful small people out in the universe, because of what I had said for a few years. You can count on me: I won't ever say that again.

An emotional or mental giant is an incredible problem-solver. A true leader of leaders is going to have many problems come their way and many people in network marketing buckle under problems and have stinking thinking.

If you are feeling bad, resisting something or feel as if you're walking on pins and needles, it's time to tell the truth to whomever you need to be clean with. It's easy to get wrapped up in emotion, because we are naturally always involved in our emotions. Randy Ward quotes in his book Tapping the Source, "The pleasant emotions make you feel good, unpleasant emotions make you feel bad. Repressed emotions create tensions." An emotional giant chooses to focus on creating the emotions that feel good to be more present. Giants are also willing to deal with, handle and clean up the other two kinds of emotions. Many times it's tough to do but must still be done. It's like having a sliver in your finger. If it is left, it will fester and become worse. It hurts to take out that splinter, but it must be done. Emotional giants are willing to tackle the tough situations for their own, and others', well-being.

An Emotional Giant delivers RESULTS.

An Emotional Jerk delivers REASONS.

An old Jewish saying that many of us know, and it's so true for me, is "You will be called to account to God for all the great things placed in front of you that you did not take advantage of."

Advantage means being willing to rise up and be accountable for everything that comes into our lives and to move forward with them. That's one of the things an emotional/mental giant does.

When someone calls me on the phone and starts up, "I have a problem," I say, "Hang on. I'm not going to listen to your problem. I know, without a shadow of a doubt, you have the power, the skills and everything you need to solve it. May I ask you a question? Are you willing to solve this situation or this problem now?"

Most of the time they are going to say "yes". If they say "no", then they are stuck in being an emotional jerk. When someone is unwilling to become unstuck, there is nothing we can do about it at that moment. It's a waste of time to be in communication with a temporary emotional jerk.

I'll say, "I'm going to end this call now. When you are ready to be an emotional/mental giant, call me back and we'll move forward then."

You might not be popular or liked for taking that stand, but you will earn respect. We need to play offense; we need to play to win. When we play defense, we are playing not to lose. A stuck player will attempt to get you caught up in their stuff to put you on the defensive— a lose-lose situation for sure.

You are not being an emotional giant leader if you continually solve others' problems and don't give them the tools, the resources and the clarity so they see the value in solving their own problems.

8. Visionary Leadership

Finally, the leader's state of being is visionary and having personal commitment despite all adversities and against all odds. No matter what it is, your commitment stays in place. On this rock I stand, and, World, you will adjust. People need to hear that from you. You need to hear that from yourself, too.

I can remember when I had made my decision, about three years ago, to write a book. I had no idea how it was going to come about, but I started telling people I'm going to write a book about this industry. I had the results in my business, but I knew nothing about writing a book. I just kept putting it out there, declaring it was something I would do within the next three years. I had no idea of the mechanics, but I had vision and commitment, and I was rock-solid about my future book.

Brian Klemmer, in his Personal Mastery seminar, has an incredible exercise on intention. He shows how intention becomes *commitment* to create an end result. Most people think it is the *mechanism*— the "how to"— that creates results. The mechanism is the "doing," and it has little to do with final creation. You could have 50 mechanisms, 50 ways to create an income of $100,000 or more a year, but vision and intention are actually going to create that result. It's not the mechanism at all.

Many people get hung up in the mechanism and then, when the

mechanism or the doingness doesn't work, they become discouraged and lose their vision.

I kept putting it out and putting it out that I would write a book. That was my vision. That was my commitment. At the Upline® Masters in San Diego, John Fogg and I were talking. I had no idea that he had been the editor-writer of more than 20 books. I asked him for some advice, and he said, "Hey, let's go into partnership. I'll help you." He has tremendous skills and years of experience and knowledge that I don't have in writing a book— and I'm not about to take years to learn all that.

A visionary leader will risk asking for coaching from someone who knows the way and goes the way. That same leader will be willing— with no ego— to reach out and ask for people's support and empowerment. John and I have been in a great partnership in creating and making this book happen. I have had this book on my treasure map for three years. It happened because I made the declaration. I kept putting it out to more and more people, and then John showed up in my life. Intention. On this rock I stand, and, World, you will adjust.

The world will adjust, the world will come forward, the world will meet your needs, your requests, your demands as long as you are unshakable, unstoppable, unsinkable. Remember those lines from Commitment:

"... the moment one definitely commits oneself, then Providence moves too. All sorts of things occur to help one that would never otherwise have occurred. A whole stream of events issues from the decision, raising in one's favor all manner of unforeseen incidents and meetings and material assistance, which no man could have dreamt would have come his way."

Stand on your rock, have your vision, and have your personal intention and commitment absolutely in place. The world will adjust— guaranteed!

Check Yourself Out

To summarize, the eight states of being are:

1. Contribution.
2. Integrity with yourself.
3. Honesty to others.
4. EnthusiASM—I Am Solid Myself.
5. Results in creating leaders, passing the baton, duplicating and creating leaders of leaders.

6. Communication for action and inspiration.
7. Being an emotional/mental giant, a problem-solver, having your attitude absolutely straight, not getting caught in negativity.
8. Being a visionary leader and having personal commitment.

You can again use the meter-reading exercise with these steps. Look at your business and rate yourself from one to eight— one being the best and eight needing improvement. Then have your people do it too. I have them list two or three action steps they are willing to take in the next 30 days to expand and improve their eighth-ranked state of being. They could need to communicate for action more effectively. If they don't have tangible action steps, they would have a hard time tracking and being accountable for their growth and improvements. The action steps keep them on top of their business rather than letting the business dominate them. How do you eat an elephant? One bite at a time. The steps are bites that show how they can stay on target for 30 days.

Here is a Leadership Quiz you can use to periodically check your personal leadership. Read through it and simply answer yes or no on the line next to each question— you'll be able to see those areas where you can focus on gaining strength.

Personal Leadership Quiz

1. Do I deal with others in an ethical, professional and sincere manner, and always look at things in a positive fashion? _____

2. Do I abide by and promote company policies and procedures and not make false or unrealistic claims about my company, products and opportunity? _____

3. Have I recognized the importance of people, and do I put them first within my network marketing team? _____

4. Do I recognize that sponsoring versus recruiting will sustain my business' growth? _____

5. Do I look for long-term success versus the fast cash? _____

6. Do I sponsor in a responsible manner and not leave people orphans once I have brought them into the business? _____

7. Do I work for the good of my team or downline and the good of the company and the industry, instead of only my own gain? _____

8. Do I welcome all representatives, even sidelines, to my presentations, training and events? _____

9. Have I recognized that the people I support and coach to become successful in their results will absolutely support me in my success? _____

10. Have I recognized and acknowledged those who have contributed to my success? _____

11. Do I see problems as challenges and, only if need be, direct them to my upline for help or solution? _____

12. Do I demand the very best of myself and others in balance with tolerance and empathy? _____

13. Do I maintain a balance in my life, fulfilling my family, spiritual and personal health needs? _____

14. Have I allowed my successes to gain the better of me and forgotten what it was like to be a new representative in this business? _____

15. Am I still coachable and do I practice genuine teamwork and leave my ego behind? _____

16. Do I act in a manner which improves the image of network marketing and sets the standards for excellence in our industry? _____

> "How you lead is a reflection of your true self."
>
> —Anonymous

Decisions

Leaders make decisions— they don't wallow around in the same issue without moving forward. Leaders make a decision now and absolutely when necessary, regardless of the outcome, because they know they can change it if it doesn't work. Most of the time, we'll make the right decisions, but even when we don't, we can always change and improve upon them. And no matter what happens, things always turn out *best* for the people who *make* the best of the way things turn out. When you are given lemons, make lemonade. Most people don't make lemonade, they make slush and fermented lemon juice, because they don't make decisions fast enough.

If you want to make an easy job seem hard, just keep putting it off. When you get into procrastination mode, the problem gets bigger and bigger. If you want to stay on purpose, don't procrastinate. Decide to decide to act.

Great leaders are like airplane pilots— we both spend 95% of the time correcting what is off course. If your team is going forward, then you're on track and have made great decisions. Here's a really simple test you can use, just a couple of questions to ask yourself, in arriving at a decision. Ask:

· Is this ethically right?
· Is it absolutely fair to all concerned?
· Is my decision based upon *what* is right, not *who* is right?
· Will this do the most for the most?

Run these four questions through your mental computer and make a decision. Richard Brooke says: *"It's not a matter of doing things right, it's a matter of doing the right things."*

Each of our acts makes a statement of who we are. What act or what decision do you need to make right now that will create greater leadership in you?

The more decisions you make, the faster you make them and the more intuitive they are, the more effective they will be. When you desire *to go far* in your business, you'll have to *stay close* to it. That means making vital decisions. Don't forget that people will judge you by your actions. You may have heart of gold— so does a hard-boiled egg. Decisions show others your leadership in action.

Good News: Bad News

Leaders keep their fears to themselves and share their courage with others. The saying in network marketing— and it is the way we truly need to be— is bad news or concerns go upline and only good news, inspiration, new positive information goes downline. Too many people start sewering and putting holes in the boats of their downline by sharing things that are not appropriate and do not follow the proper chain of communication.

I respect the saying Amway uses: "No Need to Know". Your downline has No Need to Know that your most recent product order was delayed. Coach your team early that there will be times when you will say to them No Need to Know. They must be willing to accept your coaching at this time. Many issues are not necessary for another person to know immediately, and some they may never need to know.

Being an emotional/mental giant and being a leader of leaders means being an inspiration, not a wet blanket.

Dwight Eisenhower, a great leader, said "people who value their privileges above principles soon lose both." As network marketers, we have the privilege of serving, not sewering, our team by right principles and actions. A leader of leaders cannot get caught up in the web where negative people are. They either have to totally get out of that state or they need to remove themselves from the problem.

Like I shared earlier, I actually hang up on people, because I do not need to hear their emotional and mental negativity. Negativity is not healthful for my well-being. It takes courage to hang up. I'm suggesting not to get caught in all the upset. You perpetuate that upset if you get caught up in it. The purpose is to solve it and support your team member in getting unstuck.

I used to live in Hawaii and go down to Sandy Beach on the island of Oahu, a great body—surfing beach. We'd go down on to the edge of the water with our bathing suits on and simply stand there. Pretty soon the waves would come in. Our feet would go deeper into the sand as the water rushed out with each wave. The next one would come in and our feet would go even deeper into the sand. If we stood there for quite a while, that sand would be up to our calves and then up to our knees and then up to our thighs and then up to our okoles (bottoms), and then we'd be truly stuck. It is very hard to get out of that sand then.

It's the very same with problems we face as leaders. We cannot afford to become stuck. People get stuck in the smallest things: My newsletter came late from the company; my check came in a torn envelope and it was all mutilated; the company hasn't gotten my product order processed; there are backorders. They get stuck, tell other people and they dig themselves deeper into the sand. An emotional and mental giant will, instead, communicate for action and inspiration. Leaders do not *major in the minors!*

What Would a Great Leader Do?

One of the finest ways to develop your own leadership is to associate with leaders and mentors and model them. Remember the exercise we discussed before? Find someone who you greatly desire to be more like— not in their personality, but in the way they interact with people, the way they operate, the way they communicate, the way that they are always present to people.

Then, pretend that you have the head and heart of a leader you revere and ask what they would do in the same position. When you use this technique, you tap into your subconscious, and it will be your guiding light. What would Martin Luther King do? What would Winston Churchill do? What would Mother Teresa do? What would the-great-leader-you-respect do? You will be led intuitively to a decision that is best for all involved. Trust it and act on it now.

In leadership, a pint of example is worth a barrel of talk. Too many people want to just tell, tell, tell and talk, talk, talk. It is far better to show by example, share a short story of inspiration or ask your team what leaders they respect. What does the team think those leaders would do?

Why Real Leaders Lead

Here is a revealing exercise I use when I'm coaching about leadership. Simply have your people write down three or five names of great leaders in their life. This might be a high school coach. It might be a Sunday School teacher. It might be a priest, a sports figure or a political figure. It might be a spiritual figure, like Jesus Christ or Mohammed. It might be Mahatma Gandhi, Martin Luther King, Jr., or Mother Teresa. It might be their father. It might be their neighbor.

They need to write down three names of people they respect as leaders. Then I have them write down three reasons why anybody does anything.

Ask them to call out the reasons they wrote in their notes. The first thing out of their mouths is money. I write that on a flip chart or I just say it out loud, if it's a huge room. They might say recognition. They might say to feel good. They might say to make a difference.

Then I ask them to go back to their list of leaders. What was their main thrust? They will all say making a difference, being a point of light, having commitment, having leadership, coming from contribution, putting other people first, leaving a legacy. The three reasons anyone does anything are:

#3—The least reason—Money
#2—Acknowledgment and Recognition
#1—A Cause

Look at any great leader, military, political, spiritual, educational, network marketing or medical. Jonas Salk had a goal and a dream to alleviate polio. It took him many years to come up with the vaccine, but do you think he did it for money? Do you think he did it for acknowledgment and recognition? No, he wanted to save people's lives. He did it for a *cause.*

Those who have the strongest vision and purpose in their lives will always come from cause first. The absolute truth is the money, the acknowledgment and the recognition will follow. In becoming a leader of leaders, you must put others first.

Where you find *success,* you will find *sacrifice.* Enlightened leadership is service, not selfishness. "The leader grows more and lasts longer by placing the well-being of all above the well-being of self alone. By being selfless, the leader enhances self." Then you become a shining light and that rock your team will follow. Coming from cause will create lasting successes for all.

Lombardi Time

Time is very important in developing your integrity as a leader. Time is our best insurance policy for tomorrow; we have to make the most productive use of it today. I use a concept when I'm coaching called Lombardi Time, from Vince Lombardi— one of the greatest coaches of all time.

He's the coach who took the Green Bay Packers football team to many successful seasons, and he used to tell his players, "If you are not on the field, dressed for practice, 15 minutes prior to start-up time, you are already late."

Many people in this business do not plan their time, so they are always in a rush. They scramble into a presentation or a training, huffing and puffing and apologizing. The reason to use Lombardi Time— planning to arrive 15 minutes before the scheduled start— is to avoid last-minute problems. When you get there early, maybe there's a way to use your leadership by handling a breakdown. Maybe someone forgot the overhead, and it will take ten minutes to get one. Maybe someone had a crisis and wasn't able to get there for the registration table. By getting there early, you are saying, "Hey, I'm here. Is there anything I can do to help this evening be absolutely successful?" That's part one of Lombardi Time.

The second part of Lombardi Time has to do with being at a function early so you have the time to center yourself, to ground yourself, to calm yourself down from the busy day that you've had. To forget about the children, to forget about the dishes in the sink, to forget about the traffic. To totally be present and be here now. I encourage you to use Lombardi time, so your team sees you at an event early and not running in at the last minute.

If you teach by example, that's going to set the pace. The speed of the leader determines the speed of the pack. In horse racing, when the horse is running the hardest is when the jockey uses the whip. When one of your leaders is really into momentum and full production, that is when you must keep them on purpose, on target and keep the speed growing.

Are You a Manager or a Leader?

One of the things I frequently notice is how many people fall into managing and monitoring, rather than truly leading by example and building their businesses persistently and consistently.

My mom, Betty Shumway, supports me in everything I do. She is always giving me newspaper articles that are calls to action. One source, from our Canadian community of Gravenhurst, Ontario (population: 4,000), is a weekly paper called the *Percolator*.

A coffee machine will not percolate unless there is activation, unless we push the button that will create the heat and make the coffee. Without any activation, there will be no coffee. We need to be perking like that coffee machine in our businesses, not sitting around waiting for things to happen. Without action, you will have no business.

Little Action = Little Business

Massive Action = Massive Business

My mom sent me an excellent *Percolator* article about the difference between leading and managing.

Managers and Leaders

Many people seem to assume that if someone is a manager, they are automatically a leader. This is not necessarily correct. Let's examine the functions of managers and leaders. Once we have done this, we will be in a better position to find leaders and also to become one:

- *The **manager** administers, the **leader** [inspires].*
- *The **manager** is a copy, the **leader** the original.*
- *The **manager** maintains, the **leader** develops.*
- *The **manager** focuses on systems, the **leader** on people.*
- *The **manager** relies on control, the **leader** [creates] trust.*
- *The **manager** looks at the short term, the **leader** has a long range view.*
- *The **manager** asks how and when, the **leader** what and why.*
- *The **manager** eyes the bottom line, the **leader** looks to the horizon.*
- *The **manager** imitates, the **leader** originates.*
- *The **manager** accepts the status quo, the **leader** challenges it.*

Take time to analyze these points and apply them to yourself. Be honest and then ask yourself:

*In what percentage of my business am I a **manager**?* _____%
*In what percentage of my business am I a **leader**?* _____%
                                                    TOTAL 100%

What's Managing You?

One of the most common things to pull leaders off purpose is crisis. When a crisis comes up, they run to it and become engulfed by it. They lose sight of their daily and weekly goals. Goals are the stepping stones for you to have rock-solid time and money freedom. It doesn't make sense to allow crises to determine your future. *Crises never create results, leaders, income or leverage.*

Why do we feel a crisis is so important to handle right now? One possible reason is we are not 100% committed to our goals as priorities. The second reason is people think crisis management is part of being a leader. That's hogwash!

Stephen Covey, in his great book *Daily Reflections for Highly Effective People*, says, "Efficient management without effective leadership is, as one individual has phrased it, 'like straightening deck chairs on the Titanic.'" If you are managing crisis, then crisis is managing you. It doesn't serve anyone for you to be in crisis management, so don't get caught in it.

Effective leadership is developing new leaders. Keep focused on your priorities. Completing daily and weekly priorities is a necessary action for leaders who accomplish their goals.

How You Learn

Being a leader of leaders involves four levels of learning and excellence. There are two main sections in each level: Awareness and Action. The four levels are:

Awareness	*Action*
Unconscious	Incompetent
Conscious	Incompetent
Conscious	Competent
Unconscious	Competent

When we reach the highest internal level of Unconscious Competent and our belief is solid as a rock, the external world starts adjusting. Get ready!!

Unconscious Incompetent

A baby is born totally unconscious and incompetent to do anything. They don't know what is going on around them. Their awareness is zero and their action is zero.

If you have ever been around a brand new baby, you know that. They are like a brand new prospect. Prospect are unconscious, most of them, about this industry. They are unconscious about our products. They are unconscious about the company. They are totally incompetent— the prospect can't even take any action yet. They don't understand anything about this new business we are presenting.

They do have enough value, because we've asked enough questions about what they want to do when they have unlimited time and unlimited money. The unconscious incompetent would be a prospect just turned into a brand new representative.

Conscious Incompetent

Conscious incompetents are like four-month-old babies. They are very conscious of that rattle or bottle, but they are incompetent to reach out and pick it up. They struggle and they knock it over because the muscles in their little hands aren't strong enough to hold on to the bottle or rattle. They drop it, and then they get frustrated and cry. They are conscious that's what they want, but they are incompetent to act and handle it responsibly.

A brand new representative is similarly conscious of what they have. They've gotten their starter pack and are starting to read, they are going to call workshops and presentations, they are getting on conference calls and they're getting coached. They have done their 48-hour duplication. They are becoming conscious of all the possibilities, and truly how much knowledge they need to learn and how much belief they need to gain.

Most brand new silvers, golds, associates, directors or whatever they are in your company, are still incompetent. They cannot pass that baton. They are still incompetent to draw out the sales compensation plan. They don't know all the value and the benefits of your products. So they are conscious, they are beginning to learn, but they are incompetent in their action to really be effective in showing the business.

That's why we do not send new representatives out without a backup, without a safety net, without an upline coach. As they are doing their two-on-ones, it's still important to have three-way follow-up calls. Beginners are still incompetent to answer all the questions, so they need an upline coach who can handle that for them.

This is a very frustrating spot in a lot of people's business. This is where the coach must patiently teach the representative to build new skills, to strengthen undeveloped muscles. It's a great time to remind representatives that they need to learn to crawl before they can run.

Conscious Competent

The next level our babies reach is conscious competent. At about eight months old, they are able to reach out. They are able to roll over and get that rattle if it's out of reach. They are able to hold that bottle. They are conscious and they are competent.

This is where most people in the business know all the skills. They are very conscious, they have the knowledge, they have their belief in place, and they are very competent to show it. They are doing their three-way follow-ups, they are doing all their 48-hour duplication, leading call workshops and speaking on conference calls. They now are what I call do-do machines. They are into doing, doing, doing, doing.

If they remain a conscious competent, they are going to get bored, because the joy and personal satisfaction does not come from doing— it comes from BEing. This phase is based on their own efforts again— they are not developing into a leader of leaders. Conscious competents compare themselves to someone who is moving faster in their business without recognizing that the other person has shifted from conscious competent into an unconscious competent.

For example: Let's go back to these tiny babies. They are now able to simply and unconsciously pick up that rattle. They don't have to think about opening and closing their hands to hold the rattle or the bottle. They just do it. They see it and they do it. They are unconscious of the skill, and they are competent doing it. They are even getting bored with the rattle and this action.

In our business, a conscious competent is almost always driven by cash and recognition. They think they have to do more to earn more money. The money is very big in this industry and gives people inspiration and value to join the team. They are drawn to the time and money freedom. When a team player's income isn't growing, they think they have to do, do, do more. They stay stuck in that arena and get frustrated, bored or burned out.

When a team player is not challenged or loses their passion, they could very well be on their way out. Here is where a phenomenal leader of leaders intervenes. The stalled player must be willing to receive new coaching, and, at this stage, many representatives operate out of I KNOW IT ALL. They are uncoachable— a tragedy, as I see it. You can lead a horse to water, but you can't make him drink. Being stubborn and defensive costs the whole team and is very selfish.

As coaches, we need to be all that we can to support a conscious competent in going up to the next and highest level. They need to believe and shine more deeply. Get their permission for you to hold their faces to the light even though, for the moment, they do not see the light. Your whole team will benefit each time a player responds to coaching and moves into unconscious competence.

Unconscious Competent

The babies are bored with the bottle and rattle and with crawling around. They are now conscious and aware of big people walking. They don't even think about walking, they start doing, learning and falling down many times for months in this new process of walking. They begin to say "Da-da, Ma-ma, mine, bye-bye." The stuck conscious competent needs to break through just like the toddler.

At the Upline® Lifer's Retreat in Scottsdale, Arizona, Brian Biro had us all break boards with one hand. It was an incredible and powerful experience for everyone in attendance. If we don't break through, we will absolutely stay the same. The same is not good enough for a leader of leaders.

Your team needs to see and know you are climbing new mountains. An unconscious competent is not driven by cash, but by cause or contribution. They won't allow themselves to stay the same person they are today. They are willing to pay the price of becoming more.

Laurie Beth Brooke, in her book *The Path*, talks about using WCI (What Currently Is) versus WCB (What Could Be). Programs, belief systems, old paradigms won't stop an unconscious competent. They become a stronger point of light, make a bigger difference in others' lives, commit again to a larger legacy and become more of a rock to their team. Is this level easy? No! Is it simple? Yes! Just because someone reaches the top level in a company and is earning a large income does not mean they are unconscious competent. That level simply means they have met the qualifications and they might not even be seen as an inspiring leader to others.

We see highly paid people leave one company for the next and the next, because they have not become an unconscious competent. They start the cycle again, and it is a challenge for a while. If they don't break through their wall, it will stop them short again and again. Integrity, principles and character are key elements in this level of awareness and action.

How do you know that you are an unconscious competent? Words and actions flow naturally and easily. There is no struggle in your beingness. You are on automatic pilot with intuition being the control tower.

How would your business be right now if you were ten times more courageous, bold, risk-taking, forgiving, patient, focused, acknowledging, inspiring, supporting, open, fun, etc. (add your own adjectives)? Notice these are all *being* words, and beingness lives and blossoms only in the unconscious competent level.

It is critical, as leaders of leaders, that we allow people to experience their own process and journey. We cannot force people through their awareness and action. It is our privilege and responsibility to educate and support people in becoming aware so they can see the power and the wealth in being an unconscious competent.

I am not interested in the fast runners; I am interested in the permanent runners, those who will commit to finishing the race.

In the Mexico City Olympics of 1968, John Stephen Aquara represented Tanzania in the marathon. He had diligently prepared, through years of discipline and practice, for that one race for the gold medal. As the 26-mile race began, John took off with full anticipation of winning.

During the race, a tragic fall injured his knee and ankle quite seriously. He had to take time for medical attention to stop the bleeding and stabilize his ankle. The repeated delays put him well behind the lead runners while the injuries slowed his pace too much for him to catch up.

Everyone was sure that those obstacles were extreme enough to make John withdraw from the race. Instead, he got back on the course and kept going. He was hobbling most of the way, and as he neared the finish line, hours behind all the other runners, blood was pouring down his leg.

Even though the race winners had long been decided, there were announcers and hundreds of spectators waiting for John at the finish line. The reporters were all eager to know why he had continued to run. They asked, "John, why didn't you stop? With so much pain, what kept you running and crossing the finish line? You lost all chance of winning when you fell."

John, still breathing heavily from his exertions and pain, said with total dignity and pride, "My great country did not send me here to enter the race. They sent me here to finish the race."

Will you be solid as a rock and finish your race, with your company? That is what a leader of leaders in our industry does: FINISH THE RACE!

Turning Obstacles into Victories

Leaders are going to stumble, but that isn't failure. Failure isn't simply *falling* down; failure is *staying* down.

Bad attitudes, negative spirit and know-it-all thinking are the worst obstacles to success. They're like poison ivy— it only takes a little to spread the infection. As a leader of leaders, we cannot afford *any* negativity coming out of our mouths. Every one of our actions and communications is a self-portrait. We need to autograph our duplication and coaching. Autograph your work and your beingness with excellence.

Leaders don't worry about obstacles. Worrying is like sitting in a rocking chair: It gives you something to do, but it doesn't get you anywhere. Leaders are never in rocking chair mode. They don't stay in the past. They keep moving forward, doing the best with what they are given at any moment.

I'm going to tell the story of my son James, because it was a major crisis in my life and business.

I was on my diamond run, which was the highest executive title of my previous company. I had to study the diamond qualifications, what I needed to do, the mechanics. I cut the qualification page out of our compensation plan brochure and put it with my picture my treasure map. I wrote: "Peggy Long, Diamond, June 30, 1993, UNSTOPPABLE." I put that same message everywhere— mirrors, car, ceiling.

From the perspective of my external world, it looked like I couldn't do it, that it wasn't really possible. At best, it would take a heck of a push, and I decided that I was going to make diamond absolutely happen. On this rock I stand, and, World, you will adjust.

Midway through my run, I got a call from San Diego where my oldest son, James, lived. The call came from jail. My son had been arrested, and it was going to be a very heavy, long, involved court case.

He was wrong and irresponsible. In order to support my son, I borrowed $10,000 for a lawyer to represent him, even though it made my finances more than a little thin. He was not earning enough in his networking business to hire a defense lawyer. Many people said I couldn't take time to be with Jamie *and* still reach my diamond commitment that quarter.

I just wanted to scream at them. Rather than holding me accountable, capable, they were dream stealers. I knew I had enough knowledge, skills and commitment to be with my son responsibly and still reach diamond. But the majority of people said "You won't reach your diamond this quarter— you'll have to handle your son, and we'll understand."

A leader of leaders does not do this. When another curve comes into our road, we don't go off the road and create an accident. We adjust. That's what I did.

Jamie was convicted and faced up to 16 years in a California state prison. I had made seven trips to San Diego, from Phoenix, for court, right in the middle of my diamond run. It did absolutely look like I couldn't reach my goal. But I said son-of-a-gun, I am capable of handling both responsibly.

James did end up sentenced to seven years in prison, and I made a commitment to see him at least every three months. I kept my word. No matter where I was, I would fly in, rent a car, visit him for only three to six hours. I reached my diamond the very same quarter as I declared I would.

I'm sure you're wondering what Jamie's crime was. A leader does not leave unfinished communication with listeners. Jamie has given me his okay to share the full story.

Jamie got very drunk and broke into a neighbor's home to borrow their VCR while they were away. I'm not just being a loyal mom by saying he wanted to "borrow" their video equipment— the neighbors were Jamie's friends, and they didn't press charges.

Unfortunately, that didn't make any difference. Someone saw something suspicious and called the police. Jamie was too drunk to think clearly, so he added more mistakes; he ran from the police and resisted. He was arrested next.

The district attorney was up for reelection, and he needed to show that he had put so many people behind bars. Jamie got caught in the system as an example of cracking down on crime.

Too many people, when something else enters their life, allow their first commitment to stop. They get into scarcity of time or money rather than into abundance. Crises will not ever create great results.

The good news about my son is while he was inside, I was able to send materials to him to read. I could photocopy pages from positive books and send them to him. He started reading *Upline*® to get his belief strong. He started working his network marketing business inside, behind the prison walls and he sponsored people and retailed product.

Let me tell you how James did this. He would write on a piece of paper with a little tiny, inch-and-a-half stub of a pencil. He wrote to friends on the outside who knew who he truly was. He just got off the path, and he paid his price. His friends on the outside would write back, some as customers or new representatives. The process took three months for retail selling and sometimes six months for sponsoring.

He wasn't allowed to have any catalogs, independent representative forms or product order forms. He would write to me and I would send them to each person. Talk about commitment, talk about seeing the perfect end result! He also worked the entire time he was in prison and used his time productively.

Bloom where you are planted.

He did not want to be one of those inmates sitting, spacing out, idling their time, blaming the system, being unaccountable for his own actions, and so he worked. He made a whopping 11 cents an hour. He was going to set himself up so when he got out of prison, he would be a valuable contributing citizen of society again and have money saved. He had a couple of people, when he got out, who he was ready to coach, as well as many in the funnel who said, "I'll wait until you get out to start the business, and we'll build together."

He had obstacles and steel bars— literally— to work around. The rest of us, not behind physical prison bars, still put up our own. We put up obstacles. Jamie is such an inspiration to other people today, because of what he did. Since he worked in prison and took on leadership roles, his time was cut in half. Instead of seven years, he served three and a half years.

He became the leader of the Alcoholics Anonymous while he was inside. He could make a phone call to me once every two weeks. I remember when he said, "They have asked me to become the chairman of the AA group. I'm nervous, because there are all kinds of gangs that go to AA, but it's an opportunity for me to really put myself on the line of what I'm up to in life." He wanted to serve and become a better human being, so he took the chairman position in AA.

James had vision, he had light at the end of the tunnel because he chose to be and do something positive in a very negative situation. He moved forward in faith. Most people put their own bars up, their own obstacles, and live in their smallness. They do not operate out of their greatness.

The back cover of *Jonathan Livingston Seagull* reads: "Argue for your limitations and they're yours."

Many times in a training, I share Jamie's story, because people come up with all the reasons, all the excuses, all the alibis, all the justifications for why they can't move forward in their business. That's only because they have their own bars and limitations they are creating to keep themselves imprisoned.

Jamie was not going to be my reason for not achieving my diamond. He would be an added catalyst for me to become even greater in keeping my word to myself and others. I would stay on course.

The question is: Are you going to be tossed and turned? When the seas get rough, are you going to have a strong enough ship, a strong enough belief, a strong enough commitment, are you going to have the courage to keep going on your path?

Here is a poem I love by Ella Wheeler Wilcox:

One ship drives east another drives west
With the self same winds that blow.
'Tis the set of the sails
And not the gales
Which tells us the way to go.

Like the winds of the sea are the winds of fate,
As we voyage along through life,
'Tis the set of the soul
That decides its goal
And not the calm or the strife.

Don't just talk the talk. Walk the walk, lead by example. If your example is not moving forward, you are not going to have team members who choose to follow your lead.

Reasons or results— which do you choose daily?

Making a Difference

I'll share a story about action and inspiration. It is a favorite I use at the end of my training.

There had been an extremely violent storm along the coast, and thousands of starfish had been tossed helplessly onto the beach. They were too far from the water to survive, so most would die before the next tide.

A small boy was very distraught over the death of so many beautiful sea creatures. He decided to take action. He began to scoop up armloads of starfish and toss them back into the ocean.

There were miles of starfish-covered beach, and a cynical observer asked the boy, "What are you doing, sonny? Can't you see what a waste of time and effort your puny actions are? For every few you can pick up, there's a mile of stupid starfish that will die long before you can get to them. What difference can you make?"

The young boy looked up respectfully and considered his reply.

Then he picked up a starfish and said to the observer, "Sir, it makes a difference to this one," and he gently tossed the starfish into the waves. Then he continued gathering armloads of starfish and returning them to the water.

Never forget that the first step of a leader's state of being is contribution. We need to forget ourselves— then others will not forget us. That's putting others first. That's like walking a mile in their shoes. That's having empathy and being in contribution.

I remember hearing of a billionaire business man who had a sign on his desk that he saw every minute of every day. It said: "I'm Third." He explained that with every decision he made, he put God first, the other person second, and himself third.

Don't confuse putting others first with being a chameleon— changing color, behavior, attitude, integrity or honesty to please someone else. That will never work. It will take a little chip out of you and a little chip out of anyone else with whom you are in partnership.

When you are focused and committed to making a difference, nothing will stop you, and you truly make a difference in the life of each person you sponsor and coach.

A powerful declaration of your commitment to those you sponsor is, "I'm in this business for a lifetime." Can you see how that statement will create rock-solid belief in the listening of the new person? It will make a difference to that one.

State Your Purpose

When you send letters, faxes or e-mails, choose a statement that you always sign the same way. On all my correspondence, I sign with "Keep your Vision, Peggy 'Like a Rock' Long." It keeps me focused when the times are very tough for me.

Rich and Mary Smith, great industry leaders in Oregon, close their letters with "U CAN 2," and that's what their license plate says. Personalized plates are a super prospecting tool. Jordan, my son, gave me a license plate for Christmas that says "LK A ROCK." Some people sign "on fire," or "making life happen." You may want to use your anchor word or something from your treasure map. By creating a visionary slogan and signing it continually, you reinforce the stand and declaration you are taking.

When you call somebody, use your anchor word or special phrase and ask, "What is something great that happened for you this week?" It doesn't always have to be in the business, but sharing and talking about something great that happened for them reinforces those stepping stones. You and your team will find yourselves having fun celebrating all your successes out loud. When someone can do it in one part of their life they can do it in another part. Every time someone makes a goal and feels great, their credibility and integrity grows. This is necessary in creating leaders.

What's Your Legacy?

Why do we remember Hank Aaron and Babe Ruth? We remember them by all their home runs. They had thousands and thousands of strikeouts, but it's the home runs which are their legacy.

What is your life legacy? What are you going to leave other people? What are they going to remember you by?

You know what I want on my tombstone? I'm actually not going to be buried (I will be cremated and my family knows that), but if I had a tombstone, here is what it would say:

"Used Up Fully"

I am committed to leaving a legacy on this planet. Not the legacy of Peggy Long, but the legacy of making a difference, of being a point of light, of being a leader, of working for cause. Here's an acronym to remind you of your legacy:

L stands for **Life**.
Live life joyously. It doesn't matter what happens to us, it's how we handle it.

E stands for **Enthusiasm.**
Enthusiasm is the super glue of our business.

G stands for **Goals.**
Resting on your laurels doesn't work. What are your next goals?

One of my goals was to have ten Lifetime Members for Upline® last year, and I actually enrolled 18. I have a goal for 20 in 1999. By having goals and declaring them, you open the way for people to support you, and they will.

A stands for **Accountability**.

We must be accountable for our actions. Every single one of our actions is going to make a ripple. Are you making a positive ripple or a negative ripple? Or no ripple?

C stands for **Contribution.**

What are you contributing in your business, in your church, in your family and in your community? Many wonderful teams do fund-raising events where they "run for cancer," support women's shelters, take action for the fight against AIDS or donate to a children's hospital. I have a goal in the next three years which is purely contribution. I will take a group of 50 to 100 representatives to work on Habitat for Humanity houses. What are your contributions outside of your business? Contribution is cause and creates cash.

Y stands for **Youthful.**

Always be youthful, open to new possibilities. You know the Good Book talks about being child-like, not childish. Being childish is having attitude problems, temper tantrums and stinkin' thinkin'. Being child-like means taking a child's eager, open approach to each new idea, new tool, new skill or win-win situation.

I ask you to look today at what you are doing and how you are being to create your life legacy. What message or impact are you committed to leaving on this planet? I'll have the team choose one of the l-e-g-a-c-y letters in which they need to have more skills, more action, more being and awareness. Then they practice in that area for the next 30 days. *Practice makes permanent,* not perfect.

What is your life going to be counted for? Are you just spinning your wheels, or are you making a difference? Are you a leader that somebody considers solid as a rock in your company?

Recently, one of the key leaders in our business died very unexpectedly. His funeral was packed, because he made a difference in the four years he was with our company. He left a legacy, and people wanted to acknowledge his life. I wonder if people didn't have to come to your funeral out of obligation, how many people would actually attend? Ask yourself and answer truthfully.

Are You a Cow or a Rhino?

I met Jerry Clark at the Upline® Masters seminar in Dallas. He's a wonderful man, a trainer and author in this industry, and he puts out a series of tapes. He gave me one of his tapes and, looking me right in the eye, he said, "Peggy, will you listen to this?"

He was really intent on getting my attention. I looked at him and said, "Yes." He was intent that I would listen to his tape. I said, "Absolutely, Jerry, you can count on me. I will listen to this within one week." I put in the time table for action.

I left Dallas the very next day and happened to have time on my drive home from the airport. I listened to Jerry's tape in my car. It opened many new ideas for leadership. I purchased 500 of those tapes and gave them out to every key leader on my team. The tape is called the *Murphy's Committee*, and its main thrust is there are only two ways that you or I can operate and be in life:

One, you can be a cow, which means you can play it safe. You stay in security. You have someone else feed you and take care of you. You are too complacent to even knock the flies off your back. You follow other cows, single file, to the food and the barn. Cows are very secure, safe and not spirited or assertive.

Your other choice is to be a rhino— and a leader of leaders, an emotional/mental giant is a rhino. The rhino goes into the jungle, even though the jungle is tough. I've done some studying on rhinos recently, and it takes a rhino almost five years for their hide to become so impenetrable that a poison dart cannot get through their skin. No other animal attacks the rhino, but it takes a five-year process to build that toughness. Rhinos are strong, but they will not attack another animal.

As a rhino gaining strength and going into the jungle, you face all kinds of challenges. In network marketing, you know all the failures, all the rejection, all the put downs and all the people that stare at you blankly and say, "I can't believe that you are doing this." An emotional/mental giant is a rhino who continues to go into that jungle, taking more leaders with them, and that isn't easy.

On the other side of the jungle is everything that everybody wants and deserves. Whether it's the time freedom, the money freedom, the fulfillment or your peace of mind.

Emerson says what lies behind us and before us are tiny matters compared to what lies within us. An emotional/mental giant is a rhino, not a cow; one who rises to the occasion and doesn't avoid it. You are either going to rise to it or you are going to avoid it. A true leader of leaders promptly handles what needs to be handled.

I have a request for you: When you put your head on your pillow late at night, ask yourself, "Have I been an inspiration today? Have I been an emotional and mental giant? Have I made a difference? Am I leaving the kind of legacy I want to leave in the world? Did I offer the gift of my network marketing company and product to someone today?" If you can answer those questions "Yes" with full integrity, then you are what network marketing is truly all about.

Chapter 7

Developing Leaders

Great leaders truly are prepared, ready, willing and absolutely happy for others to surpass them. That's the sign of a leader: Your team, your followers, the people you are coaching and training can move past you. Then you are not the superstar and hero, you're just one of the industry's many success stories.

When leaders are the heroes and superstars, they outshine the teaching and system. Their attitude and action never allow the development of strong leaders on the team, so duplication never happens. This might appeal to those who are power hungry, but it kills lasting success. Give yourself and your team the great gift of putting your team and your up-and-coming leaders ahead of yourself. Let them be the greatest, and the teaching and coaching for duplication will radiate and resound for everyone everywhere.

Identifying New Leaders

I frequently ask the team's key leaders, "Who are the next people you are grooming to become Directors?" I always want to know, who are the leaders that this leader is developing? I'll find out who those people are and use our company's great toll-free voice mail system to call or fax them just to let them know, "Hey, I know you are on the team. I know you are getting ready in the next two months to become a Director. I'm here for you. You have a great coach. You have an incredible leader taking you to the top."

I acknowledge the person coaching them, so I am not disempowering or butting into that coach's leadership. This is something so many people in this industry think: I have to do it all hands-on, by myself. That is not developing leaders and passing the baton. The way to be a leader of leaders is to empower your leaders, to encourage them, to let them know that you will be available for them at any time.

This business is like that old dance game, still done in the Caribbean, called the limbo. In the limbo, two people hold a stick and the dancers start going underneath it. As they go under, the stick is moved lower towards the ground. The winner of the limbo game is the one who can go the lowest without knocking the stick down. In developing leaders of leaders and communicating for action and inspiration, it's how "low" in our downline we can go— how much we can empower each other.

As I said before, leaders identify *themselves* when they are ready for the baton. I'm going to share with you the characteristics of a real leader, but remember, "A leader is one who knows the way, goes the way, and then shows the way." The leaders you are developing are going to duplicate the good and the bad things that you do, say and be.

1. A leader is very goal-directed and goal-achieving.

Setting goals means yak, yak— it means nothing unless the achievement is there. It's important— not for ego or recognition— for a leader to be able to state what they have done and what they are committed to achieving.

An example would be attending your company's convention with key leaders of 200 and their teams. Another example is having two guests at a presentation, one guest on nightly introduction conference calls or leading a call workshop this week. When you are developing leaders, they need to hear and see that you, as the coach, are achieving your goals.

2. Leaders must be persistent and consistent.

Some representatives go pell-mell for a few months. They get in front of a lot of people and do training, call workshops, presentations and one-on-ones, but they're not consistent. They take a sabbatical, they take a break for the next two or three weeks. Their personal momentum slows down. That example does not serve them or their team.

If you get on a bicycle, which is harder, to get it up and going, or to maintain your speed? Once your business and leaders are up and going, they will maintain and move along very well with relatively little effort. If you are not consistent, you have to keep putting all that start-up effort into your work again and again.

3. A great leader has a strong self-image and is self-confident.

That's the reason to take personal growth classes and do the exercises that are on all the different tapes. Many people don't stop to do the exercises in the books and tapes they buy. They cheat themselves by skipping those learning opportunities.

Carol McCall's manual, in the *Empowerment of Listening* tape set, has some awesome exercises. Many people read those and say, "I know that." That person is not open to receiving any more knowledge, and that's a shame.

To be self-confident, a person needs to be continually open to growing in more areas. We are kind of like bananas, we're either green and growing or we're rotting and decaying. There is no middle ground.

4. A great leader is a perpetual learner.

Leaders always share with their teams what they are reading and what seminar they are taking. I have four of my key leaders coming to a Brian Klemmer seminar with me here in Arizona this month. A leader doesn't just send somebody somewhere. They're right there with the troops. We're in a foxhole together, becoming network marketing warriors.

5. A great leader enjoys the business and is driven by passion.

If you don't love what you are doing, it will seem tedious— it will be work. It's very important to shift ourselves into passion.

Peter Hirsch's book, *Living With Passion*, is one of the best out there. If someone doesn't have much passion, I'll have them read that book. When they are on the phone talking to a prospect or right before they give a presentation, I'll have them in another room doing jumping jacks, getting their passion and energy up. When someone has motion and energy, passion and emotion are going to follow.

We can change our behavior, which will change our feeling. It will be temporary, like excitement versus enthusiasm, but a temporary change can be repeated until it becomes a new habit. The real key for inner and long-lasting passion is to change your belief systems— which increases your vitality.

6. A great leader has the ability to attract and energize people.

Rate yourself on a one to ten scale (one low, ten high) on how well you attract and energize people. Are you an individual people want to be around? Do they call to ask, "How can I spend more time with you? Will you coach me?" Energy creates movement forward. Do you have that energy?

When you are prospecting, what are you attracting? Are people looking at you? How you walk, how you talk— are you whispering or do you have boldness in your voice, which attracts and energizes people? That's how it is to be around a leader.

7. A great leader is caring.

So many people in this industry have all the knowledge, all the skills, all the information, all the facts, all the data. So what? In this industry, people don't care how much you know until they know how much you care. That doesn't mean baby-sitting, that doesn't mean a doormat, that doesn't mean being walked on, that doesn't mean feeling less than. That means that the outside world knows that you are putting their best interest at heart, and sometimes that means tough love. They know how to call the tough shots with compassion.

8. A great leader is courageous and inspires others to action.

This is not a business about show and tell, like kindergarten. In the chapter on prospecting, I shared the Initial Interest Questions. Going out to malls, supermarkets, the bank or anywhere, and asking someone a question takes a lot of courage. When you take two or three representatives out with you and have a contest, that takes even more courage.

Two network marketing leaders in New York, Jacob Bickel and Jack Rosen, both diamonds on my old team, decided to test the mall prospecting tool for themselves.

Now, these have been highly paid people who earned their cars and coached thousands on their teams. They went out to the mall together, and on seven out of seven of these Initial Interest Questions, they got a positive response, names and phone numbers. That inspired others on Jack and Jacob's team to have the courage to use the Initial Interest Questions themselves.

9. A great leader keeps on keeping on in spite of failure, rejection, and frustration.

Remember, those are the critical three in our business as well as in our lives.

Marion Anderson, one of America's greatest singers, was quoted in *Guide Post Magazine* saying, "Failure and frustration are in the unwritten pages of everybody's record." At her first big concert, she was behind the curtain waiting to go out when she was told that the hall was completely sold out. She was in a daze, delighted and ready to go on. Then the manager said there would be a slight delay, so she sat behind the curtain waiting five, ten, 15 minutes and she decided she would peek through the curtain. She peeked through the curtain and the concert hall wasn't even half-full. Internally, her attitude just sank, but she decided to still sing.

The critics the next day said she was horrible. She allowed herself to be sewered by that criticism, and was so crushed in spirit that she didn't even sing for a whole year after that concert.

She finally decided singing was one of her God-given talents and she would get up and sing again. She persisted and stayed consistent, even with other failures and frustrations, and went on to become one of America's greatest singers.

Continuing in the face of failure, rejection and frustration is what an emotional giant does. It doesn't matter if there are changes in the compensation plan, it doesn't matter what your upline does, it doesn't matter what your downline does, it doesn't matter what your crossline or sideline does. What matters is: Will you keep moving? Nobody is ever defeated unless they stay down, still, quiet. Jump up and sing your song!

10. A great leader supports, encourages and acknowledges the successes of others.

That can be very hard, because people want the acknowledgment and the recognition for themselves, but that is not what makes a great leader. That will come naturally when you are supporting, encouraging, and acknowledging the successes of other people.

When you treat your team like thoroughbreds, you won't have any old nags on your hands. It does take practice in acknowledging others. Your ability and skills can take you to the top, but it takes character to keep you there. You will gain more respect from others and character in yourself through encouraging, supporting and acknowledging your team. This creates loyalty to you, your company and our industry. Acknowledgers and empowerers are producers and winners—and highly respected leaders.

Coyotes and Vultures

There are many unique animals around my Southwestern winter home in the beautiful Sonoran Desert in Arizona. Coyotes look like scrawny, scruffy dogs and run in packs. I can hear them from my poolside as they yelp after their prey. They will surround a weak or small animal and keep closing in until they can attack and kill it.

Vultures are the big black ugly birds that start circling above anything dying. Once something is dead, they swoop in to eat the remains.

Why do I mention these two predatory creatures? There are people in this industry who prey on representatives in other companies—these people are *not* leaders, and you don't want them in or near your business. The coyotes gang up on representatives who are still developing their belief. The vultures start circling companies which appear to be in trouble or dying.

Coyotes usually leave one company for another, although that alone does not make them predators. When an ex-representative starts spreading rumors, poison ivy and gossip, then they have crossed the line into coyote or vulture. I lose all respect for them at that point. They have just become part of a difficult problem that makes our industry look bad.

Heavy hitters out to make the fast cash are not usually leaders of leaders. That baton has been passed to them and they have not passed on the skills, the knowledge, the belief. In that case, if they're not doing the business, nothing is happening. A heavy hitter is someone who can do the business— inside and out— and they can earn fast cash, but a person's paycheck does not mean anything in regard to an Enduring Empire— an EE. What you look at is how many leaders of leaders are on your team or in your network. I'm not impressed if someone says, "I earned $10,000 last month." What I want to know is how many platinums, how many directs, how many ambassadors, how many high-titled leaders do you have on your team? What is your answer to that today? What will it be one year from now? Five years from now? One thing I've seen and experienced and heard from so many master network marketers who have been around for years and years is that *fast cash usually leads to a fast crash.*

If you encounter a problem with coyotes or vultures, as a leader, you need to tackle it head on. When a person leaves your company, it is crucial to contact your key leaders and tell them the truth of the situation. Realign yourself with them and stay in communication. While the coyotes and vultures are howling and attacking, the best defense is team unity. From that, you and your leaders will grow stronger if you allow yourself to become *better* instead of *bitter*.

Weathering Hard Times

At times of conflict, we need to coach, console or cancel. Jan Ruhe, the key leader with Discovery Toys, says, "Train, tolerate or terminate." You have to be in full communication with your team to do any one of those, and you have to be rock solid in your own integrity to know which one to act on.

Sometimes we need to let team members go, and that's hard to do. That's one of the prices a leader of leaders must pay. When facing tough situations, ask yourself:

1. What do I need to understand *now*?
2. What am I committed to achieving *now*?
3. What action do I need to take *now*?
4. How do I need to use my leadership *now*?

By asking and answering these questions for yourself, you will gain clarity and know what steps you need to take. Your character and integrity will rise higher with your leaders by staying solid as a rock.

Beverly Sills, the great opera singer who has faced severe personal challenges, says, "There are no shortcuts to anyplace worth going." Her path led through the disability of her child. Your path may lead to parting ways with someone you've coached and trained and cared about.

I know that every great leader has the resources, capability and knowledge to draw from within. The stronger you become in your company, the more you are going to have issues come to you as a leader of leaders.

I ask people I am developing into leaders, "Do you realize to earn more money you are going to need to become stronger in problem solving? You must learn to handle situations that are very heated."

Some are willing to take on that responsibility and some aren't. It's very important to ask the question periodically. Certainly not in the first week or sometimes not even the first year in a business. When the time is appropriate, when they start having leaders really come up underneath them, then it is time to ask if they are willing. If someone is unwilling to become responsible, to be that anchor, to be that rock, then another upline leader must intervene and pick up the next leaders.

If you don't go down to the next up-and-coming leaders, you are going to have holes in your boat. Too many holes and your boat will sink. They might be a coach on duplication, they might be a coach on prospecting, they might be a coach on how to do a presentation or call workshop, they might be a coach on how to do three—way calls, they might be a coach on how to do a training, but they need to have a coach on how to become— again that word BE— a leader of leaders who knows how to handle the tough issues.

I had no idea, when I started network marketing seven years ago, that would be part of the price. There are prices to be paid, but the payoff is absolutely awesome. Some people are unwilling to pay the price to become a leader of leaders. And that's okay. They can still be fully duplicated by the system, they can do all the steps and earn great money.

How do I get through the tough times? No, I don't go shopping. I get regrounded in three ways: Prayer and meditation— often with reading; Contribution; Spending time in nature.

I often pick up a good spiritual book. My father's most recent book, *The Power of Purposeful Living,* is about prayer being our greatest privilege in the world. I meditate and clear my mind and restore my soul.

Contribution is like the boomerang I got in Australia— it comes back each time you throw it out. The difference with contribution is that it comes back multiplied. A motto I strive to live by is to bring more life wherever I go, and by contributing, I know I am serving others while I support myself.

In 1982, I participated in and worked for the EST seminar which is now called Landmark Education. Werner Erhart said a great person will always leave a person, place or thing in better shape than when they found it. How about in public restrooms: Do you wipe off wet counters and pick up paper towels that have missed the wastebasket? Do you smile at people you don't know and acknowledge grocery store clerks and bank tellers? The more you put out, the more will come back from some source, sometime.

Grounding myself in nature can be as simple as walking out into the desert behind my Arizona home. During the summer, I take walks into the Canadian woods or ride my pontoon boat on the lake. Nature gave us two ends— one to sit on and one to think with. Our success or failure is dependent on which one we use most. Your vision/purpose always supports you regaining your solidness.

Your leaders need to have their vision/purpose done within the first month they are in the business. Then they'll have it as a foundation for their belief when the going gets rough. All you have to do to get them back on track is ask, "Are you living your purpose right now?"

Leaders are always under construction.

Leaders are readers. In the last six months, how many good inspirational books have you read? Reading keeps visions in place. The Bible says, "People without vision will perish." Visionary leadership is not easy, but it is worth it.

Emerson once said, "A hero is no braver than an ordinary man, but he is braver for five minutes longer." I change the word "hero" to "shero," and they both mean "leader." It's that extra five minutes of listening without an agenda, of listening with empathy, of persevering. Five minutes more of follow up, inviting, listening to inspiration. When you most want to quit the task at hand, remember to go *just five minutes longer.*

Successful people do what unsuccessful people are unwilling to do, even if it is simply doing five minutes more. Notice the "unwilling" part again. It isn't a matter of being *unable.* A team player who is unwilling to receive coaching from someone with greater results is trapped by that unwillingness. The team will also get stuck in that trap.

The Alcoholics Anonymous Bigbook says "There are only two sins: The first is to interfere with the growth of another human being; the second is to interfere with one's own growth."

In January, I was duplicating and coaching in Bozeman, Montana, an absolutely gorgeous mountainous area. The town is in a valley, and the whole area was blanketed in snow during my visit. If there was a blizzard, and someone left their front door open, we would immediately go over and shut that door or all the snow would come in the house. It's the same in being able to control our feelings and our thoughts. A leader of leaders controls their feelings, thoughts and actions. They don't interfere with their own or someone else's growth by letting snow sift in through a carelessly open door of negativity.

Getting the Monkey Off Your Back

If someone is stuck and their belief level is low, I have a series of questions that I ask them to answer honestly, openly and simply. KISS: Keep It Simple Sweetheart— not stupid. Here are the questions I ask. Simply lead them through the process— it absolutely works.

1. What are you feeling right now?

They might say, "I'm really feeling upset. I'm really feeling put upon. I'm feeling burned out."

2. Where do you feel it in your body?

Our bodies always tell us what is going on. Take time to read your body. "I feel it in my head or my head is spinning or my heart is beating real fast or I'm kicking all the time or I'm talking real fast."

3. What is your body telling you?

"My body is saying I need to quiet down. I have to let this issue go or my body will just speed up more."

4. What do you dislike about what is happening to you?

(Not the story, not the bad product, not the change in the compensation plan, not da, da, da, da— what do you dislike that is happening to you?)

"My belief is down. I'm unsure of where to go next. I'm allowing myself and my business to get in VCR pause. That means stopping."

When you put your VCR machine on pause, there is no picture, there is no action. You need to act, push the button with the arrow pointing forward. We need to push that button in order to get our picture again and move forward.

5. What are you tolerating?

"I'm tolerating what other people are telling me. I'm tolerating the gossip I'm listening to." Whoever gossips to you will gossip about you.

6. What are you settling for?

"I'm settling for staying where I am, rather than doing what it takes to get over it, to get through it, to get under it."

They need to get clear about what they are settling for and what price they're paying.

7. What are you committed to instead?

They are beginning to get unstuck, because they talk about possibility, which will bring them back on purpose. Many people get off the path of life. What do you want instead? What are you committed to? I'm committed to getting unstuck. I'm committed, if someone jumps out of my team or out of our company, to not let it affect me. They begin to express what really matters. The words are coming out of their mouth. I am not telling them, I'm drawing them out. We are really in the business of education for network marketing, personal leadership, contribution, integrity and courage. The Latin origin of educate means "to draw out". The more a coach can draw people out, the better. Ask questions. They know their truthful answers and solutions.

8. What will you do differently to have what you've said you are committed to?

"If someone calls and starts being negative, I'm going to say, 'Please stop. I'm not going to listen to this. If you continue to be negative, I'm not going to listen. I'll hang up.'"

The person you are coaching to get unstuck will have the answers and know the next step to take for herself.

9. What do you need to take that next step to get you back on the path of productivity, back on your path of purpose, back on your path of contribution?

You need to re-ground your people until they know how to do and be it for themselves. It is critical to have them communicate why they have chosen to do this business. A great next step is to have them share their purpose statement and describe what's on their treasure map.

When you are working with someone to get the monkey off their back, if you solve the problem for them you are not empowering them. You are not holding them capable, and you diminish them. By asking these questions without story, without drama, without history, without circumstances, they get clear and are quite capable of removing the monkey from their back.

10. What kind of support (or what do you need) to take your next step?

Perhaps they need a phone number for the home office, or the product department, or the return department. Perhaps they need a tracking number. Perhaps they need to talk to someone else who might be a part of that particular problem.

The important thing is the commitment to their next step.

At this point in the process, they are jazzed and juiced up, because they know they have solved this themselves. As a leader, they are getting stronger and clearer. They are able to share what they need to do to support themselves.

11 Is there anything else I can do for you at this time?

I have never had anyone say yes to this question. They have the monkey off their back, and you have not taken it onto yours. They have reclaimed their personal power and focus, and you have not lost yours in the process. Win-Win!

By asking these enabling questions, you have given them new light to guide them. A coach in this process simply asks the questions and uses listening skills. Take a tip from nature— your ears aren't made to close, but your mouth is! Demonstrate that for your team, and they will learn an important part of leadership.

The final and critical part is acknowledgment. This is not complimenting them on what they did, but recognizing who they are being. "You were very open during this process. I respect you for your commitment to solve this yourself, while staying open to coaching. That shows me you are a great leader. I'm proud to have a person of your caliber on my team."

This clearing process, with others on your team solving their own issues, is a necessary step in developing leaders of leaders. After you have done the "monkey off your back" process a few times with someone, they will be able to complete it on their own. They will also be ready to pass the baton and use the process for people they are coaching. You are out of the loop, becoming non-essential— a sure sign of leadership and residual income!

Time Out

It is always necessary to continue to get permission to intervene and coach. Here is a tool I use to stop behavior or communication that isn't for action or inspiration: Put your hands into a T, like a referee signaling time-out. When you use this, it means an immediate cease and desist. *Time out and trust.* Use it when a team player starts to ramble, fails to answer a questions directly, interrupts, loses their train of thought or blanks out when listening. That is when the lights are on, but nobody is home. As a compassionate coach, you need to call a time-out to gently guide them back on purpose.

The Chain of Communication

Communication for action always goes through the chain of communication. That is not a chain of command, like the military. It's a chain of communication which lets your leader know you are going to be contacting one of the people they are coaching. When you have great respect from your team, they will be so gracious and grateful that an up, up, upline leader will reach down deep into the organization to touch, inspire, acknowledge and empower someone coming up through the ranks.

Communicate for relationship-building action by asking downline leaders to take specific actions. Have them call you when they reach a certain level, lead their first big event presentation, earn a vehicle, find a new leader for their team or take their first all-expense-paid tax-write-off vacation. Repeat the process of establishing a new relationship just as you would with one of your sponsored leaders.

Remember the schoolyard trick of Pete and Repeat? Pete and Repeat went down to the river to swim. Pete fell in, so who was left? Repeat. Pete and Repeat went down to the river to swim. Pete fell in, so who was left? Repeat.

When you are communicating for inspiration— sharing in a way that will cause people to ignite and stay focused on their purpose in their business— the process is the same over and over. Repeat what works and don't reinvent the wheel. Make a difference through your communication whether or not it adds to your pocketbook. There are two kinds of leaders in the world: Those who are *interested in the fleece* and those who are *interested in the flock*. Where do you place your attention— on cash or on contribution? How would your network honestly describe you? What ripples are you sending out?

Sometimes, when I reach the people that are far downline from me— it might be over in Australia or way up in the Yukon— you would think the Queen of England or the President called. But to me, the only things that are different between me and them is my time table— I've been doing this longer than they have— and I didn't quit. Those are the only two things that are different.

This business is relationship marketing; the relationships we build today will last for years. Residual income comes through those long-term relationships. Team players downline from you will tell their network how you reached out to them. They'll tell people, "You'll never believe who called me today! It's a miracle that Rick Ryder . . . Linda Reese Young . . . Ken and Karen Long . . . Jason and Donna Haugh . . . Shirley Carmack called me." (Fill in the name of someone important to you— then fill in your own.) "I had no idea they even knew I was in their network! I'm probably thousands of people down, and he/she still cared enough to call."

Just like the song says, it's the little things that mean a lot.

Communication to Avoid

There are two kinds of communication that can be incredibly destructive to your relationships and your network: Gossip and advice.

People gossip in network marketing just like they do in any other area of life or work. There is no inspiration in gossip. You know, whoever gossips *to you* will be a gossip *about you*. I do not allow people to come to me to gossip, because I don't want people gossiping and being rumor mongers about me.

Advice is not communication for inspiration, either. Many people *want to* give advice, but it is simply someone else's opinion. You must speak up to be heard, but sometimes you have to shut up to be *appreciated*. Giving unsolicited advice will kick you in the butt. DON'T GIVE IT!! It cuts off listening and connection, diminishing partnership for a lose-lose situation.

If someone asks me a technical or mechanical question, I guide them to where the answer can be found. Whose business is it? Theirs. We are not passing the baton or developing a leader if we solve or answer everything for them. View them as capable of finding their own answers and solutions as soon as they know where to look.

Advice creates difficulty in relationships. Only trouble comes out of combining a narrow mind with a wide mouth. Troubles are like babies— the more you nurse them, the bigger they grow.

Use your words as tools of communication, not as substitutes for action. People may doubt what you say, but they are always going to believe what you do. That is communicating for inspiration and communicating for action. Coaching and training needs to be full of inspirational stories. Just remember:

People with tact have less to retract.

That's something you will find very, very useful.

Don't Look Back

We have a rear view mirror in our cars, and that's the only place we need it. A leader who communicates for action and inspiration does not spend time and communication looking into the rear view mirror. The past is as small as a car mirror when we get into a story of emotion, garbage, gossip or drama that has no power, it doesn't move people forward. Rather than looking in the rear view mirror, let's look out the front window. That's the bigger, clearer view. That's the future, the vision of what's out there.

Leaders who communicate for action and inspiration are always looking and moving themselves. The people they are coaching in leadership move forward through leading by example and not being in the past. Leaders come from the point of view we discussed earlier, Be Here Now. They don't live in the past, and they don't live in the future. They are being present, right here, right now. If you stare into your rear view mirror too long, you either lose your present or crash into your future.

That's a tough skill to learn, and it's going to take some time. Sometimes it will take a year or two for people to be fully present with someone else. Whether you are duplicating, prospecting, coaching someone to become a stronger leader— it takes time to be fully in the present.

Many native North American cultures share legends and traditions which predate "Western" culture. One I know from living in Arizona is the dream catcher. They have become popular souvenirs, so you have probably seen them as jewelry or window ornaments.

A dream catcher is a loop made of feathers, grasses and leather. There is an outer hoop with a web-like pattern woven inside. Sometimes there are beads and feathers hanging from the center of the web.

One tradition says a dream catcher should be placed above an infant's cradleboard to filter all the baby's dreams. Good dreams find the open center of the web and slide down the feathers to land softly on the sleeping baby. Bad dreams stick to the web where they get burned off by the light of morning.

Wow! What a great lesson for network marketers! Let everything negative from yesterday be filtered out of our sleep and be destroyed by a new day's dawn. Many team members use dream catchers as PDTs (remember? psychological trigger device). Leaders are able to support prospects and new represen-tatives to recatch, rekindle and reclaim their good dreams through network marketing.

Two things deprive people of their peace of mind: Work unfinished and work not yet begun. Action and accountability leave nothing to chance— you begin what needs to be accomplished and complete it. You don't stray into areas that interrupt your momentum or distract you from your purpose.

Productivity vs. Activity

As a coach, one of your most important roles is to support people to stay productive, not just active. What's the difference? PIPing is productivity. Busy work is activity. Managing is activity. My son Jordan provided a wonderful example when I called him on the phone.

He was just beginning to build his business. He was a representa-tive for three years before he actually started working his business. He had no belief in the industry. He had no belief in the company. He had no belief in the product. And he had no belief in himself doing this business. Those four cornerstones of belief must be in place in order to reach success.

I called him one day and asked, "Jordan, what are you doing?"

He said, "I'm filing."

I said, "I have never heard that filing creates financial freedom, Son."

He just went, "Aw, shoot, Mom. It is so easy to get pulled off, to get on the internet, to get on e-mail, to file, to make all these huge lists."

I said, "May I coach you?" (A leader continues to ask "may I coach you" because when our people stall or stop, we need to ask permission to coach, so that they are willing and open to hear.) I said, "Jordan, you need to be productive and work on your belief. Will filing help with that?"

He had to get out of filing and managing his office in order to go back into productivity. Productivity is prospecting, inviting, presenting and retailing the product. Too many self- or team-managing activities keep leaders away from being with people. Remember this is a reach out and touch, eyeball-to-eyeball, belly-to-belly business.

Whenever we talk to someone on the phone or in person, in our consciousness, our intention, our voice, our attitude must be a call to action for them. What is their next step forward, and by when will they take it? Ask why this step is important or necessary.

By keeping your eye and heart in the present, you will be more focused on productivity. Here is a rhyming list to keep you in productivity with people:
- Possibilities Must Be Weighed.
- Priorities Must Not Fade.
- Plans Must Be Laid.
- Commitments Must Be Made.
- The Price Must Be Paid.
- Timing May Be Delayed.
- The Course Must Be Stayed.
- The Trumpets Will Be Played.

Smart Notes

In developing leaders in training, one of the things I do is always make sure people have materials for taking notes. I will not start a training until everybody in that room has pen and paper. Many trainers will just get up and start rocking and rolling without giving every person the best possibility to learn by writing notes.

I had a great mentor share with me, 22 years ago, that notes were my second set of brains.

I suggest you have a set of ground rules for everyone of your training. The rules of football are different between Canada and the United States. Imagine how the game would be played if a Canadian team used their rules to play an American team using American rules. Total chaos! Have everyone in your training play by the same set of rules.

Here are the ground rules I use and suggest:

1. Take notes.

2. Listen as if your life depends on it— it really does.

That also means BE HERE NOW! Keep your thoughts in this room. Alcoholics Anonymous has a saying, "Just get your butt in a meeting and your mind and soul will follow."

3.No side talking.

Don't pull the person next to you off purpose by talking while the trainer is speaking.

4.Participate 100%.

Play full out. Play to win.

After people have heard the rules, I have them declare their willingness to accept and abide by them. I also ask, "Do I have permission to coach you?" I have them raise their hands, and I scan the room to be sure they have all agreed to coaching.

I start training only after we are all in agreement on the rules. If you do not set the ground rules, it is like winking at a girl in the dark: You know what you're doing, but she doesn't. Proper preparation and agreement solves 99% of the problems which could arise. The importance of a training is not what you get from it (content), but how you will put it into action immediately (context). The discipline of following rules is a necessary initial action to take, and everyone is on the same songsheet page in the training.

One Liners

Many people talk in clichés or cute little statements. Personally, I like one-liners. Here's a list of one-liners I give to new representatives two to three weeks into their business. By that point, they are seeing the day-to-day reality of RYBLAB, and these help them hit their stride.

- The largest network is built one leader at a time.
- The biggest mistake is wasting your time with the uncommitted people.
- Once they are sponsored, more people will do nothing than those

who choose commitment.

- •Commit to work this business two to five years. After that, you may not need to work at all.
  - Set big goals and little problems won't stop you.
  - You're in this business for yourself, not by yourself.
  - This is not an easy business, but it is a simple one.
  - Nothing worthwhile ever came easy.
  - This is a business of duplication, good or bad.
  - Treat everyone on your team as if you personally sponsored them.
  - This business requires self discipline.
  - Never quit— it's just a matter of time.
  - This sounds to good to be true, but in fact it is true.
  - This is a big business without big business headaches.
  - Nothing will ever take the place of enthusIASM, I Am Solid Myself.
  - Build and keep your belief 100% unshakable.
  - This is really a business of a lot of people doing a little bit well.
  - Don't take rejection personally; remember it's their loss, not yours.
  - Keep offering the gift of this business and products.
  - Your success is gauged by the people in your downline earning paychecks.
  - Your work is temporary and the income can be permanent.
  - The residual income is from your direct coaching at first, then it has nothing to do with your effort and all to do with duplication of leaders.
  - You could not afford to hire the people in your upline who are offering you their total support and skills for free.
  - Too much analysis causes paralysis.
  - Remember productivity not activity.
  - Leaders are always under construction.

As a leader of leaders, you never stop growing and learning. As your income continues to go up, you keep investing to become more!

Help Your "Followers" Surpass You

By the time someone is ready to become a leader of leaders, they have all the skills down. They have all the knowledge, and their beliefs are rock solid. They have their commitment in place. They are living their vision and purpose. They are Unconscious Competents. They know the way and have gone the way. The key is to show the way by example, by tremendous contribution and tremendous commitment to other people.

Like my dedication says, "This is not a dress rehearsal." You cannot control the length of your life, but you can control its breadth, depth and height. I can't understand why people don't choose to play full out, moment by moment in personal life and their business.

It is extremely difficult, if not impossible, to lead farther than you have gone yourself. You could have a great team player show up on your team and run right past you. That happens due to that person's skills, commitment, belief and efforts. Don't fool yourself that your leadership gets the credit; that attitude will haunt you. Always give credit where it is due, and don't be too ready to take it for yourself. In my training, I use an overhead that says:

> *The task of a leader is*
> *to take their team where they*
> *have never been before.*

People all come into this business at different places in their own personal growth, knowledge and willingness to expand and improve. It's a gradual process, and you can't rush it. Remember, this is network marketing, it's a way of life, not a destination. It's the journey and the process that moves people.

The best and only way to gauge a leader is to look at his or her results. This can be a hard one for people to swallow and tell the truth about. Another way to say this is: The best and only way to gauge a leader is to look at his or her duplication, look at the team, the results and the leaders they are developing. Some people have tremendous resistance to creating or supporting their people to grow in quantum leaps because the team might then bypass its leader.

I again have representatives do a meter-reading on themselves. When they answer for themselves honestly, we can coach in areas needing strength. It creates very personalized coaching. Meter reading means evaluating performance on a scale of one to ten (one being low, ten being high):

Ask:

Where are you today with duplication?

I'm doing a three— my duplication skills have improved, but they still need work.

Where is your belief in network marketing, your company and your products?

My belief is up to ten— I love networking, my company is strong (with a great compensation plan!), and the products are really working for me and others.

You can look at the meter reading and know exactly where to work on improving and where to acknowledge successful development. It honors each person's rate of growth while keeping everyone on the path to successful leadership.

I also frequently use the same leadership quiz I shared in Chapter Six for advanced coaching to support team players. Your results and the way you lead are reflections of yourself. When someone is not being all they can be, I ask them to take out their Leadership Quiz and identify which of the numbered questions they are not using in their business this moment. Always allow them to decide before you ask what they need from you in the way of support. If someone is stuck, being an emotional/mental jerk, rather than listening to their drama or telling them what to do, I show them a way to get *themselves* unstuck. I have them pull out their leadership quiz and see where and with which of these commitments they're off base.

Once they discover that, I'll say, "What do you need to do, or how do you need to be to get yourself unstuck and move forward?"

I think you'll find the leadership quiz extremely useful. It's okay when developing leaders— as I said before about sinning— to make mistakes, to miss the mark. I don't care if people make mistakes as long as they don't stay stuck or beat themselves up.

When leaders *take care of their business,* the results of the *business will take care of them.* At the end of any phone call, the seven most important words I always say are: *"What else can I do for you?"* Three more important words are *"you call me."* Support representatives in being accountable for calling, faxing or emailing you.

Pitfalls

What are some of the pitfalls to being a responsible sponsor?

1. **Wanting success for a representative more than that person wants it.**

When you use a clarity and commitment page, it helps eliminate confusion by having the new representative write and speak their fundamental values. You paint the picture of preparation so the new person knows exactly what it will take and what time commitment they need to make. Share with them that network marketing is a roller coaster, and the ride can get a bit rough. If you try to stand up and jump off during the bumpy parts, you risk a tragic accident.

You cannot jump-start anyone who doesn't want to ride the roller coaster. You also can't drag someone over the finish line. Keep your vision and faith, but don't waste time trying to make the ride for someone else.

2 Forgetting KISS— Keep It Simple Sweetheart.

When a prospect asks you a simple question, like where your company began, you might say Melbourne, Florida. That's the simple answer to their question. Then they'll ask another question. The more a prospect is asking the questions, the more they are moving forward.

What if you answered their question with where the company began, who started it, what financial backing it had and how much the company grew in the first year? They didn't ask for all that. That is data-dumping; they don't need to know that. They just need answers to their questions.

Answer questions very simply and to the point. Then ask, "Do you have another question?" If you are doing more than 30 % of the talking, you are talking too much. The prospect has an invisible sign on their forehead saying, "Make ME feel important!" Listening does make them feel important. Data dumping doesn't.

In the Sixties, there was a very popular song, "You Talk Too Much." One line said, "You even worry me to death." Too much talk or extra data scares prospects off. They think or feel that they couldn't ever learn all that information. So please don't talk too much.

3. Driving your network legs or lines on your own effort.

It will last and feel great for a while, and then, most likely, you'll burn out and your income will drop. Your business won't move unless you're moving it, so you lose all the benefits of leveraging your time and effort.

When you build a house, the most important part is the foundation. While I was building my new lake cottage in 1997, it took more time, planning, people and equipment to build the foundation than all the other sections. It's an object lesson for network building— build the leaders on your legs or lines, don't drive them yourself. Driving can be playing hero and boasting. Building leaders is boosting.

Boast less and boost more. Boosting is a representative's foundation and staying power.

4. Pushing a team player.

Imagine you have a piece of rope on the floor. If you push it to move it forward, it will buckle. It is far more effective to gently guide the rope toward you.

We all have sitters and squatters in our network. Chances are they were pushed into signing before they were ready, or they lost belief and commitment after they came into the business.   Pushing them will simply make them buckle. It won't move them in the direction of leadership and success, it will just set up resentment and resistance.

In The Tao of Leadership, John Heider says, "Whatever is flexible and flowing will tend to grow. Whatever is rigid and blocked will atrophy and die."

5. Forgetting to RYBLAB.

Is that Running Your Big Lips And Blabbing? Could it be Run Your Bank Account Larger And Bigger? Maybe it's Risk Your Business Life And Boost. Return Your Brains Like A Boomerang?

None of the above.

RUN YOUR BUSINESS LIKE A BUSINESS!

Many networkers don't treat their businesses like businesses, so their returns are not profitable. They fall into the pit of managing and monitoring instead of focusing on leadership. Management is a liability and leadership an asset. Keep PIPing and lead others by your example of RYBLAB.

Have each new prospect see clearly that regular jobs, trades and careers are simply income generators. If someone isn't working, they are not earning. In network marketing, we are wealth creators by leveraging our time with the efforts of many.

My parents always said, when it was time to do our chores, "Many hands make light work." I didn't like that or believe them as a kid, but networking has shown me the truth of that saying. On our teams, we have many hands, minds, hearts and spirits doing and being the business.

6. Being unwilling to hold representatives accountable for their communication.

If someone says, "I'm going to try to talk to two new prospects this week," you need to intervene and ask, "Does that mean you will call two new prospects?" When communication from a new representative is weak and non-committal, you need to step in and give compassionate coaching. They must say their goals aloud, speaking what they will be accountable for. This level of accountability can be shaky ground for new networkers, but it is the only way to produce lasting leaders.

Goethe wrote, "Treat a man as he is and he will remain as he is. Treat a man as he can and should be, and he will become as he can and should be."

I would rather have someone be accountable for one guest than to be pushed into resistance and have no guests show up. Standing firmly on even a small stepping stone starts creating a lasting foundation.

7. Telling people this business is easy.

Once someone actually starts doing this business, they find out it takes work; dedication and time. They need to know, up front, what effort will be necessary to make their business succeed. Please tell the truth always.

8. Lacking credibility.

When I started with my first network marketing company, it was only 13 months old. Although it had leadership and commitment, it didn't have any videos, audio tapes, brochures or other sales aids. I had to find materials from outside the company until it produced its own line of top-quality professional materials.

One outside source for validating most well-managed companies is, as I mentioned earlier, a Dunn and Bradstreet report. Check also to see if the company is registered with the Better Business Bureau, Multi-Level Marketing International Association and the Direct Selling Association.

Another way to develop credibility is to establish a reference file of letters from different professionals who are in the network. You can give copies to prospects in the same profession, so they can learn about the business from one of their own. I recommend letters from:

ministers, lawyers, rabbis, doctors, accountants and celebrities. Sometimes people with extensive education tend to be skeptical, and the letters ease their concerns.

People who accomplish big things do small things well. Avoiding the pitfalls and being prepared is part of that. You must practice ways to overcome the pitfalls for yourself— you can't hire someone else to practice for you. A leader of leaders will coach on the pitfalls and their solutions.

9. Loading people with inventory.

Many companies have a quota, and if you don't make your sales, then you have to buy more and more. People become discouraged about spending a lot of money out of their own pockets.

It's important to work with your people to retail the product early in the month, so that they are not struggling to move all their product in the last few days at the end of the month. If you have a quota, don't hide it. Let representatives know that it's part of the business. If they are unwilling to purchase the active distributor minimum volume of product, then just have them as a retail customer and don't put them in as business builders.

Anchoring Leaders

Are you skilled in duplication, can you do the two-on-ones, the call workshops, the one-on-ones, the 48-hour duplication? Can you do the group conference calls, training and home/hotel presentations? Do you have the knowledge and the belief in the industry, your company and your products?

I have an advanced training for team players who have reached the upper titles or levels. I can move them further and faster because of their willingness, results and leadership, using an excellent exercise for awesome results in achieving new goals.

In their notes, I have them write down one tough goal they achieved. Some of the ones I've seen are: obtaining pilot's license, getting off drugs or alcohol, graduating from college or medical school, purchasing their first home, becoming a lay minister in church, immigrating from another country and becoming a US citizen, winning a sporting event, finishing a marathon, etc.

I'll share one of my personal examples, the one I use most often involves my younger son.

James, my older boy, was almost five years old, and we'd been trying to have another baby. After three miscarriages, I realized I wanted to adopt. My husband and I applied through the Orange County Adoption Board in California. We asked for a hard-to-place baby. They said it would be about a year before we got matched with a child.

Six months later, we received a call, on a Friday, that a four-week-old baby boy was waiting for us to bring him home to our family on Monday. We were so thrilled! We decided to name him Jordan Kirk Ledgerwood.

My husband shared from the pulpit on Sunday that our baby was to be with us the next day. Our church rejoiced with us, and Jamie was completely excited about having a new brother.

On Monday, we received another call from the adoption agency telling us they had made a mistake. That particular baby boy wasn't to be ours.

Can you imagine our disappointment? Our church and all our family knew we were picking up that baby. What were we supposed to do?

We got very clear that the baby was ours. We decided to go up against the State of California and claim Jordan Kirk as our son. It took unshakable faith, constant communication and refusing to take no as the state's answer, no matter how often we heard it.

We had the support of hundreds of friends and family, and three weeks later, we placed little Jordan Kirk into the small, eager arms of his big brother Jamie. What a joy to bring our new son home! Some people say it is easier to adopt than give birth. I have done both. One involved physical pain and the other emotional challenges. I paid prices for both equally and can't say that one was any easier or harder than the other.

Jordie and Jamie have matured into incredible, responsible young men and are again in partnership with their mom and 11 other family members in our new visionary company Legacy USA.

When I share my story of Jordan's "birth" into our lives, I become emotional as I relive the process, and I often finish the story through tears. I ask leaders to sit back, close their eyes and get emotionally involved with their own process of achieving their goal by replaying in their minds and hearts. After a few minutes, I have them open their eyes and write in their notes what qualities, characteristics and talents manifested in them to bring their goal into reality.

I have four to six leaders, who are emotionally in touch with their process, stand and share with the rest of us. It is a very hushed and attentive time. When people are being authentic and sincere, all ears are listening. This exercise can truly move an entire group to a much higher awareness and action state of being.

At this point, I have the leaders call out the qualities, traits and talents they needed to achieve their goals. I write them on an overhead or whiteboard as they shout them out. Then I have each leader look over their lists and intuitively choose the one quality they drew upon the most. They circle the one characteristic or skill that jumps out as the strongest. That trait supported them in reaching a major goal in their lives once, and it can do it again. I call it their *anchor word*.

Some of the anchor words are: Persistence Pays, Trust, Discipline, Go Beyond, Never Give Up, Paying the Price, Like a Rock, Be Bold, No Fear, Unstoppable and Action Counts. You will hear many more from the participants.

Leaders need to be sure that word is big on their treasure maps, in red lipstick on their bathroom mirrors and posted on the ceilings above their beds. It will anchor them through the rough seas of their business.

Get an agreement that they will call another team member or coach when they have their anchor word up. This is holding them accountable. Use this process and I believe you will be awestruck by the connection and acceptance of your team leaders. Individuals are heroes, sheroes and superstars, but it is always teams that win the championships.

Goals become commitments when they become results and realities. The moment you truly commit and quit holding back, all sorts of people and things will rise up to support you. The simple act of commitment is a powerful magnet for receiving what you need.

When we are open and real, it wins people over. Sometimes when I share the story of Jamie in prison, there isn't a dry eye in the room. Do you know how many people come to me to share about their family members in prison? "I have a daughter, brother, father, sister in prison. I never thought I could be open with my team and let them know this. By your example, Peggy, I can see what a difference it makes to be open and authentic. I now have the courage to share this. Thank you."

The success of your business is in direct proportion to the quality relationships you make. You are going to have either reasons or results. Like oil and water, they do not mix. You will have to choose which price to pay. There are prices a leader pays for reasons, and prices a leader pays for results. Why not go for the gold medal and pay the price to win big?

The Network Marketing Warrior

Martin Luther King, Jr., a great mentor and inspiration to me, said the ultimate measure of a person is not where he or she is standing in moments of comfort and success, but where he or she stands in times of challenge, change and discovery. True leaders continue to move forward in faith. They become network marketing warriors.

Faith *with* action is a FORCE.

Faith *without* action is a farce.

A warrior is willing to conquer the enemy. What is *the enemy?*

The enemy is mediocrity, "stinking thinking," not being your best every day. That's where most people lead their lives. Network marketing challenges us to look at ourselves and be more than average. Becoming a stronger leader of ourselves is an awesome wake up call: What is your life about? Why are you breathing on this planet? What difference are you going to make? This is something that you and all the leaders you are developing should be focused on.

One network marketing team in Oklahoma uses a motto to keep them being warriors. They have each team member put the motto on their mirrors, dashboards, their ceilings, all their stationery and even on their toilet lids. Their motto:

See It Big.

A warrior is going to see what is at the end of the war. We can lose a lot of battles in network marketing without losing the war. The only way to do that is to quit.

Develop a team of leaders who are *network marketing warriors:*

1. Warriors keep their dreams alive daily.

They are champions of good news. They don't spread gossip, rumors or negativity. Great warriors stop communication that isn't inspiring.

2, A network warrior goes to war on their belief system and is dedicated to keeping that belief system in the highest order.

There are tons of changes that go on in any company, no matter what company you are with. A great warrior will always keep their belief level high and be able to share that with other people.

3. Warriors honor the network marketing industry, and its virtues of loyalty, integrity, dignity and courage.

We are all in this industry together. Network marketing is the road and the road leads all over the world, in 125 countries with over a $100 billion worth of goods and services were moved through network marketing and direct sales in 1997. The road is strong and sure and will continue to grow. Your company is the vehicle that moves down the road, and your products are the gas that moves the vehicle. It's very important as a warrior to have dignity towards any company, not to be knocking another company, not to be knocking another product. That is one of the worst actions that some people take, and it gives our entire industry a bad name.

Always empower and acknowledge other companies that are legal and ethical. Yes, we do have scams and pyramids, and they will be shut down or they will not stand the test of time. It normally takes the FTC or an attorney general one and a half to three years to finally shut down a company. A company may fold or shut itself down due to bad management, not enough capital or a product that has not been accepted and approved by the FDA.

4. Warriors live in self-mastery, through patience and practice.

I've just finished reading Randy Gage's latest book. Randy is certainly one of the great leaders in our industry, and he is constantly developing himself, as any other great leader in this industry does. Self mastery through patience. He shares that he was in a number of companies that didn't make it, and he could have totally lost his belief, but he knew the industry, that the road was strong, he just needed to find the vehicle and the gas to move that vehicle.

Think of the astronauts in the movie Apollo 13. They were stuck in space, and no one knew how to bring them back to earth safely. Their lives were on the line, but they needed patience while the professionals on the ground searched for a solution.

Floating around in space, not knowing if they would ever return to earth and their families, those three astronauts declared that failure and quitting were not an option. On this rock I stand and, World (or "universe"), you will adjust. They came back safely.

They had to follow very specific coaching and do things they had never done before. The astronauts had to trust the space control center on earth to give them knowledge, skills and instruction. They had to patiently follow instructions and believe in a successful outcome. They were true warriors.

5. Warriors commit to improving themselves.

Not so much as a means to achieving external goals, but to expand themselves being better human beings. Please hear that word being. The qualities of persistence, consistency, passion, vitality, purpose, vision, contribution, acknowledgment and integrity are important ones to constantly improve in ourselves. A warrior will always be expanding.

6. Warriors are willing to take risks to realize their greatness.

In doing so, they further the general good of the entire network. It's important to verbally share what risks you are taking. This book has been a gigantic risk and challenge to me. There have been so many times I have wanted to shut this puppy down and not go forward. It is on my treasure map, so I see it every day and I've made myself a commitment to do a book. I've also declared this to hundreds and thousands of people. It would be simple and easy for me to say it just didn't happen or it wasn't the right timing. My word is good, so I didn't quit on this book.

Many young parents choose network marketing for their family's financial freedom. Then they use their children as reason not to attend call workshops, presentations and training. "My baby-sitter canceled at the last minute." "Tommy was late getting home from soccer, so I'm not coming out tonight." Our children need to be the REASONS WHY parents do this business— not an excuse.

If you are not as successful as you desire to be, you need the call workshops, conference calls and presentations. If you are successful, the call workshops, conference calls and presentations need you. We all need to show up! Disciplined working means going all out until you are all in!

There was a big monthly presentation and training here in Phoenix, Arizona, and I went. You have no idea what a difference it makes when I show up. I have the financial freedom and time freedom, but I show up to support local presentations. People know that I have not gotten too big for our britches, that I can humble myself to go sit and empower and learn from a new kid on the block or a new leader who has accepted the baton.

7. Warriors are 100% accountable for their actions.

There is no pointing the finger out there. If developing leaders get into blame or lack responsibility or use reasons, justifications, excuses or alibis, I will simply say, "For what part of this do you take accountability and responsibility?" It has nothing to do with the outside world— as within so without. Warriors become willing to take full accountability for their action.

I was on a conference call recently— all over the United States, Canada, Australia, the Virgin Islands, Hawaii— and it lasted for a long 40 minutes. Just afterwards, a lady called me with an upset. I had just put in over half an hour of intense communication, and I was drained. A leader gets drained sometimes and needs to restore or replenish her soul and spirit. The lady called me and started to be a poison-ivy-monger, started to dump stuff on me. I was inappropriate with my response. I make mistakes, I said things that are not appropriate, and I was off with my communication to her. I knew it immediately because of the way she reacted. When people tighten up, leaders need to lighten up. I said, "Hang on a second, let me get myself grounded. (I took a deep breath or two.) I apologize."

A leader will always apologize. It was not my intention to be short with her, but I was. I realized I was totally off my purpose, because I was not coming from contribution and inspiration. I was drained, so I was inappropriate. I needed to clean it up with her by apologizing.

She heard my sincerity and thanked me for it, and the 100-pound ball of upset energy totally dissipated between us on the phone. It disappeared, because I took 100% accountability for my communication.

When there is an upset, most people will just go on like bulldozer and not stop, because of ego and being right. When we are driving down the street and there is a traffic light, if it's green, we can go ahead. If it is yellow, it means warning, it means slow down. If a warrior and a leader can read themselves, they know when they get into that yellow zone by their energy, tone of voice, how their body feels. They slow down and realize that the yellow zone means caution.

We can avoid many accidents in our business if we slow down and get grounded. If we don't stop in the yellow zone and keep going into the red light zone, we'll get into accidents in relationships, in communications, in developing leaders. People will drop out of our network. Whether in green light, yellow light or red light zones, warriors are aware of where they are and take accountability when they slip over the line into the wrong one.

It is a good technique to set green, yellow and red zones with people you are coaching. When they are communicating for action and inspiration, say, "Green light," so they know it's working. When they are resisting your coaching, arguing or not following, let them know they've reached the yellow zone. "Red light" means you will stop coaching at that point. When these parameters are in place, you both know the rules and can use them for effective communication. Use it for 30 days and then decide if you will keep it in your coaching.

8. Warriors are committed to empowering their company, its officers, and employees.

Remember these are people, human beings who do not walk on water. They make mistakes. They get in that yellow zone, and it is very important that we still empower them. Remember if it wasn't for the company, its officers and its employees, we would not have a vehicle to move to time freedom and financial freedom. Whenever I hear somebody become negative about anything with my company, its officers or its employees, I stop that conversation. The person who is talking might get very upset with me and feel I'm not listening. The truth is I won't allow that external negativity to affect my internal belief. I say, "Do you have a problem with this?" They usually say, "Well, yes."

"Are you going to be accountable to communicate it to the person who can do something about it? Don't come to me with it. I can't change what our company president is doing. I can't change the refund policy. I can't change which new products get released. What I can do is be accountable for my response and my reaction to the communication."

9. Warriors respect and value each team member. They serve others and are honest.

To give freely is the warrior's biggest challenge. Sometimes giving means tough love, calling a spade a spade, not being afraid that you're going to lose one of your team members. That is never the intention, but if someone crumbles under tactful truth, they won't ever rise to be a leader of leaders. A huge network warrior's challenge is to communicate openly and honestly with other team members so everyone wins. This is a vital necessity.

10. Warriors are committed to doing the right things— rather than doing things right.

We herd sheep, we drive cattle, and we lead people. By doing the right things, we earn respect. Character is made by many acts; it may be lost by a single act. When you get stuck in "doing things right," you risk losing all the respect you have earned over the years. Our actions are our own—their consequences are not.

In any endeavor—religion, education, science, network marketing, politics—leaders have egos, but they don't allow ego to get in the way of leading. When your ego is getting in the way, you are not energizing and attracting people. Chances are, you are stuck in doing things right rather than doing the right thing. A great warrior is able to shift—it's like flipping the coin, like turning on the light switch, that simple. It's not easy, but it's very simple to change an action, an attitude or a behavior for the good of the masses rather than the good of only yourself.

11. Warriors cherish life.

They conduct their business affairs to be ready for change at any moment and willing to change when needed. This is a big one.

I go canoeing on our lake up in Canada, and it is much easier to paddle the canoe in the direction of the current or the wind. When someone is unwilling (it's not a matter of being unable), I could say, "For $10,000 a month, you are going to need to change this," and I guarantee you they'd change it. If they are not flexible within themselves, they stop their business, stop their leadership, stop their contribution.

In order to keep trust with your team, you must flow and embrace change. By accepting new situations and ideas, you encourage your team to follow your lead. You don't have to enjoy the change, just accept it gracefully. The only person who really likes change is a wet baby!

12. Warriors are committed to being leaders of leaders.

Just being a leader of themselves would be operating out of ego, out of "I look good, I'm great, look at me." A leader of only themselves who is not developing the leaders on their team will soon not have a team.

13. Warriors fully realize that being a warrior doesn't always mean winning.

It does mean putting your life on the line. It does mean risking and failing. A warrior risks and fails, risks and fails, risks again as long as they live.

Risking is like a rubber band that is made to be stretched. The more we risk, the more we grow as leaders. Risk is a great teacher for showing how much more is available for us in life.

The other day, I sponsored some new people into the business. We set up their first two-on-one, and I went with them. They set an appointment at a beauty salon with a husband and wife who own 12 nail clinics all over Phoenix and Las Vegas. They have the headaches of employees, and if the alarm goes off, they have to go and check it out.

I asked the owners if they would be open and they said yes. They were right with me as I was sharing, and the new representatives I'd sponsored were listening and learning. That is what new people need to do on a two-on-one, not talk but listen, take notes and learn.

After about ten minutes, the man just exploded. He got up off his chair and started swearing. He said, "This is a *@#&% pyramid!"

I said, "What makes you think that?"

I could have adopted his same energy and become very defensive, but that would have put me into that yellow zone of danger. I backed off and asked a simple question. Then I started listening.

He had been in a couple of companies, and they had gone under. He had a tainted history. I said, "Are you willing to stay open?"

He replied, "Absolutely not! Get up and get out of my shop."

That was the first time in years I had somebody so blatantly resistant and angry. I said, "I'm very sorry that you're feeling like this. We simply came here to share with you something that could support and assist you in your life. I will respect you and we'll get up and leave."

It was such an eye-opener to my brand new representatives. They were thinking "Is this how this business is?" I knew I needed to coach them on what had happened.

We went over to a little restaurant and had coffee together. I was able to debrief them on what happened in that two-on-one presentation. They became very clear that it had nothing to do with what I said, that this is the way that this man and woman were in their lives. They had a huge turnover in their employees, and their reaction to me suggested it has to do with how fast they fly off the handle and operate in the red zone.

I didn't win. The new representatives didn't win, as far as having a new person to sponsor. And, of course, the people we were showing it to certainly didn't win.

When I left the shop, I just did an internal blessing. I said to myself "I wish you well and pray some day you are open to leveraging your time, rather than trading time for dollars with all these salons." They were literally working themselves to the bone.

My new representatives have been in real estate, so they know that people sometimes overreact. My representatives are fine, but it was very important to debrief them. When we walked into that salon, the new sponsors felt those people were going to be great. Many people who you feel would be great for this business don't want it.

A warrior won't always win, but will always pick themselves up and be ready to go back onto the battlefield.

14. Warriors live by the idea that "If it is to be, it is up to me."

Your success is not up to the downline or the upline or the company. Many people are looking for someone to do what they are unwilling to do, and that just does not work.

Network marketing warriors get beaten up, because we are face-to-face with people's lives and belief systems. If you don't climb the mountain, you can't see the view. When we have climbed one mountain, we had better be ready to climb the next one. If we don't, we could become complacent and slide back into mediocrity. As far as I know, we only go through this life once. Let's risk living life to the fullest. Believe in everyone and count on yourself to make it happen.

Barbara Walters, of television interview fame, says, "When you come to the edge of all the light you know, and are about to step off into the darkness of the unknown, faith is knowing one of two things will happen: There will be something solid to stand on or you will be taught how to fly."

I absolutely love that because there have been many times in my network marketing history that I found myself in the dark. That's when I simply look down at my feet and look for my rock— the one I stand on. My rock is my belief in my being and my faith in God.

Sometimes, when it's dark, I can't see it. I can always feel my being and faith. And when I do, when I know its there— and my being is always there— I can bend my knees a little and spring up high and fly.

Find your rock— your being— and stand on it.

I promise you, the world will adjust.

APPENDIX A: Resources

Seminars

Personal Mastery, Basic & Advanced	Brian Klemmer 2529 Laguna Vista Novato, CA 94945 (415) 898-0848
CLASS	Brian Biro 204 Weston Way Ashville, NC 28803 (704) 654-8852
Empowerment of Listening Possibility of Woman	Carol McCall The World Institute Group Tracy Cooke, Enrollment tracycooke@aol.com
The Start of Something Big Millionaires in Motion	John Kalench 6821 Convoy Ct. San Diego, CA 92111 (800) 388-1748
Masters' Seminar Lifers' Retreat (Upline® Lifetime Members only)	Upline® 106 South Street Charlottesville, VA 22902

Books & Tapes

Being the Best You Can Be in Network Marketing *17 Secrets of the Master Prospector*	John Kalench
Living with Passion	Peter Hirsch
The Greatest Networker in the World *Money, Money, Money, Money*	John Milton Fogg
Dynamic Spiritual Laws of Prosperity	Katherine Ponder
Developing the Leader Within *Developing the Leader in Others*	John Maxwell
Wave 3	Richard Poe

Who Stole the American Dream	Burke Hedges
You Can't Steal Second with Your Foot on First	
Winning is the Greatest Game of All	Randy Ward
The Path	Laurie Beth Brooks
Power for Purposeful Living	Dr. Kermit Long
	Vision Hill Press
	9654 W. Rosemonte
	Peoria, AZ 85382
	PH (602) 566-1575
	FX (602) 566-5840
A Hero in Every Heart	H. Jackson Brown, Jr.
The Seven Laws of Money	Michael Phillips
Power Calling	Joan Guiducci
Future Choice	Michael S. Clouse
The Science of Getting Rich	Wallace D. Wattles & Dr. Judith Powell
Tapping the Source	Randy Joe Ward
Your First Year in Network Marketing	Mark & Rene Yarnell
A Zoo With a View (children's)	Steven Vollaro
Don't Sweat the Small Stuff	Richard Carlson
Organize Your Work Space	Odette Pollar
Bread Winner Bread Baker	Sandy Elsberg
Fire Up	
Nuts and Bolts of MLM	Jan Ruhe
Daily Reflections for Highly Effective People	
7 Habits of Highly Effective People	Stephen R. Covey
Escape the Rat Race	Randy Gage
As A Man/Woman Thinketh	James Allen Jonathan
Living Synergistically	Thomas D. Willhite

The Celestine Prophecy	James Redfield
Jonathan Livingston Seagull	Richard Bach
Men Are From Mars/Women Are From Venus	John Gray
The Road Less Traveled	Dr. M. Scott Peck
The Richest Man in Babylon	George S. Clason
The Seven Spiritual Laws of Success	Deepak Chopra
Unlimited Power	Anthony Robbins
Simple Abundance	Sarah Ban Breathnach
You Were Born Rich	Bob Proctor
7 Minute Sizzle	Diane Gustwiller

Ellen Kreidman, Ph.D.

Mega Systems, Inc.
521 East 86th AveSuite G
Merrillville, IN 46410

WMLM Tapes

Upline®
(see info above)

The Heifer Project

Heifer Project Int.
Box 808
Little Rock, AR 72203
(501) 376-6836

Peggy Long can be reached at;

winter
9006 W. Escuda Dr.
Peoria, AZ 85382
ph: (623) 825-1994
fax: (623) 825-3003
likearock@uswest.net

summer
RR #1 Box 14A
Kilworthy, ONT P0E-1G0
Canada
fax: (705) 687-7792
ph: (705) 687-1625

APPENDIX B: Standard Welcome/Training Letters

Letter #1

Welcome to [Your Company] TEAM

Congratulations on your wise decision! You now own a business that has the potential to create a residual income of $1,000-$100,000 per month over the next one to five years.

Are you tired of trading your time for dollars? You now have the opportunity to enjoy time freedom, control, flexibility and achieve you dreams.

It's all up to you and your 100% commitment!

While this business moves at your own pace, if you want to see success and create a significant, permanent income for yourself, you need to run your business like a business (RYBLAB) and be committed to it. In that light, I ask the following things of you:

1) Be coachable. Keep it simple. This business is based on the concept of duplication. Our system is simple —and it works! Our Company has everything in place for you to Win Big. KISD— Keep It Simple and Duplicable!!

2) Order your product when becoming a Distributor by purchasing one of the Leadership Paks or Quick Start Paks immediately. Your Personal Sales Volume requirement is $100/$82 a month and have all your customers, including yourself, on Autoship. Your TEAM will do the same. This is simple and will create the residual monies you deserve. Be a Product of the Product!! It also gives you credibility when sharing Autoship with new Distributors. We all can retail from our Autoship and receive $$$ back.

3) Make a commitment to build your business over the next 18-24 months. You cannot create a business that will allow you to retire with a permanent income overnight. Please stay focused on your long-term vision.

4) Know why you are doing this business and what it will do for you and your family. Write down your goals on the Vision for Success sheet and fax or mail them to your sponsor. Fax or call your sponsor every week to tell them what you've accomplished and what your goals are for the next week. Schedule this business into your life. Remember RYBLAB—Run Your Business Like A Business. And you can count on your upline TEAM!!

5) Read through your materials in the first 24 hours. Watch the video and listen to audios. Make a list of questions and call your sponsor to answer them or guide you where to get the answers. Make a list of the first 100 people you think of (no pre-judgement). Call, fax or e-mail your sponsor when you have completed this. Set up a time to complete your training within the first two days you are in the business. Ask your sponsor for the names and phone numbers of your upline people for three-way calls, and put them in your training binder. Go over your prospect list and choose the top 15 for business builders, and the top 15 for retail customers in the first week.

6) Make a commitment to yourself to pass out five to ten audios each week. Plug your prospects into all the support the Company offers.

7) Do not attempt to present this whole business to someone in five to ten minutes. Use the systems 100%. Over the first month or two, you will become comfortable presenting the whole business in your home. You are in the sorting and sifting mode at first. You want to expose this idea to enough people until you find those people who are really serious in building a massive worldwide empire. Then teach them to do the same thing. Don't waste your time or energy on negative people. Use your time efficiently.

8) Remember QTIP — Quit Taking It Personally. Not everyone is going to want to do this business, and honestly, not everyone would be good at it. There are over 6 billion people waiting out there for just you. Are you willing to have 100 people tell you no to find those serious, determined people who will lock in for you a six figure income? You are looking for leaders, people who will out-earn you in this business. You want strong, successful people with an entrepreneurial spirit on your team. You are building a large, international business. But if someone tells you no, ask them to be your customer, and ask for referrals from them. This

is your business and financial future!

9) Learn the Success system, follow it, and teach it to your downline. Duplicate it fully!

10) Use all of your products and share their results. Always have audios, your talking business cards, in your purse or car. Remember you have a product of superior value to improve the well-being of people everywhere in the world.

11) Subscribe to *Upline®* *Journal* (network marketing's trade magazine; 888-875-4631). Use it to become an expert in this industry. Did you know that network marketing produces many of the multi-millionaires in the world? Learn from the best. Your attitude is everything. The only way to build a milti-million dollar network is to believe in what you are doing. Leaders are Readers.

12) Place three-way calling on your phone. Use your upline TEAM to coach you and do three-way calls with you while you learn. Listen to all training calls and invite prospects to listen as well. Your belief and knowledge will come from these calls. If you wanted to become a successful physician, you would mentor and train under the best in that filed, not under someone who knew nothing about it or had failed at it, right?

Success in this business is built on your belief, knowledge, and determination!

Have fun!

This is a great business. Coach people you care about to earn money and achieve their dreams, and then you'll have your financial and time freedom as well.

Congratulations on Your New Business!!!

Keep Your Vision,

Peggy Long
Like a Rock

Letter #2

You have now reached our highest earning title!

WOW!!! You're a great leader based on results. Coach and train your TEAM to do the same. Continue being a leader of leaders. Your potential earnings are now unlimited, and you'll share in the company's leadership bonus. This is big $$$!

Your task is to stay out of monitoring and management of your TEAM and work diligently with those committed representatives to win. Lots of people will give you excuses. Run with the runners, walk with the walkers and stop with the stoppers!

Always continue to PIP — Prospect, Invite, Present — and then sponsor. Your TEAM is watching you. Build leaders in your network. You can't do it all by yourself. DUPLICATE! Pass the baton! A few serious duplicators on your TEAM, and you'll be on your way to financial freedom. It's a matter of time!

The world needs more people like you — people of principle, people who care about something beyond themselves. In a world where having power and looking good are so important, you're someone who has a higher vision and who inspires others to share it. You have made a difference in the lives of many others, and I deeply acknowledge you.

See you at the convention, on stage, being acknowledged. You truly deserve it!! Now the true leadership is developing leaders on your legs: Be a continuous leader of leaders!!

Congratulations again,

Keep Your Vision!!

Peggy "Like a Rock" Long

APPENDIX C: Inspirational Quotes

Hold or Roll

Rocks hold firm while water's might
Sends pebbles rolling left and right.
Call pebbles rock? Set firm their goal?
First flash flood, still pebbles roll.
Not name, nor goal divide the two.
It's how they act. It's what they do.
Size dictates to stone, but you're in control.
Are you rock or pebble? Will you hold or roll?

–Manly Grant
Rhymes for the Land

The Bee Team

Somethimes we wonder whether the little we do can make a difference in the grand scheme of the network. I read that in a beehive producing 100-200 pounds of honey a year, a single bee produces only a teaspoon of honey in its lifetime. Yet with each bee's contribution, the hive accomplishes tremendous production. It happens because they work together and attack only their enemies, not each other. Though the hive may have as many as 80,000-90,000 bees, it operates almost as a single organism. You can see that TEAMWORK makes a difference for bees, and it can do the same in your life by creating leverage and residual income.

– Peggy Long

Persistent or Stubborn?

Sometimes in an attempt to be persistent, we become stubborn. That's a mistake, because there's a big difference between the two. Persistence is the ability to keep your eye on the goal; to continue plowing ahead despite the challenges; to doggedly work your way past any obstacle. Yet persistence also demands flexibility. Stubbornness, on the other hand, is a refusal to accept reality and an unwillingness to adapt to changing conditions.

To reach any goal requires that we be unyielding about where we intend to go, while at the same time remaining flexible about how to get there. Unfortunately, many times we get it backwards— we persistently do the same thing every day, out of a sense of habit or comfort or lack of knowing what else to do, even if it is not taking us in the direction we want to go.

Few things ever come to pass in exactly the way that we plan them. The ability to adapt is very much a part of relentless persistence. When you're persistent about what you intend to accomplish, and flexible as to how it will happen, anything is possible.

– Ralph Marston

Pass It On

He was driving home one evening, on a two-lane country road. Work, in this small Midwestern community, was almost as slow as his beat-up Pontiac. But he never quit looking. Ever since the factory closed, he'd been unemployed, and with winter raging on, the chill had finally hit home.

It was a lonely road. Not very many people had a reason to be on it, unless they were leaving town. Most of his friends had already left. They had families to feed and dreams to fulfill. But he stayed on. After all, this was where he buried his mother and father. He was born here and knew the country.

He could go down this road blind and tell you what was on either side, and with his headlights not working, that came in handy. It was starting to get dark and light snow flurries were coming down. He'd better get a move on.

He almost didn't see the old lady, stranded on the side of the road. But even in the dim light of evening, he could see she needed help. He pulled up in front of her Mercedes and got out. His Pontiac was still sputtering when he approached her.

Even with the pleasant smile on the stranger's face, the old lady was worried. No one had stopped to help in the last hour or so. Was this man going to hurt her? He didn't look safe; he looked poor and hungry.

He could see that she was frightened, standing out in the cold and gathering dark. He knew how she felt. It was that chill that only fear can put in you.

He said, "I'm here to help you, ma'am. Why don't you wait in the car where it's warm. By the way, my name is Joe."

The problem was simply a flat tire, but that was bad enough for a lady her age. Joe crawled under the car to find a place for the jack, skinning his knuckles a time or two before he found what he needed. Then he changed the tire, further dirtying his hands and adding a bruise to the scrapes.

As Joe was tightening the last lug nut, the old lady rolled down her window and began to talk to him. She told him that she was from St. Louis and was only passing through. She couldn't thank him enough for coming to her aid. Joe just smiled as he closed her trunk.

She asked him how much she owed him. Any amount would have been fine with her, considering all the awful things she imagined could have happened if he hadn't stopped or hadn't been a gentleman.

Joe never thought twice about the money. This was not a job to him, it was helping a woman in need. God knows there were plenty who had given him a hand in the past! He had lived his whole life that way, and it never occurred to him to act any other way. He told her that if she really wanted to pay him back, the next time she saw someone who needed help, she could give that person the assistance that they needed. Joe added, ". . . and think of me."

He waited until she started her car and drove off. It had been a cold and depressing day, but he felt good as he headed for home, disappearing into the twilight.

A few miles down the road, the old lady saw a small cafe. She went in to grab a bite to eat and take the chill off before she made the last leg of her trip home.

The restaurant was a dingy-looking place with two old gas pumps out front. The whole scene was unfamiliar to her. The cash register was like the phone of an out-of-work actor— it didn't ring much.

Her waitress came over and brought a clean towel to wipe the lady's wet hair. The waitress had a sweet smile, one that being on her feet all day couldn't erase. The lady noticed that the waitress was about eight months pregnant, but she didn't let the aches and strain change her attitude. The old lady wondered how someone who had so little could be so giving to a stranger. It made her think of Joe.

After the lady finished her meal, while the waitress was making change from a $100 bill, the lady slipped out the door. She was gone by the time the waitress came back. As she stood near the table with a $90 tip in her hand, the waitress noticed something written on a napkin. Tears came to her eyes as she read, "You don't owe me a thing. I've been there, too. Someone once helped me out, the way I'm helping you. If you really want to pay me back, here's what you do: Don't let the chain of love end with you."

There were tables to clear, sugar bowls to fill and people to serve, but the waitress made it through the day with a happy heart. That night when she got home and climbed into bed, she was thinking about the money and the old lady's note. How could she have known how much the waitress and her husband needed that money? With the baby due next month, it was going to be hard. She knew how worried her husband was, and she gave him a soft kiss as he lay sleeping.

"Everything is going to be all right. I love you, Joe."

Pass it on.

–Author Unknown

Mile by Mile . . . It's a Trial
Yard by Yard . . . It's Hard
Inch by Inch . . . It's a Cinch!

Inspiration
Inspiration is fuel for the soul.
Without it we would never reach our goal.
To be inspired by someone is truly a gift,
Gives our whole life's pupose a tremendous lift.

That "Point of Light" comes from only a few,
But settles on people like morning dew.
To shine on others, you don't have to be smart.
True inspiration always comes from the heart.

—Bobby Nelson

How Do You Live Your Dash?

I read of a pastor who stood to speak
At the funeral of his friend.
He referred to the dates on her tombstone
From the beginning to the end.

He noted that first came the date of her birth,
And spoke of the second date with tears,
But he said what mattered most of all
Was the dash between those years.

For that dash represents all the time
That she spent alive on earth,
And now only those who loved her
Know what that dash is worth.

For it matters not how much we own;
The cars, the house, the cash.
What matters most is how we live,
And how we spend our dash.

So think about this long and hard,
Are there things you'd like to change?
For you never know what time is left;
You could be at "dash, mid-range."

If we could just slow down enough,
To see what's true and real,
And always try to understand
The way that others feel.

And be less quick to anger,
And show appreciation more,
And love the people in our lives
Like we've never loved before.

If we treat each other with respect,
And more often wear a smile,

So when you eulogy's being read,
Your life's actions to rehash,
Would you smile at the things being said
About how you spent your dash?
— Author Unknown

Your life is not a dress rehearsal!

APPENDIX D: Tools and Exercises

AAA

Coaching for Action and Accountability Assignments

Name _____

Anchor Name _____

Week Ending _____/_____/_____

	Action	Achieved
1. # of tapes samples to send out	_____	_____
2. # of prospecting calls	_____	_____
3. # of prospects on 800#	_____	_____
4. # of Life Style Intros	_____	_____
5. # of prospects on conference calls	_____	_____
6. # of prospecting faxes to send/E-mails	_____	_____
7. # of follow ups	_____	_____
8. # of three-way calls	_____	_____
9. # of website responses	_____	_____
10. # of in-home videos	_____	_____
11. # of new retail customers to develop	_____	_____
12. # of new personally-sponsored reps	_____	_____
13. # of TEAM support sponsored	_____	_____

TOTAL_____TOTAL_____

% of Accountability _____

What I discovered about me:

_____

_____

_____

As within, so without!!!

How will I Be/Do different next week?

_____

_____

On this rock I stand, and, World, you WILL adjust.

Who Do You Know?

Dedicate at least two hours exclusively to making a written list of everyone you know everywhere. Include acquaintances from years ago. Names of people who live over 150 miles away and whom you do not see frequently should be written on a separate "long distance" page of your list. Married people should "brain storm" together in making the list. (Your sponsor will guide your search for PEARLS after the list is made.) Since your mind stores names by categories, systematically start your list the same way.

One of the easiest ways to think of names is by occupation. Take each of the occupations below and list everyone you know that is in the same occupation, no matter where they live.

If your list does not contain at least 100 names, you are probably pre-judging, and you should consult your sponsor for help and other techniques. Your first list will continue to grow rapidly for several days as you see or recall other people, so keep your list with you at all times. This list becomes a starting point for both building an organization and developing your retail business. It will continue to grow as you meet new people.

RELATIVES
Name   Phone

_____   _____
(give yourself 15-20 lines, minimum, for this part of your list)

CURRENT FRIENDS & NEIGHBORS
Name   Phone

_____   _____
(give yourself 10 lines, minimum, for this part of your list)

CHURCH ACQUAINTANCES
Name   Phone

_____   _____
(give yourself 15-20 lines, minimum, for this part of your list)

PREVIOUS FRIENDS & NEIGHBORS
Name   Phone

_____   _____

(give yourself 15-20 lines, minimum, for this part of your list)

WORK ASSOCIATES
Name   Phone
_____   _____

(give yourself 15-20 lines, minimum, for this part of your list)

ORGANIZATIONS, TEAMS & CLUBS
Name   Phone
_____   _____

(give yourself 15-20 lines, minimum, for this part of your list)

CHRISTMAS LIST
Name   Phone
_____   _____

(give yourself 15-20 lines, minimum, for this part of your list)

WHO IS YOUR . . .

- · Dentist
- · Doctor
- · Obstetrician
- · Pharmacist
- · Veterinarian
- · Accountant
- · Architect
- · Builder
- · Congressman
- · Insurance Agent
- · Lawyer
- · Minister
- · Mail Carrier
- · Newpaper Delivery Person
- · UPS Driver
- · Other

PEOPLE YOU KNOW:

- Landlord
- Babysitters (Parents)
- Wedding Party
    Best Man
    Maid/Matron of Honor
    Ushers
    Bridesmaids/Groomsmen
- Car Pool Members
- Whoever Cuts Your Grass
- Dry Cleaners
- Fraternity Brothers/Sorority Sisters
- Health Club Members
- High School Teachers

The important thing is:

What's your message?